THE *SCANDALOUS* MR. BENNETT

THE *SCANDALOUS*

MR. BENNETT

by *Richard O'Connor*

ILLUSTRATED WITH PHOTOGRAPHS

DOUBLEDAY & COMPANY, INC.

GARDEN CITY, NEW YORK

1962

Preface

"A great editor is one who knows where hell is going to break loose next and how to get a reporter first on the scene."

JAMES GORDON BENNETT, JR.

If a montage of the daily life of a modern newspaper publisher could be assembled, it would probably be composed of scenes showing an unexceptional citizen fretting over the price of newsprint and the latest demands of a dozen unions, conferring with his lesser executives on how to outmaneuver the local television stations (unless he has been quick-witted enough to grab off his own channel), addressing businessmen's luncheons, buttering up some of the larger advertisers and worrying about the overlapping tendency of his color presses. In contrast to the intellectual fireworks set off by his great predecessors, his professional life is dominated by statistics, surveys, and techniques. No longer can he persuade himself that his editorial columns can frighten evildoers or shake the city. He is simply another businessman.

As for the editorial departments of his organization, they have also succumbed to an almost pathological lethargy. Editors, fearing a visit from the grievance committee, speak softly to reporters. News gathering has become a drab routine in which reporters phone their stories to rewrite men, who process the stuff as mechanically as a pulp-shredding machine, thereby depriving it of what once was its most valuable attribute—the freshness and individuality of a reporter describing what he has observed. Newspapermen, with the exception of a few odd throwbacks, are workaday citizens who hasten to suburban homes, rather than the nearest barrel house, and whose deepest concern is whether the Guild will get them another pay raise this year. There is a general acceptance that an advertising salesman hurrying back to the office with a double-truck ad is a lot more glamorous than the reporter who has just discovered that the city manager has eloped with his secretary and a half a million in municipal funds, and who knows that when the news breaks he will probably be elbowed into the background by television camera crews.

Journalism has been lying dead in the water for many decades. The last sizable innovation was the development of the photoengraving process, which permits editors to plaster their pages with pictures in the belief that television-obsessed readers' eyeballs will glaze over when confronted by the sight of more than a few inches of type. In a hundred years the dimensions of journalism have changed much less than those of the other marginal professions. The few efforts to expand them have been short-lived. Except for necessarily brisker writing, more attractive typography, and a proliferation of "columns" in today's newspaper, a reader would feel perfectly at home with an issue dated sixty years ago.

The best of the American newspapers, with a few honorable living exceptions, are either dead or sadly diminished—some of them suicides, some of them slaughtered in the offices of newspaper brokers, many fallen from the nerveless hands of weak-willed or disinterested heirs.

Considering this dismal situation, it may be a relief

to turn back to the days before the newspaper business succumbed to senility, despair, and general incompetence —back to the long, lively, and enterprising years of James Gordon Bennett, Jr., of the New York *Herald,* between the Civil War and World War I. There has been no more hectic or picturesque career in American journalism—not even Hearst's, nor Bonfils and Tammen of the Denver *Post,* nor Colonel McCormick of the Chicago *Tribune,* nor any of the other vanished Cyclopean figures who were fortunate enough to live in a day when the printed word possessed an unchallenged potency.

Between them, Bennett and his father, who founded the New York *Herald,* "invented almost everything, good and bad, in modern journalism," as the late Elmer Davis wrote. Before the Bennetts made the *Herald* the greatest newspaper in America—possibly, for a time, in the world—journalism was dedicated to the politics and personalities of the editor-publishers, with the tastes and interests of their readers entirely disregarded. With the Bennetts came the development of society, sports, shipping and financial news, of telegraphed and cabled dispatches from all parts of the world. Police stories and court cases were exploited for the first time. The reader was able to find what interested *him* in the columns of his newspaper, instead of the personal concerns of its editor.

By sending Stanley to find Livingstone, dispatching expeditions to the North Pole, and other enterprises, Bennett Junior pioneered the anticipation or exclusive fabrication of news. "He liked the novel and bizarre and he did not mind if people ridiculed him and the *Herald,*" as Oswald Garrison Villard wrote; "what he dreaded was their not talking about his papers." He was the first editor who developed to the utmost his talent for seeing

around the corner and beyond the horizons of daily
events and, as Villard pointed out, "it was not by accident that a correspondent from the *Herald* stood beside
Dewey on that memorable morning in Manila Bay when
he said to Gridley, 'You may fire when you are ready.'"
He expanded on the ground-breaking achievements of
his father by making the New York *Herald* not only the
biggest and most prosperous in the United States between the Civil and Spanish-American wars, but the
one American newspaper respected abroad and read in
all the foreign chancelleries.

Like Greeley, Dana, and Pulitzer, his father was one
of the several authentic geniuses of American journalism.
Bennett Junior, because of his erratic and wayward
temperament, his scandalous personal life, and above all,
perhaps, the fact that he had inherited his position in
the newspaper world, has generally escaped classification.
His contemporaries feared him or envied his lordly style
of living, truckled to him or hated his tripes (often with
good reason); none took a particularly objective view
of his achievements; he was Bennett the Terrible, the
mad Commodore, the autocrat of the transatlantic
cables. His escapades, as will be seen below, were more
fascinating than his sober accomplishments.

Perhaps—though it seems doubtful at this remove
from journalism-as-it-was—he deserves a more serious
biography, a determined effort to assess his contributions
to the American newspaper. If so, it must be admitted
at the outset, this isn't it. To take a solemn or scholarly
view of Bennett Junior would be an imposing task indeed. What makes him interesting isn't merely his over-
lordship of the New York *Herald* and the forgotten
headlines he reaped, but the personality of a man who
somehow managed to live like one of the lustier doges
of Venice several centuries after such behavior went out

of fashion. There was no one quite like him in the social history of the United States.

Memoirs, diaries, magazines, and newspapers of his era amply testify to the fact that of all of the sports, playboys, rounders, and profligates produced by the Gilded Age, none was more spirited and less inhibited by convention than James Gordon Bennett, Jr. He spent an estimated thirty to forty million dollars as an internationally famous yachtsman, sportsman, womanizer, and boon companion of some of the more raffish members of the European aristocracy. He introduced polo to the United States, skippered the winner of the first transoceanic yacht race, established the first English-language paper in Paris as a personal plaything. He never stifled an impulse, whether it was to yank off every tablecloth in a Paris restaurant, fire a dozen men merely because his executives claimed they were indispensable, ride his horse into Newport's most exclusive club, run down an American warship, kidnap beautiful ladies on his yacht, or acquire the most disagreeable woman in Paris as his mistress.

In between pranks and duels, scandals and binges, hunts and cruises, he somehow managed to supervise every detail of the publication of three metropolitan newspapers.

He didn't need readership polls to tell him what people wanted to read; he created their desire for information himself, and then satisfied it in full measure. He faced no competition from television, radio, motion pictures, automobiles, communal cookouts, or other modern distractions. He could afford to tell his staff that he intended to please only himself and would print the paper upside down if he wished. He could even afford, until the last few years of his life, to live up to his own image of himself as one of the lords of creation.

Contents

Part One:

The Naked Coachman
and Other Stories

1: An Unpopular Truthteller

In the middle 1830s, when James Gordon Bennett, Sr., made his publishing debut on what was loosely known as Park Row, there were fifteen daily newspapers circulating on the streets of New York—the *Sun*, the *Transcript*, the *Jeffersonian*, *The Man*, the *Star*, the *American*, the *Evening Post*, the *Gazette and General Advertiser*, the *Mercantile Advertiser and New York Advocate*, the New York *Daily Advertiser*, the *Morning Courier and New York Enquirer*, the *Journal of Commerce*, the New York *Times*, the *Commerical Advertiser*, the *Business Reporter and Merchants' and Mechanics Advertiser*.

Few of these journalistic trade-marks are recognizable now to any but newspaper historians, most of them dying like dragonflies in the midsummer heat of competition; poisonous little puffsheets, most of them, mourned only by their erstwhile proprietors.

They had little to offer of general interest. The journals of those days, when the whims and prejudices of the editors dictated what was to be found in their smudgy columns, were either excruciatingly dull or excessively shrill. It was the heyday of personal journalism. An editor's feud with one of his competitors, who may well have horsewhipped him the day before, was considered far more interesting than, say, a fire that wiped out a tenement block uptown, and a war in

Europe or a plague in China was worth no more than a few lines. The ink-smeared sheets that issued from basement print shops were simply a series of broadsides, venting the editor's opinions of his rivals, contributing more heat than light to political controversies, airing personal grievances, "puffing" the several merchants, barkeeps, and restaurant owners to whom the editor was beholden. On the social scale the editor, who was usually also the publisher, rightly was rated somewhere below the proprietor of a Bowery flea circus.

News, as such, simply hadn't been discovered in the first third of the century. A good juicy murder was described in a few lines, if it was mentioned at all. There were unbreakable taboos against covering court actions, social affairs could not be mentioned, and it was libelous to report bankruptcy proceedings. Financial matters, if considered at all, were treated with the greatest circumspection. The daily life of the metropolis might have been taking place on another planet.

Bennett Senior, the original genius and only true pioneer of modern journalism, changed all that, bringing with him not only the sense of what people wanted to read, but the ability to communicate it in terms they understood and relished. He made the newspaper "impudent and intrusive." He conceived of reporting, rather than editorial writing, as the newspaper's mainstay. He made the newspaper readable for ordinary people by "discovering and encouraging the popular taste for vicarious vice and crime."

Comparatively easy as it was to start a newspaper in those days, Bennett did not get around to establishing the New York *Herald* until he was almost forty years old. Born in Banffshire, Scotland, in 1795, he migrated to the United States when he was twenty-four years old, apparently in revolt against his Catholic family's deter-

mination that he become a priest. Ever after, his attitude
toward both his family and the Church was that of the
renegade, a misanthropic viewpoint that was soon to
widen and include most of human society. Of his family,
he wrote with scant respect: "Every record of the
Bennetts was lost in a great freshet, previous to the year
of Our Lord 896, when they were a little band of free-
booters in Saxony. I have no doubt that they robbed
and plundered a great deal, and, very likely, hen roosts,
or anything that came in their way. When William the
Conqueror went to England, they were always ready for
a fight, and crossed the seas. . . .

"Another branch went to Scotland with an ancestor
of the present Duke of Gordon, and all, I believe, were
robbers on a great scale. Latterly, however, they became
churchmen, but never abandoned the good old Catholic
Church, till I became graceless enough to set up for
myself, and slap the Pope and Bishop Dubois right
and left. I have had bishops, priests, deacons, robbers
and all sorts of people in my family; and, what is more,
we were bright in ideas and saucy enough in all conscience."

Bennett Senior's career in America lacked little in
variety if much in success. He taught school in Addison,
Maine, read proof in a Boston print shop; translated
news from foreign journals for the Charleston (S.C.)
Courier, and finally, at the age of twenty-eight, made
his appearance in New York as a free lance, selling his
stuff to various newspapers. In 1827, for a pittance, he
joined the staff of the New York *Enquirer* and in his
spare time was an enthusiastic heeler for Tammany Hall,
until "I found out the hollow-heartedness and hum-
buggery of these political associations and political men;
but yet I was so fascinated with the hairbreadth escapes
and adventures that I could not disconnect myself from

it until the revulsion took place between me and my partners. . . ."

Subsequently, he boasted as Washington correspondent for the *Enquirer,* "I changed the whole tone, temper and style of Washington correspondence," which until then had consisted of "heavy, flat, stupid and disagreeable" accounts of what was said on the floor of Congress. "All the political, gay, fashionable, witty, beautiful characters that appeared in Washington during that winter were sketched off at random, without being personal or offensive to any of the parties."

Two years later he became associate editor of the newly combined *Courier and Enquirer* and continued his efforts to breathe a little life into contemporary journalism. His coverage of a murder trial in Salem, Massachusetts, over the protests of the attorney general, developed into an unsuccessful trial of the rights of the press to report whatever it chose. "It is an old, worm-eaten Gothic dogma of Courts," he wrote, "to consider the publicity given to every event by the Press as destructive to the interests of law and justice." Nevertheless the judge at the trial ruled that no accounts of the proceedings before him could be sent out of Massachusetts, and he made his ruling stick.

After several years of working at cross-purposes with the *Courier and Enquirer's* hot-tempered editor in chief, James Watson Webb, Bennett struck out on his own. He started publication of the New York *Globe,* which folded after one month, and was forced to return to free-lancing in New York, Philadelphia, and Washington. Returning to New York with five hundred dollars he had managed to save up from these efforts, he rented a cellar office at 20 Wall Street and on May 6, 1835, brought out the first issue of the New York *Herald,* which was to sell for one penny and to appeal, in read-

ing matter as well as price, to the untapped thousands
of the working classes.

"Our only guide," he wrote in that first issue, "shall
be good, sound, practical common sense, applicable to
the business and bosoms of men engaged in every-day
life. We shall support no party, be the organ of no
faction or coterie, and care nothing for any election
or any candidate from President down to a Constable.

"We shall endeavor to record facts on every public
and proper subject, stripped of verbiage and coloring,
with comments when suitable, just, independent, fearless, and good tempered. If the *Herald* wants the mere
expansion which many journals possess, we shall try to
make it up in industry, good taste, brevity, variety, point,
piquancy, and cheapness. It is equally intended for the
great masses of the community. . . . There are in this
city at least 150,000 persons who glance over one or
more newspapers every day. Only 42,000 daily sheets
are issued to supply them. We have plenty of room,
therefore, without jostling neighbors, rivals, or friends
. . . we commit ourselves and our cause to the public,
with perfect confidence in our own capacity to publish
a paper that will seldom pall on the appetite. . . ."

Right from the start the *Herald* was saucy enough to
whet the appetite of New Yorkers with its irreverent,
realistic coverage of the news. The circulation of the
little four-column, four-page sheet, which soon expanded to six columns, gradually reached the 20,000
mark, close to that of the pre-eminent *Sun*. Bennett
himself covered Wall Street and wrote the daily financial
column. "Our journal," he promised, "shall tell what
Wall Street really is and what is done there." Until then
the financial pages had been "accessory to the swindling
of the sharpers," whom Bennett set about exposing. As
he recalled some thirty years later, "War was made

upon us right and left by the men whose little games were spoiled whenever the public came to know what they were at." But it was in the treatment of police and court news—crime and scandal—that the *Herald* began to pull away from its competitors.

Thousands of new readers were attracted by the way Bennett handled the murder of Helen Jewett, a beautiful young whore (even then a murder victim, if female, automatically was ascribed beauty) whose body was found in a house of assignation in Thomas Street. She had been killed with a hatchet, and Bennett, covering the story himself, did not spare the gore which spattered the death scene. A young clerk whose cloak was found in the room and who admittedly had "visited" the girl was accused of the murder. Bennett's stories showing there was no other evidence against the clerk succeeded in absolving him, and pointed to a jealous woman as the slayer. The *Herald's* colorful and detailed coverage of the crime, coupled with its rivals' charges that Bennett had taken a thirteen-thousand-dollar bribe to establish a case for the initial suspect, increased its circulation by 10,000 copies a day.

Success came rapidly to Bennett Senior in his early forties, but the "better people" managed to withhold their approval. To them he was a vulgar, grubby fellow, engaged in the most degrading of pursuits. Physically, too, he was graceless, with a jutting nose, a wide, thin mouth, deep-set, squinting eyes, and a lank, ungainly figure. The celebrated diarist Philip Hone, a former mayor of New York and a snob of snobs, recorded (in what was subsequently published as *The Diary of Philip Hone*) early in 1836: "There is an ill-looking, squinting man called Bennett, formerly connected with Webb in the publication of his paper, who is now the editor of the *Herald*, one of the penny papers which are hawked about the streets by a gang of troublesome, ragged boys, and in which scandal is retailed to all who delight in it, at that moderate price." The mocking note in Bennett's columns, slyly poking fun at those who considered themselves his betters, was particularly irritating to the gentry, especially since, it may be inferred, it induced a similar disrespect among the lower classes.

Bennett himself was too absorbed in his vision of the future power and influence of the newspaper to be distracted by the disapproval of Hone and his friends. "This is the age of the Daily Press," he believed. "The *Herald* is producing and will produce as complete a revolution in the intellectual habit of daily life as steam-power is doing in the material. . . .

"I mean to make the *Herald* the great organ of social life, the prime element of civilization, the channel through which native talent, native genius, and native power may bubble up daily. . . . I shall mix together commerce and business, pure religion and morals, literature and poetry, the drama and dramatic purity, till the *Herald* shall outstrip everything in the conception of man."

Bennett must have realized that he was succeeding, in a measure, when the assaults which were visited upon him almost from the beginning of his publishing career mounted in wrath and frequency. Editorial impact could almost be measured by the number of welts and bruises a newspaper proprietor displayed. Assaulting an editor, generally with a whip, was rarely out of season on the streets of New York, and Bennett, being the most gaudily successful, collected more than his share of wound stripes. A particularly vexed and enthusiastic assailant was his former employer, James Watson Webb of the *Courier and Enquirer*. Besides being engaged in a circulation battle, Webb and Bennett differed radically in their approach to Wall Street reportage. Webb made a specialty of touting certain stocks, for which he was presumably rewarded; Bennett devoted considerable effort to exposing flotations of stocks and bonds which, in the absence of any regulatory agency, were offered the investing public with larceny aforethought.

A Bennett editorial casting aspersions on Webb's integrity as a Wall Street weather vane so irked the latter that on January 19, 1836, he flailed away at Bennett with fists and cane when they met on the street. In reporting the encounter, Bennett claimed that Webb sneaked up behind him and "cut a slash in my head about one and a half inches in length. . . . The fellow, no doubt, wanted to let out the never-failing supply of good humor and wit, which has created such a reputation for the *Herald,* and appropriate the contents to supply the emptiness of his own thick skull. He did not succeed, however, in rifling me of my ideas. . . . He has not injured the skull. My ideas, in a few days, will flow as freshly as ever, and he will find it so to his cost." In his own account of the assault, Webb added the slightly nauseating detail that he had also forced Bennett's jaws open and spit down his throat.

During the following May, despite a warning from Webb not to mention his name in the *Herald's* columns, Bennett commented editorially that Webb "from his habits, education, temper, and talents . . . was utterly unfit to have control of a newspaper" and that "sooner or later he would disgrace the press and destroy his own reputation." On May 10 Bennett again had to report an encounter with the editor of the *Courier and Enquirer.* The two men met in Wall Street, Bennett said, and Webb "commenced fighting with a species of brutal and demoniac desperation characteristic of a fury." This time, he assured his readers, his only injury was a scratch "on the third finger of the left hand," whereas "his loss is a rent from top to bottom of a very beautiful black coat, which cost the ruffian $40, and a blow in the face, which may have knocked down his throat some of his infernal teeth. . . . Balance in my favor, $39.94."

A broker named A. A. Clason, infuriated by some of Bennett's comments on the *Herald* financial page, assaulted the editor with a horsewhip. The whip broke at the first blow, however, and fell to the sidewalk; Bennett politely picked up the pieces and handed them to his assailant.

A short time later another reader with a grievance, Thomas S. Hamblin, manager of the famous Bowery Theatre, invaded the *Herald* offices with a group of bibulous friends and had just started to smash up the place when the police arrived. "Civilization is yet defaced with traits of barbarism," Bennett sadly commented. "We are only half civilized."

With the coming of steamship service across the Atlantic and the development of the telegraph, the enterprising Bennett made every possible use of the speed-up in communications and not only showed up his rivals consistently, but widened Americans' view of the world. He began reporting social functions, hitherto banned from the columns of newspapers, since such publicity was regarded as vulgar. Polite society was further affronted by the mocking tinge to the *Herald's* reportage, its slyly satirical comment on the social exclusiveness of nabobs a generation removed from the family butcher shop or tallow chandler's. Even less amusing to certain readers was the *Herald's* innovation of publishing the list of bankruptcies, which had an unsettling effect on the more venturesome fringe of the business community.

But it was Bennett's campaign against prudery which really stirred up the moralists, professional bluenoses, religious fanatics, and neo-Puritans of the city. In May of 1840, Bennett outraged the prissier sections of the community by denouncing the custom of referring to arms and legs as "branches of the body," by calling trousers "inexpressibles" and shirts "linen." Petticoats, of course, could not be mentioned at all—not even as "unmentionables." Any properly reared young lady was supposed to plead for smelling salts if some vulgarian uttered the word "pants" within range of her delicate ear. All those dainty circumlocutions, ordained to conceal any hint of the body's natural functions, drew Bennett's wrath.

"Petticoats—petticoats—petticoats—" he taunted the bluenoses in an editorial, "there, you fastidious fools, vent your mawkishness on that."

The reaction was uproarious. The *Evening Signal,* the *Courier and Enquirer* (whose editor swore like a divekeeper), the *Evening Star*, the *Journal of Commerce,* the *Express*, the *News,* and the *Mercury* all fired up rockets of outrage and indignation. Bennett should be tarred, feathered, and run out of town. The *Herald* should be exorcised. Groups of busybodies visited the *Herald's* advertisers and demanded that they withdraw their patronage from "that Devil's print shop." Committees were organized to boycott the *Herald* and all its works. Encouraged by these manifestations of outrage, rival editors outdid each other in applying epithets to the *Herald's* proprietor. Some of those collected by Frederic Hudson, long Bennett's managing editor (and author of *History of Journalism in the United States*), were "obscene vagabond," "leprous slanderer," "profligate wretch," "gallows rogue," "venal wretch," "infamous Scotchman," "contemptible libeller," "pestilential scoundrel," "common bandit," "vile nuisance," and "turkey-buzzard."

On June 2, 1840, Philip Hone gloated in his diary,

"The career of the infamous editor of the *Herald* seems at last to have met with a check, which his unblushing impudence will find some difficulty in recovering from. Some of his late remarks have been so scandalous and profane as to have drawn out the editors from the contemptuous silence which they have hitherto observed toward the scoundrel. . . . Bennett is absolutely excoriated by the *Signal*, and all the other papers, without regard to party, have joined the righteous crusade. This is the only thing to be done; the punishment of the law adds to the fellow's notoriety, and personal chastisement is pollution to him who undertakes it. Write him down, make respectable people withdraw their support from the vile sheet, so that it shall be considered disgraceful to read it, and the serpent will be rendered harmless; and this effect is likely to be produced by the united efforts of the respectable part of the public press."

Despite Mr. Hone's optimism, the thundering from press and pulpit, the attempts to force advertisers to boycott the *Herald,* all had little or no effect on the *Herald's* revenue.

As Bennett himself wrote, "These blockheads are determined to make me the greatest man of the age."

One leading advertiser, on being visited by a delegation of boycotters, doubled his appropriation to the *Herald.*

As for his enemies' campaign to make reading the *Herald* "disgraceful," as Mr. Hone put it, the effect was just the opposite. A month after the uproar began, Bennett published a table showing that the nine newspapers which had joined in condemning him and which he dubbed "The Holy Allies" had a combined circulation of only 36,550. The *Herald's* circulation had risen to 51,000.

During the mid-century agitation for women's rights, carried on by such angrily eloquent voices as those of

Lucy Stone, Sojourner Truth, Lucretia Mott, and Susan B. Anthony, the *Herald's* circulation spurted forward again through Bennett's vigorous denunciation of their cause, which was generally unpopular. The vulgarity of his editorial attack, however, dismayed even those who disagreed with the bloomer-clad females who were demanding social and political equality.

In his editorials Bennett expressed the hope that Lucy Stone, while pleading her cause from some platform, would suddenly give birth to "a fine, bouncing boy." As for the stridently pro-feminist physician Dr. Harriot K. Hunt, it was Bennett's dearest wish, so he said, that while treating some gentleman for hemorrhoids she would have to send posthaste for a midwife, who would be called upon to deliver her of twins. Since Dr. Hunt was not married, Bennett's taste in suggesting these remedies was regarded as deplorable.

Bennett replied to criticisms of his coarse-grained humor by citing the case of Mrs. Jane Grey Swisshelm, editor of the Pittsburgh *Sunday Visitor* and once a rather noisy advocate of women's rights, who "formerly ran about to such gatherings, but now stays at home because, after weary years of unfruitfulness, she has at length got her rights in the shape of a baby." Motherhood, he proclaimed, was "the best cure for the mania, and we would recommend it to all who are afflicted."

The "tomfoolery" over women's rights would soon run its "farcical" course, he believed, and even the fanatics would return to their rightful place in the kitchen.

From these bumptious beginnings the *Herald* continued to be a journalistic storm center, even after great prosperity blessed its endeavors. Politically, socially, and personally, its editor was a born outsider, a maverick, a continual irritant, all the more encouraged in his intransigeance by the fact that nonconformism was paying

off. It wasn't too long before Bennett joined the ranks of
the millionaires, yet it made little difference in his attitude, habits, or style of living. "American Society," he
once observed, "consists of the people who don't invite
me to their parties." His whole existence was bound up
in the *Herald,* and even marriage to a socially inclined
young lady hardly distracted him from his purpose.

To charges of atheism, which abounded after every
oblique assault launched by the *Herald* on the established
churches, he replied that true religion consists "not in
hanging about the apron strings of rich old women—not
in presuming to judge the opinions of others beyond
what their acts will justify. . . . The Bible is before me.
Have I not a right to read that book—to draw out from
it religious opinions—and to create a belief and a church
of my own?" When the militant Catholic Archbishop
John Hughes demanded that parochial schools be given
a share of the public revenues, Bennett commented that
"his mind must be blinded to all facts—to all truths—
save the dogmas and drivellings of the Catholic Church
in the last stage of decrepitude." With both Catholic and
Protestant clergy united against him, Bennett, tongue in
cheek, expressed fervent sympathy for the Mormons and
with mock gravity accepted a brevet commission as a
major general in that sect's Nauvoo Legion.

An "unpopular truthteller in a wildcat age," Bennett
was so successful in exposing the schemes of get-rich-
quick promoters that the *Foreign Quarterly Review* of
England wrote that "The New York *Herald* has been
one of the most powerful instruments in the United
States in exposing frauds, bubbles, and stock-gambling
machinery, which our fund-mongers had organized in
America for robbing the land and labor in that country,
as they have robbed since the days of Walpole."

On the increasingly critical divergence of the North

and South over the slavery issue, Bennett, for once, was
something of a fence straddler. His view seemed to be
that the abolition of slavery was hardly so pressing a
matter as to be worth endangering the Union, and he
was a firm supporter of the temporizing administration
of President Buchanan, who wrote Bennett that he was
"gratified to know that you have ever been my friend."
On the eve of Sumter he wrote that the wisest course
would be to "yield to the Confederates and to all the
slave-holding communities their just rights as co-equal
partners in the Union." Abraham Lincoln, to him, was
the "pliant instrument" of a "destructive sectional party,"
as well as an "imbecile," a "smutty joker," and a "traitor."
Only when Virginia joined the secession movement did
the *Herald* come out against the Confederacy and charge
it with "wantonly and wickedly" bringing on the Civil
War. President Lincoln made a special effort, through
Thurlow Weed, who he understood had "considerable
experience in belling cats," to obtain the *Herald's* editorial support "in view especially of the influence the
Herald was exerting in Europe."

By now Bennett was accustomed to being courted
by men of national prominence, and he was reluctant
to abandon his original estimate of Lincoln as a back-
woods politician jumped up to the presidency, but
through the persuasions of Weed and other emissaries
from Washington he swung around to supporting the
Administration, although he placed most of the blame
for starting the war on the abolitionists and was always
critical of that faction in the Republican party. Once a
mob formed in front of the *Herald* building and would
not disperse until the colors were displayed, and Bennett
was so fearful of the wartime temper that he installed
a secret arsenal, with plenty of rifles and ammunition,
behind the walnut paneling of the library and conference

room next to his office. The first battle of Bull Run, at which the Union Army was routed, finally convinced Bennett that Confederate military power, not the machinations of Radical Republican leaders, was the most serious threat to the maintenance of the Union. Nevertheless, throughout the war, the *Herald* was more inclined than any other influential journal to take a cool and objective view of events. It was said to be one of the few papers Lincoln himself read regularly. In 1864 it supported Lincoln's candidacy for re-election.

Politically grateful, the President wrote Bennett on February 20, 1865: "I propose, at some convenient and not distant day, to nominate you to the United States Senate as Minister to France."

Bennett, however, "respectfully and positively declined."

Meanwhile (according to managing editor Frederic Hudson) the *Herald* was spending half a million dollars, an enormous sum in that day, for covering the war on all its fronts. It maintained forty correspondents in the field at all times. No other newspaper reported the war in greater detail, with greater accuracy or enterprise. But Bennett's heart was never in it, though he gave lip service to federal war aims—largely, it may be believed, because it might have endangered the existence of his newspaper to oppose them. A brilliant young war correspondent who met him early in 1865, John Russell Young (*Men and Memories*), recalled that his chief "did not have a cheerful view of the war; he could see no result but irretrievable bankruptcy, against which, as he said with a smile, he had provided by keeping a special deposit of gold in the Chemical Bank."

In the seventh decade of his life Bennett was a thoroughgoing cynic, his outlook verging on misanthropy. Both his hard-scrabble years as a reporter and writer and his exceedingly prosperous years as a publisher had taught him only that there was money to be made in the newspaper business through catering to popular tastes. He had discarded whatever principles informed his youthful years, and he regarded his newspaper purely as a retailer of news and a merchandiser of advertising. Lofty editorials and public-spirited crusades, in his view, were a lot of nonsense. All men were selfish, greedy, and intrinsically worthless; the human condition could never be bettered, certainly not through the medium of journalism, and he did not propose to waste his time in uplifting gestures—that was the crackbrained domain of Horace Greeley, who published weekly letters from Karl Marx, participated in the women's rights movement, and took a serious view of contemporary literature. Bennett concerned himself solely with getting out the liveliest sheet in town and watching his acumen reflected in the balance sheets, the circulation tallies, and the advertising revenues. He was now in the top rank of New York's millionaires, he who once had denounced John Jacob Astor as a "self-invented money-making machine" and recommended, on Astor's death, that half his fortune be returned to the people of New York from whom he had squeezed it. And he now had no intention of sharing the proceeds of his own money-making machine with the ignorant populace.

That machine, the New York *Herald*, would be entrusted to his only son, who both as his heir and as the future publisher of the paper must have caused him considerable misgivings. Neither marriage nor paternity had brought Bennett any great amount of personal satisfaction.

In his scramble for success, and in the pitiless self-knowledge that he was not particularly well favored for romantic pursuits (he once recalled that he had been chased out of a whorehouse by the girls, who told him "you are too ugly to come amongst us"), Bennett had waited until his forty-fifth year before falling in love.

One day in the spring of 1840 he attended the wedding of the *Herald's* society editor, William Atree, and there he was introduced to a charming and attractive young woman, Henrietta Agnes Crean, who had migrated from Ireland several years before and supported herself by giving piano and elocution lessons. Miss Crean was only half his age, but Bennett tumbled head over heels. In his account of the Atree wedding the next day he gave Miss Crean more space than the bride, describing her thus: "Her figure is most magnificent—her head, neck and bust, of the purest classic contour. There was a quiet and finish in her sweet looks."

It was a headlong courtship; Miss Crean had wearied of teaching fumble-fingered offspring of prosperous merchants their piano exercises, and Bennett had sickened of his solitary life and decided he could spare some time from his mistress, the *Herald,* for a comely young wife. Naturally he shared his ecstasy with the *Herald's* readers and proclaimed his love in a headline that less exuberant people found exceedingly vulgar:

DECLARATION OF LOVE—CAUGHT AT LAST
—GOING TO BE MARRIED—NEW
MOMENT IN CIVILIZATION

In the story beneath, he managed to list both his fiancée's charms and those of her rival, largely financial, in the same romantic paragraph. He would be married in a few days, he announced in that declaration of June 1, 1840, to "one of the most remarkable, accomplished, and beautiful young women of her age. She possesses a fortune. I sought and found a fortune—a large fortune. She has no Stonington shares or Manhattan stock, but in purity and uprightness she is worth half a million of pure coin. Can any swindling bank show half as much? In good sense and elegance another half million; in soul, mind and beauty, millions on millions, equal to the whole specie of all the rotten banks in the world. Happily, the patronage of the *Herald* is nearly twenty-five thousand dollars per annum, almost equal to a President's salary. . . ."

The beautiful Irish girl and the squinting, prematurely aged Scot were married June 6 at Saint Peter's Catholic Church in Barclay Street.

Almost from the moment the priest pronounced his benediction on the infidel head of the bridegroom, the marriage was attended by an almost incredible showering of abuse, scorn, and contempt. The former Miss Crean quickly learned that she was not only sharing the bed and board of the city's most successful publisher, but the hatred of his colleagues and the isolation of a social leper. She had married her way into Coventry, and it was no discredit to her that she did not choose to endure an involuntary pariahdom, which scarcely affected her husband, for the rest of her days. She was libelously attacked in the columns of Bennett's journalistic rivals, who accused her of "snobbery," "extravagance," and misconduct with other men before and after her marriage; the *Star* and the *Sun* were particularly abusive.

When the couple returned from their honeymoon, Bennett's enemies exerted all the pressure they could muster on the proprietor of the Astor House, then New York's finest hotel, to refuse them accommodations. Some of the papers falsely reported that Charles Stetson, the owner, had turned them away from his doors as briskly as a pair of baggageless nonentities living in sin. Stetson, however, demanded and received retractions of the canard. And when James Gordon Bennett, Jr., was born on May 10, 1841, by which time the Bennetts had moved to a house at 114 Chambers Street, the *Sun* greeted the event with an insinuation that Bennett Senior was not the child's father. Bennett sued the *Sun* for libel and won his case, a matter of greater satisfaction to him than it was comfort to his wife. In the next ten years Bennett fathered three other children, including a son who died at six and a girl who died even younger, but only his daughter Jeanette survived to share the nursery with James Junior.

Despite Bennett's high hopes for marital happiness, he found that his wife, lacking a nature calloused by his years in the rough and tumble of New York journalism, simply could not endure the ostracism and violence which enclosed his existence. Society's contempt was so outspoken, so inexorable, that she made no attempt to win its favor, as a lesser woman might have done. She had her own pride, coming from a West of Ireland family that had known better days. For ten years she shared her husband's isolation, apparently without protest.

It was only when the activities of his enemies increased in deeds as well as words that she decided she could not raise her children in such an atmosphere.

On November 9, 1850, she was strolling on Broadway, near White Street, on her husband's arm when a group of men, some of them carrying whips, approached the couple. The gang was headed by John Graham, whose candidacy for district attorney the *Herald* had helped to defeat, and his brothers, DeWitt and Charles. While Mrs. Bennett watched in "helpless agony," her husband was beaten to the ground and mercilessly lashed with the cowhide whips. Two policemen watched the assault without attempting to interfere. All of which drew from Philip Hone, as a spokesman for a supposedly polite society, the comment that he would be "well pleased to hear of this fellow [Bennett] being punished in this way, and once a week for the remainder of his life, so that new wounds might be inflicted before old ones were healed. . . ."

Two years later a box labeled "For Mr. Bennett Only" was delivered to the *Herald* offices and found to contain a black-powder bomb, ingeniously rigged to explode when the top was removed. Its recipient became suspicious when a few grains of powder leaked out and summoned the police, who soaked it in water for several days before opening the box. Bomb experts said it was powerful enough to "blow Mr. Bennett to smithereens."

That was the last attempt to inflict physical harm on Bennett, his enemies apparently deciding that he was indestructible.

By then Mrs. Bennett, badly shaken by the Graham brothers' assault on her husband and equally so by the callous attitude of polite society toward the brutal affair, had removed herself and her two children to France. She would rear her children "out of the sphere of calumny, misrepresentation, and reckless wit" in which her husband necessarily operated. Bennett Senior could have sold the *Herald* for enough money to keep himself and his family in luxury abroad, but the gaiety and splendor of Paris were drab in comparison with the daily excitements of publishing a New York newspaper. He would return to bachelorhood, relieved occasionally by trips to France or visits from his wife and family to America.

With little apparent stress he reconciled himself to

becoming one of the first of many successful entre-
preneurs whose wives would expatriate themselves to
escape the atmosphere made noxious by their husbands'
pursuit of money and power.

2: A Princeling on Park Row

From the moment that James Gordon Bennett, Jr., first became conscious of life around him, he was made aware that he was a very special human being. It was all but inevitable that he would be imbued with the idea that the world was shaped for his pleasure and convenience, an idea that even maturity would not eradicate.

The young master was surrounded by people who seemed to exist only to satisfy every whim. Nurses and governesses fussed over him in three languages. Private tutors tactfully and not too insistently tried to impart a certain amount of education, but he was never forced to rub elbows with schoolmates, and the inescapable democracy of the playground and schoolyard was denied him. There was never any other boy to rub his nose in the dirt once in a while to give him a sense of proportion; the only friend of his boyhood, in fact, was an office boy employed by his father. If anything went wrong in his well-insulated world, he had only to bawl for his nanny or his mummy, and everything would be put to rights. His pretty young mother petted, spoiled, and cozened him, when she was not too busy securing a place in Parisian society. His largely absentee father, with more money than affection or real concern at his disposal, simply gave him an allowance larger than the salary of his best reporter.

His native New York made the acquaintance of Junior

in his middle teens, when Mrs. Bennett returned on a visit with her children. After that the boy spent about half of the year in his father's care, to use the word loosely, and the rest of the time in Paris with his mother. The Bennetts were not separated in the legal sense, nor even estranged; they had simply come to the understanding that she would continue to live abroad, as she preferred, while he devoted all his attention to the *Herald*. Occasionally Bennett Senior would visit Paris briefly, and Mrs. Bennett would return to New York even more briefly, usually around Easter time, but they never again attempted to establish a home together.

Given his servant-sheltered upbringing, Bennett Junior should have turned into a proper little sissy. Instead, through some native toughness of fiber, he was a broth of a lad, large for his age and as ready to use his fists as any stripling from Hell's Kitchen. Someone, possibly a servant, had led him astray when he was very young, and he was experienced in matters of sex and alcohol soon after reaching puberty. Life in Paris had not only given him command of the French language, which in that day—particularly in an America conscious of its frontier crudities—certified a person of awesome culture and gentility, but left him with a sophisticated air that his American contemporaries viewed with envy and despair. To them, with his tall, erect frame, his blade of a nose, and his haughty eye, he was a young grandee. E. P. Mitchell, who grew up in the neighborhood and later was an editor of the New York *Sun*, wrote (in *Memoirs of an Editor*) that he was "admired reverently" as "the beau ideal of the man of the world and all-around daredevil."

He was allowed to remain with his father when it became apparent that Society would welcome him as a peer, much as it detested his father. The tutoring, the

French lessons, the riding lessons had paid off handsomely, given the boy a cosmopolitan manner, even an
air of condescension, that the smart set could not resist.
(Not including the Astors as yet; they found it hard to
forget that Bennett Senior had suggested that half the
fortune be given back to the city of New York.) Invitations to the Bennett home at Fifth Avenue and Thirty-
eighth Street were now welcomed on behalf of sons and
daughters of people who would not speak to Bennett
Senior, even though the behavior of Bennett Junior,
with so little parental discipline, was likely to be erratic
at best.

Frank Squier, the Brooklyn park commissioner, recalled dropping in at the Bennett mansion one day in
1857 when Bennett Junior was acting as host at a party
for the gilded youth of the neighborhood. The young
man, Squier said, "gave an exhibition of himself such
as his father, even in the unregenerate days of the penny
Herald, would hardly have cared to publish." Young
Bennett, more precisely, was reeling from the effects of
alcohol. He was then just sixteen years of age.

A few months later the boy was elected to membership in the New York Yacht Club, which along with
the Union Club and the Jockey Club was the most
exclusive organization in the city. He was, in fact, the
youngest member ever admitted. His father, generous
with everything but paternal guidance, indulged the boy
endlessly. He bought his son the trim, fleet sloop
Rebecca (and later the 160-ton yacht *Henrietta*), en-
gaging the renowned Captain Samuel (Bully) Samuels,
to take professional charge of the vessel. Possibly he
hoped that Samuels would also acquaint Junior with a
touch of seagoing discipline, but the latter wasn't having
any. On at least one occasion the brawny Samuels, who
could put down a mutiny with one hand, almost placed

him in chains to discourage interference with the sloop's navigation.

When the Civil War broke out and Bennett Junior felt a craving for naval glory—on his own terms and amid familiar surroundings—his father naturally exerted every effort to enable Junior to have his fling at saving the Union. This was arranged only after Henry Villard, then representing the *Herald* in Washington, was summoned to New York and ordered to open negotiations with President Lincoln, Secretary of State William H. Seward, and Secretary of the Treasury Salmon P. Chase. Three of the nation's highest officers were required to give time and thought to finding a suitable place for an untrained, twenty-year-old officer candidate in order to gain Bennett Senior's editorial support. Villard wrote that he found the assignment "rather amusing," but he must have penned those words with gritted teeth. With due solemnity the application of James Gordon Bennett, Jr., was passed through channels from the Secretary of State to the President to the Secretary of the Treasury. On May 6, 1861, Lincoln wrote Chase:

"The Secretary of State this moment introduces to me Mr. James Gordon Bennett, Jr. who tenders to the U.S. the service, a fine Yacht of 160 tons burthen. If you allow him an interview, which I ask for him, he will talk with you about putting some other vessels of the same class into the service. We send this subject to you because we believe these vessels may be made most available in the Revenue service."

History does not record whether young Bennett succeeded in persuading his fellow yachtsmen to join their cause and their craft to the defense of the Union at sea, but within a week he was commissioned a third lieutenant in the Revenue Cutter Service, which was assisting the navy in blockading the Southern ports.

He was everlastingly proud of his Civil War service, but judging strictly from the record it was nothing to promise that another John Paul Jones was in the making, had his interest in naval affairs survived his first year of duty. That summer of 1861 the *Henrietta* cruised along the peaceful shores of Long Island. By then the yacht had been converted into a cutter with two six-pound rifled bronze guns and a twelve-pound brass cannon to dismay any Confederate raider daring to venture into Long Island Sound.

In February of 1862 the prospects of action for the *Henrietta* quickened when she was ordered to join the blockading squadron operating off Port Royal, South Carolina. She served with the squadron exactly two months before the businesslike naval commanders, like Bully Samuels, found young Bennett a trifle presumptuous for a mere third lieutenant. On April 29, for unspecified reasons, the squadron commander decided that the Union Navy could handle its assignments without any further assistance from the *Henrietta*. The cutter was ordered decommissioned.

Lieutenant Bennett, of course, could have remained in the service and been transferred to another vessel—but, really, could an heir presumptive to millions of dollars be expected to pig it as a very junior officer on some deck not his very own? And what of the food and wine aboard one of the ships of the regular navy? Substandard, undoubtedly. Furthermore he would have to take orders from people who were inferior in everything but rank. If they wouldn't have his boat, they couldn't have Bennett the Younger.

On May 11, 1862, a few days short of a year after he entered the service, Lieutenant Bennett tendered his resignation, which was hastily accepted.

He then resumed a desultory apprenticeship which he

had been undergoing at the *Herald* since his middle
teens. His father had installed two desks, one on each
side of his own, in his office. One was for his son, the
other for Edward Townsend Flynn, who had been an
office boy until Bennett Senior promoted him to the
position of companion, co-worker and friend to his son.
Flynn was a bright lad with red hair and a lively mind;
he also had a sense of balance and responsibility which
his employer evidently hoped might rub off on Bennett Junior. The two boys were supposed to absorb the
principles of newspapering at the side of a master, and
young Flynn was a diligent student. Later, as the elder
Bennett had undoubtedly intended, he held down various
executive posts at the *Herald* and performed faithfully
as the younger Bennett's chief New York representative
while the latter was sojourning in various parts of the
world. Bennett Junior had never been required to learn
anything, and although he was attached to the *Herald*
payroll at a salary the managing editor would have envied, he paid little attention to the business he would
one day inherit. Early in life he had formed the notion
that he could hire all the brains he needed at ridiculously
low prices—hardly cigar money for a man about town.

Young Mr. Flynn, in the delicate position of being
both friend and hireling, was called upon to extricate
Bennett Junior from situations in which he frequently
became involved through a combination of alcohol and
arrogance. The two young men customarily adjourned
to Delmonico's at noontime for food and drink, after
spending the morning in Bennett Senior's schoolroom-
office. A few hours of attendance at the Bennett School
of Journalism usually induced a considerable thirst in
Bennett Junior.

One afternoon at Delmonico's he became irked when
the waiter was delayed in bringing a bottle of cham-

pagne over to his table. Young Bennett shouldered his way through the crowded room, jarring elbows and spilling drinks in his progress toward the bar.

"I ordered a bottle of champagne fifteen minutes ago," he snapped at the bartender. "Where is it?"

A small but compact man whom Bennett had elbowed aside commented in a loud voice, "You would have thought he'd ordered a case."

Bennett wound up and launched a blow that would have torn a hole in the wall, had it landed. The little man it was aimed at, however, quickly landed a left hook on Junior's jaw and knocked him flat.

Flynn had been watching his ill-mannered companion's bull-like rush through the barroom, noted the dispatch with which he had been laid low, and decided that his duties did not extend to rescuing young Bennett from brawls he started out of sheer cussedness. He quickly and discreetly vanished from the scene, leaving the job of bringing Bennett around to Delmonico's efficient waiters.

Next day at the office Bennett, with his bruised jaw and a knot on the back of his head, inquired whether Flynn hadn't been with him at Delmonico's when he was slugged. Flynn said he had been called away on urgent business just as Bennett headed for the bar.

"A little fellow knocked me out," Bennett said, nursing thoughts of revenge. "Find out who he was."

Flynn's investigation showed that Bennett had indiscreetly picked on Billy Edwards, a prominent lightweight boxer. Always unpredictable in his reactions, Bennett was positively delighted when he learned who had knocked him witless. It pleased him that it had been done by a professional, which removed any stigma attached to being beaten by a smaller man. Through

Flynn he arranged a meeting with Edwards. Most spoiled young men respect a left hook when smartly applied, and Bennett took a liking to Edwards. For some months the prize fighter and the millionaire's son were the best of drinking companions. Bennett the Younger's outlook could change from that of the grand seigneur to the barroom equalitarian with amazing speed and with an apparent lack of motivation that alarmed more conventional people.

His changeability was observed with professional interest by Dr. George Hosmer, who practiced medicine and journalism with equal success. (One of the *Herald's* outstanding war correspondents, he had spotted a large Confederate force moving up on Cemetery Ridge during a critical phase of the battle of Gettysburg, and his warning alerted the Union command in time to save the key position.) Dr. Hosmer remarked that Bennett Junior was Scottish on his father's side, Irish on his mother's, and concluded that he had inherited the worst features of both strains.

"When sober, he displays the worst qualities of the Scotch," was Dr. Hosmer's diagnosis, "and when drunk the worst qualities of the Irish." It could have been the other way around, of course.

Whatever the accuracy of Dr. Hosmer's estimate of his character, Park Row learned over the years to fear both sides of his nature. His reactions were always unpredictable, except that they were predictably perverse. Given his mother's indulgence and his father's preoccupation with his newspaper, and the latter's tendency to react only when disgusted by his son's rudderless behavior, Bennett really had little chance of turning out differently. For almost sixty years his flagrant self-centeredness, his escapades, pranks, and exploits were to produce a Park Row legend at the extreme opposite of his hardheaded father's. The long-vanished street of newspapers witnessed a procession of frisky individualists in its day, but never a more extravagant character than the heir to the New York *Herald*.

3: Scenes from Sporting Life

Despite his bumptious youth and his odious father, James Gordon Bennett, Jr., was welcomed into New York's "fast set," a high-living and pleasure-loving group of largely middle-aged brokers, sportsmen, clubmen, scapegraces, rounders, and all-around good fellows which flourished on the postwar inflation, the rising stock market, and the industrial boom following the Civil War. Entry into this lusty circle was obtainable through the possession of various qualifications: (1) money and/or social connections, but especially money; (2) a proper respect for fast horses and trim boats; (3) a proper disrespect for middle-class morals and virtues; (4) an appreciation of wine and women that approached connoisseurship; (5) a hearty if not particularly refined sense of humor; and (6) a lordly contempt for those who "did not belong," which included moneygrubbers who gave too much attention to business, men who went home to their wives at nightfall, and others unwilling to accept the principle that having a good time was all that mattered in life, especially if it was carried off in style. Style, form, and dash were very important to the Victorian gentleman, in America as well as in England.

In addition to possessing most of these qualifications, Jimmy Bennett came well recommended.

Young Bennett's acceptance by these roistering gentlemen was largely facilitated by the Jerome brothers, who were born on a farm near Syracuse and had established one of the leading brokerages in Wall Street. Leonard, Lawrence, and Addison Jerome, as Anita Leslie (*The Remarkable Mr. Jerome*) has written, annoyed their fellow financiers by "mingling ruthlessness with frivolity. Their failures could be jeered at, but the steel-hard tycoons found their successes hard to stomach. In Wall Street it was lese majesty to laugh about money."

Leonard Jerome, in particular, became Bennett the Younger's patron and took an almost brotherly interest in the young man, although he was twenty-three years his senior. He owned a quarter interest in the New York *Times,* was married and had three beautiful daughters, was usually successful in any financial ventures he undertook (when he could spare the time), but his real interests lay in horses, women, good food and wine. By the time Bennett Junior became his protégé, he had already run through ten million dollars. "One rode better, sailed better, banquetted better when Mr. Jerome was of the company," as an admiring contemporary wrote. Another said that he "outdid all who were bent on cutting a figure." He drove his own runabouts with teams that were trained to rear and prance as they turned the street corners; he organized the first steeplechases and racing meets in the United States; and he had a devilish eye for the ladies. Ward McAllister wrote that "he turned out daily with his drag or coach loaded with beautiful women, and drove to every desirable little country inn in and about the city, where one could dine at all well, crossing ferries, and driving up Broadway with the ease and skill of a veteran whip, which he was." People cheered when he drove by with a whole bouquet attached to his buttonhole, his hands encased in white gloves, his whip cracking, "gay and laughing ladies in gorgeous costume" spilling over the seats behind him. That was the way to live, if you were lucky enough to be rich! He made a career out of being a gentleman, and when he lay on his deathbed with his three daughters gathered around him, he tried to make them smile by saying, "I've given you all I have. Pass it on."

It was this kind of *bon vivant,* rather than his workworn, grim, and ascetic father, on which Bennett Junior was determined to model his life.

He was bored stiff by formal society, disdainful of those who yearned to be "classy," embittered by those who considered him a wealthy fop who would inherit his father's money but never his brains or ability.

With the Jerome brothers and his friends of the Union, Jockey, and New York Yacht clubs, as he said, he "found the companionship of real men at last."

His father had already made the *Herald* the most prosperous newspaper in America, and there was little he could do downtown at the *Herald* offices but watch the old man run things.

Somehow he had to make his mark in something that mattered to *him,* not the elder Bennett, who saw virtue only in the balance sheets of the *Herald's* bookkeepers.

Sports might be condemned as frivolous by the stuffed shirts, the reformers, the pulpit-pounders, and other grim specimens of humanity, but to young Bennett and his friends they made life worth living. The sheer achievement of speed, on or behind horses or on boats, made a man feel godlike. The J. P. Morgans, Jay Goulds, Daniel Drews, Commodore Vanderbilts and the rest of that piratical crew down in Wall Street might get the same feeling of power out of stealing railroads and pumping out watered stock; wasn't this cleaner, more sporting, and more manly?

One of the more fashionable sports revived in the

post-Civil War years was coaching. It was all the rage in England, where the Duke of Beaufort had taken to driving a four-in-hand up and down the island's roads and the Marquis of Blandford was whipping up his coach-and-four as a "public vehicle" between London and Dorking. And what was good enough for English aristocrats was more than good enough for their imitative admirers across the Atlantic. Leonard Jerome, DeLancey Kane, August Belmont and other magnificos took up the sport, and Bennett Junior, of course, joined in enthusiastically when they organized the Coaching Club. To these swells, being a good "whip" and observing the proper form were all-important; it wasn't simply a matter of sending four horses and a carriage bucketing down the roads; you had to observe the amenities. You wore a silk topper, a large boutonniere, bright green coat with gilt buttons, yellow-striped waistcoat, and patent-leather boots. You folded your driver's apron *outside* out when it was not in use. You fastened a bunch of artificial flowers to the throatlatch of each horse. And that made you a "howling swell."

But Bennett, an extremist always, was not satisfied with merely tooling his coach around the streets for the admiration of the populace or conducting excursions along country roads.

He drove like a madman, grew so intoxicated by speed that some of his friends, observing him wild-eyed and shouting on the box of his coach, were convinced that he was more than slightly insane and was being chased by Headless Horsemen visible only to himself. Sometimes at coaching races he would tear across the finish line and just keep on going, driving his horses until they dropped. Often, with Gunning S. Bedford and other reckless aficionados, he would go charging off on expeditions into New England, driving night and day for two or three weeks at a time, buying new coaches-and-four along the way as his teams foamed with exhaustion, until whatever demons spurred him were exorcised.

"I want to be able to breathe," he once said of his lust for wild driving.

This reach for breath sometimes took startling forms. On midnight rides, careening down country roads, he would often strip off all his clothing. Stark-naked in the box, he would drive his four-in-hand along the turnpikes, cracking his whip and yelling his head off in delirious pleasure. Many an old farmer, peering out his bedroom window at this apparition, must have sworn off applejack the moment Bennett and his equipage bounded out of view.

Bennett's reckless driving was the talk of New York society, but Leonard Jerome took a tolerant view of his high-spirited protégé. Jimmy boy just had to go to extremes. Didn't that prove he had the stuff of champions? His sporting blood ran a little faster than that of tamer citizens. Jerome was a trifle less affable about Bennett's driving, however, when his dark-eyed Jennie, the loveliest of his three beautiful daughters, had to report that while coaching with Bennett and other friends "we came to grief and were nearly killed" through Bennett's reckless handling of his four-in-hand. The whole party was spilled out on the pavement, but nobody was seriously injured. Had Jennie lost her life in that tumble, history would have sustained a serious, if not calamitous loss— especially British history. Jennie Jerome was to marry Lord Randolph Churchill and one of her sons was to be Winston Churchill.

In addition to reviving coaching as a fashionable pastime, Leonard Jerome also organized the American Jockey Club and established a race track called Jerome Park on an old estate at Fordham where the Bathgate family had been breeding thoroughbreds for half a century. Jerome, having bought a race horse for $40,000, was determined to exclude the low lifes from American racing and keep it a sport for gentlemen. The purpose of his organizing committee, it was announced with high-minded emphasis, was "to promote the improvement of horses, to elevate the public taste in sports of the turf, and to become an authority on racing matters in the country." Jimmy Bennett joined this idealistic movement wholeheartedly, and was among those present when the Jockey Club held its first meeting at the opening of Jerome Park in September, 1866—as were such assorted personalities as the German-born banker, August Belmont; Boss Tweed, the hetman of Tammany Hall; John Morissey, the Bowery gang leader who controlled a large share of the Irish vote; a Mrs. Ronalds, whose growing friendship with Jerome would be mentioned only in whispers; Josie Woods, who operated the city's most exclusive and high-toned house of assignation; Jim Fisk, whose career as a financial buccaneer was just beginning; William Travers, "the stammering wit of Wall Street," who wondered aloud what insignia could possibly be engraved on the silver buttons of the liveried footmen attending Miss Woods, and the most imposing figure of them all, Lieutenant General Ulysses S. Grant.

For Jerome and his friends, it was a matter of some relief, considering the elevated plane on which the Jockey Club hoped to sponsor sports of the turf, that Madam Restell, who had made more than a million dollars with her little knives, did not choose to attend the opening of the race meeting. The Frenchwoman operated an abortion mill, well known to people with more money than discretion, in her fashionable brownstone at Fifth Avenue and Fifty-second Street. Like Miss

Woods, she would have met many of her best customers at Jerome Park's opening.

Bennett himself was soon to take his place beside Jerome as an innovator and developer in the field of sports. He was the first (and last) man to ride his horse into a Newport club, thereby winning a wager but outraging the resort's matrons. He also introduced a sport called "Bennetting" in honor of its founder. One afternoon, gazing out of one of the front windows of the Union Club, he observed the decorous procession of young ladies from a nearby boarding school who were taken out at four o'clock every afternoon for an airing. At their rear marched a stern duenna, as E. P. Mitchell (*Memoirs of an Editor*) recalled. Bennett's game was to rush out of the club and gallop down on the young ladies, "plunging between the foremost couple, enfilading the entire line and throwing it into confusion, and then dodging to escape the duenna at the rear." His fellow clubmen—and this may have been a measure of their intellectual capacity—thought this a most amusing way to enliven an afternoon. Soon every young buck in the Union Club was taking his turn at stampeding the boarding-school promenade, until finally it had to be forbidden—not because frightening schoolgirls was considered undignified, but because one of the children might be injured by some intemperate follower of Bennetting, with consequent lawsuits against the club. A more seemly sporting venture of Bennett's was his challenge to John Whipple, the champion pedestrian, for a walking contest from Fifth Avenue and Thirty-eighth Street to the gates of Jerome Park. Bennett won the race and a $6000 purse.

Somewhat later, in 1876, Bennett introduced polo to the United States. The game had been played in India for centuries and was imported to England by officers of

the Indian Army. Watching a game being played by
retired pukka sahibs while on a visit to England, Bennett immediately was fascinated and begged for instruction from his hosts, among them a Captain Candy,
who soon became one of his best friends. Steaming with
enthusiasm, he brought the captain and a collection of
polo mallets and balls back to the United States with
him and taught the rudiments of the game to William
P. Douglas, Frank Gray, August Belmont, and others
at a riding academy in the city, then moved from the
tanbark to a field at Jerome Park and kept drilling them
until they were skilled enough to make their public
debut. Polo matches were held after the racing meets at
Jerome Park, and the sport began to catch on among
people well heeled enough to maintain a string of
ponies. Bennett and several of his friends then founded
the Westchester Polo Club, built a clubhouse, and hired
one of the Delmonicos to take charge of the cuisine.
There is no cloud to Bennett's title as the Father of
American Polo.

The sporting passion that absorbed him throughout
his life, however, was yachting.

Ever since his middle teens he had spent most of his
summers on the seventy-ton sloop *Rebecca,* or her successor, the 160-ton *Henrietta,* which he named for his
mother. At seventeen, only a few months after he had
been admitted to membership in the New York Yacht
Club, he was inadvertently involved in charges of unsportsmanlike conduct by cutting corners in a race,
though investigation disclosed that he had done so on the
insistence of his sailing master. In a race around Long
Island on June 24, 1858, the *Rebecca* breezed across
the finish line ahead of three other sloops and four
schooners. It was discovered, however, that the *Rebecca*

had taken a short cut through Plum Gut instead of sailing the prescribed course, which disqualified her.

Race officials decided that his performance was "not due to sharp practice but to bold seamanship," since the Plum Gut short cut had been eliminated from the course only because of the risk involved in negotiating it. Nothing more would have been said, in all probability, except for the fact that the *Herald's* competitors got hold of the story and used it as an excuse for an attack on the Bennett family.

Bennett Senior was so annoyed with his son, though his fellow yachtsmen had not censured him, that the boy was banished to Europe for several months until the scandal died down. It was a prime example of the father's misapplication of discipline.

Racing across the Atlantic was only an unfulfilled challenge until one evening in October of 1866, when a yachtsmen's dinner was held at the Union Club. It was regarded as too risky, particularly during the winter storms on the Atlantic. But now sporting blood rose to the challenge, helped along by liberal doses of brandy.

Lingering over cigars and after-dinner drinks, Pierre Lorillard, George Frank Osgood, the Jerome brothers, and Bennett were debating the merits of the centerboard yacht. Lorillard's *Vesta* was outfitted with a centerboard. Osgood's schooner *Fleetwing* and Bennett's *Henrietta*, that unscarred veteran of the Civil War blockade, both were built with keels.

Finally Lawrence Jerome wearied of listening to the argument and blurted out:

"Don't blather so much—put it to the test! Race 'em across the Atlantic."

All three accepted the challenge immediately, although Lorillard and Osgood argued it wouldn't be fair to include Bennett's *Henrietta* because she had been beaten by both *Vesta* and *Fleetwing* in shorter previous races. Bennett, then twenty-five years old and unaccustomed to being thwarted in any desire, pleaded so vehemently that he was allowed to participate.

Before day broke through the drawn draperies of the Union Club's dining room, it was agreed that the three yachts would race for a $90,000 purse, to which each participant equally contributed, and that the course would be from Sandy Hook to the Needles Rocks off the south coast of England. Furthermore the race would be held in December, when "there was wind enough for all."

For the next six weeks Bennett busied himself with preparations, displaying an energy and an attention to detail that should have amazed his father, considering how lackadaisically Junior performed around the *Herald* offices. Both he and his rival contestants scurried around the water front, trying to round up the finest seamen available to fill out their crews.

Several weeks before the ships were to be put out to sea, both Lorillard and Osgood reconsidered their brandied boasts of the night the challenges were issued. Driving their sleek but frail craft, little over a hundred feet in length, through December storms, had lost its appeal. They had agreed that all three vessels would be skippered by their owners, but Osgood and Lorillard begged off. Their yachts would be commanded as well as staffed by professionals.

Bennett insisted on sailing his own ship. He'd agreed to it, hadn't he? And why should he ask other men to take risks for that $90,000 purse that he wasn't man enough to accept himself? He was a very firm believer in the unwritten code of the gentleman, which was as mythical, for all except him, as honor among thieves.

Nothing could dissuade him from taking command

of the *Henrietta.* Bully Samuels, who had once driven the clipper ship *Dreadnaught* from New York to Liverpool without ever shortening sail, would accompany him, as usual, as the *Henrietta's* sailing master.

Other men involved in the race began having second thoughts, too, about the dangers confronting them.

"Some difficulty was experienced," according to the weekly magazine *All the Year Round,* "in securing seamen to cross the Atlantic in such vessels, and in such weather. The men were willing enough but their mothers, wives, and sweethearts interfered and persuaded them not to sign articles."

The carefully selected crew of the *Henrietta,* in fact, decided against boarding her and "their places had to be taken by a lot of landlubbers. . . . Invitations to prominent yachtsmen were declined for various reasons, and the gentlemen who served finally in this capacity were almost all volunteers."

Among the landlubbers who cast their lot with Bennett were three of his best friends, Charles Longfellow, the poet's son; Stephen Fiske, the playwright and drama critic, and Lawrence Jerome, "a very large man, full of humor and wit and a practical joker."

Bennett, according to the *All the Year Round,* took no chances that even these boon companions would desert him. "From seven A.M. on Dec. 11, the day of the start, no communication was permitted between the yacht and the shore, partly to prevent any further difficulties in regard to the crew, and partly because several kind but frightened friends had conceived the idea of subpoenaing some of the yachtsmen as witnesses in trials of which they knew nothing, in order to preserve them from the perils of the sea."

Fleetwing, also troubled by defections among the crew, had to round up nine whaling-ship captains at the last moment at what must have been enormous fees.

As the three vessels got under way, Bennett was loudly cheered as "the only man who goes in his own boat." The cheers, however, found no echo from Bennett Senior, who was enraged by the charges of his competitors that the race was foolhardy in the extreme and the lives of close to a hundred men were being endangered by a contest conceived in alcohol by the idlers and triflers of the Union Club. Bad publicity, which had rarely troubled the old man in the past, now bedeviled him; it was bad enough to collect his own black eyes, but now his damn-fool son was doing it for him.

The three yachts headed into a brisk wind, with *Vesta* taking an early lead. It was noted that both *Henrietta* and *Vesta* had decked over their cockpits to afford a greater measure of protection for their crews, but *Fleetwing's* cockpit was open to the Atlantic's icy gales.

For two weeks all three vessels disappeared from sight and sound, lost in the fight against strong westerly winds, which blew all during the race, allowed no beating to windward, and sometimes rose to gale force. They bucked heavy seas and drove on through snows which crusted the decks and rigging. On December 19 a heavy sea swept over *Fleetwing*, picked up six crew members from its open cockpit, and carried them off to their deaths. In the annals of ocean racing, it is still considered one of the greatest, if not the greatest, race ever held under sail. "Ever since," as Alfred Loomis, the yachting historian, recorded, "in a score of ocean races, have seamanship and dogged determination and inscrutable luck mirrored the greatness of the historic match between *Henrietta, Fleetwing,* and *Vesta.*"

The *Henrietta's* log, which has been preserved by the New York Yacht Club, shows that during the first week of the race the vessel made from 203 to 280 miles a day. Then, on December 19, it ran into heavy seas. The day began with a comparatively light south-southwest wind, which increased to gale force by midafternoon. Soon a full gale was blowing and Bully Samuels ordered that the *Henrietta* heave to under close canvas, overriding protests from Bennett, to whom discretion was definitely not the better part of valor. The *Henrietta's* log during this crisis read: "The storm trisails happened to be stored in the cabin, and as the sailors came silently down, coiled the tackle, and carried up the sail on the deck, the scene reminded one of the bringing forth of a pall for a funeral. A pause in a race like this seemed the burial of all our hopes. Nevertheless, it was some consolation to be informed by Captain Samuels that, in his thirty years experience, he had never seen a vessel that could face a gale for so long."

With Bully Samuels' wisdom prevailing, however, the *Henrietta* managed to ride out the storm without losing a member of its crew. *Fleetwing* meanwhile was mourning its six lost crew members. *Vesta,* unable to heave to because of its centerboard construction, made 222 miles that day.

As the three contenders picked up the lights of the Scilly Isles on Christmas Eve, the *Vesta,* thanks to having plunged on through the gale of December 19, was almost an hour's running time in the lead.

But there was still a 200-mile stretch of the English Channel to be negotiated, and *Vesta* was hampered by "poor pilotage." *Henrietta,* meanwhile, was beating her way up at the Channel at a good thirteen knots and making good the day lost when she was forced to heave to during the gale.

At 5:32 P.M. on Christmas Day, *Henrietta* anchored in Cowes Roads, having covered a distance of 3106 miles in thirteen days, twenty-one hours, and fifty-five minutes. *Fleetwing* dropped anchor eight hours and fifteen minutes later, *Vesta*, finishing third, forty minutes after *Fleetwing*.

Newspapers on both sides of the Atlantic had fastened international attention on the race. Representatives of all the major yacht clubs in Europe were waiting to greet the storm-battered craft as they were piloted into Cowes Roads, and members of the Royal Yacht Squadron ceremoniously escorted their crews ashore. Bennett and his comrades relaxed, basked in universal admiration, and soon were playing practical jokes on each other that astounded their English hosts. To turn the tables on the middle-aged but frisky Lawrence Jerome, his friends obtained a sheet of royal note paper from Osborne House and wrote out a command from Queen Victoria for Jerome to appear as her guest for dinner. Jerome was thrown into a panic by such a formidable summons. For several days he fretted over his costume, consulted experts on court etiquette, and worried himself sick over the impression he would make on the starchiest of queens. His friends didn't let him off the hook until the moment he stepped into a gig which was supposed to take him to the Royal Yacht Landing. Far from being annoyed at the joke played on him, Jerome was so relieved that he wouldn't have to face the ordeal of dining with the Queen that he danced an elephantine hornpipe on the deck of the *Henrietta*.

One happy result of the *Henrietta's* hard-earned victory was the paternal esteem that flowered in the cautious heart of James Gordon Bennett, Sr. The yacht race, which he had viewed with disapproval a few days before it started, but which he now regarded as the *Herald's* own feat of seamanship, gave the paper a tremendous boost in circulation—and nothing could be more pleasing to its publisher than booming street sales. A break in cable transmission had delayed the news, but on December 30 the *Herald* was able to proclaim with proprietary pride on its main news page:

HENRIETTA THE WINNER
OF THE OCEAN RACE
Her Arrival at Cowes on
Christmas Day
YACHTSMEN TO VISIT QUEEN
*A Challenge Is Hurled
to the Old World*

A few days later, having second thoughts about his son's ability to handle success, he sounded an unmistakable parental warning on his editorial page: "We hope that the young gentlemen concerned have borne and will throughout bear themselves in a manner worthy of all praise."

When the *Henrietta's* skipper and crew were honored at a banquet in Paris, where enthusiasm for their victory was an exhilarating foretaste of the acclaim Charles A. Lindbergh would receive sixty-odd years later for flying the Atlantic, the *Herald* published full accounts and reprinted editorials from French and English newspapers praising young Bennett and his crew.

Almost giddy with the unaccustomed sensation of paternal pride, the elder Bennett was quite justified in hoping that his son had changed for the better, according to the young man's companions. Bennett Junior was finding himself praised from all quarters, while formerly he had been written off as the idle and brainless son of an illustrious father.

Obviously what he had needed more than anything else, after spending disgruntled years in his father's shadow, was a dose of any kind of success on his own. Much of his instability was undoubtedly traceable to the feeling of unworthiness that overwhelmed him whenever he compared himself—as every son must—with his father. Bennett Senior was always too busy and too self-centered to cope with the psychological circumstances he had wished upon his son, so the latter, admittedly in a haphazard manner, had solved the problem for himself with the help of a yacht and his brave companions.

"This ocean race," wrote Stephen Fiske, one of the *Henrietta's* gentleman sailors, in his *Off-Hand Portraits of Prominent New Yorkers,* "was the turning point in James Gordon Bennett's career. When he returned to New York he began to devote himself to business. . . . The acquaintances Bennett [Junior] made as a yachtsman became of the greatest service to him as an editor." Shortly after his son returned to New York, Bennett Senior was so impressed by the change in him, by a partly illusory glimpse of maturity and a developing sense of responsibility, that he turned over control and direction of the *Herald* to him.

The financier and yachtsman J. P. Morgan himself laid down the dictum, "You can do business with anyone, but you can go sailing only with a gentleman."

"Right," commented Leonard Jerome, "although it depends on what you mean by a gentleman." According to his biographer and kinswoman, Anita Leslie, "he was thinking of hard-driving Captain Samuels, and of the stout crews of flush-decked *Henrietta* and *Vesta,* crouching half-frozen in the lee of weather cloths during long hours of watch, and putting all their heart into the handling of canvas in shifting freezing winds, and of *Fleetwing's* six sailors lost in the roaring ocean."

In 1870 Bennett participated in another historic yacht race. By this time he was as pre-eminent in yachting as his father was in the newspaper world; he had been elected Vice Commodore of the New York Yacht Club, and the following year would be elevated to Commodore. He had abandoned *Henrietta* for the schooner *Hirondelle,* which he bought from Dexter Bradford, Jr., lengthened it by fifteen feet and renamed it *Dauntless.* The *Dauntless,* as refitted under Bennett's instructions, was 120 feet long, spread 7000 square feet of canvas, required a crew of thirty-seven, and was described by one who saw it sweeping down the Hudson under full canvas as "a thing of beauty aglow with brass, the deck polished until it shone and every strand of cordage as taut as the strings of a fiddle."

Soon after *Dauntless* was in shape to meet any challenges, Bennett became involved in a rather boastful correspondence with Commodore James Ashbury of the Royal Harwick Yacht Club. Ashbury was convinced that his 108-foot *Cambria,* smaller but possessing the priceless boon of British seamanship, could take the measure of *Dauntless.* It would be the first international transoceanic race, and Bennett could not resist the challenge. It was agreed that *Cambria* and *Dauntless* would race from Daunt's Rock off Queenstown, Ireland, to the Sandy Hook Lightship.

Among those who sailed with Bennett when the blue peter was hoisted on July 4, 1870, and the two vessels went scudding away before a brisk westerly were Bully Samuels, Richard Brown, and Martin J. Lyons, the latter two both Sandy Hook pilots. This time Lyons served as sailing master, and Samuels and Brown were enlisted as "advisers." Along with the strong-minded owner, this made four men struggling for command. Also aboard were Leonard and Lawrence Jerome and Charles Longfellow. Right from the start there was acrimonious feeling between the "professionals" and the "gentlemen." *Dauntless* was not a happy ship, although it may have been taut enough.

Cambria headed straight across the Atlantic, while *Dauntless*, according to the experts, made the tactical error of taking a more southerly course. Three days out, too, *Dauntless* ran into a gale and was delayed by a tragic mishap. According to her log for that day, the wind and sea began rising before dawn. At 7:30 A.M. it became necessary to take in the flying jib. "In furling it, two men—Charles Scot and Albert Demar—were washed off the boom. Hove to the yacht for two hours, lowered foresail and got out boat, but failed to see anything of the missing men. At 9:30 the wind increased to a gale, we reluctantly gave them up, took the boat on board, and kept on our course."

Meanwhile, as Loomis (*Ocean Racing*) recorded, "*Cambria* had worked north to 54–79, her highest latitude, and from the seventh she slanted slowly down, taking what current there was on her port beam until she came within the helpful influence of the Labrador current."

As the two schooners approached Sandy Hook on their different courses, there was great excitement, and not only from the wealthy sporting class, over the outcome of the race. On July 27, with *Cambria* and *Dauntless* piling on all their canvas for the approach to Sandy Hook, the operators' room on the lightship was crowded with ship-news and sports reporters. In midafternoon the first of the two contenders hove into sight, but its colors could not be made out at that distance.

"The speck rapidly approached," the New York *Times* reported, "and assumed plainer proportions until it was discovered to be the sails and spars of a schooner. Nothing was visible of her hull, which seemed to be a part of the sea on which it floated. Exactly forty-one minutes elapsed . . . before she passed the lightship, seven miles outside of Sandy Hook. The wind was blowing off her port quarter due east, and she scudded along under full sail. The flags which she carried at her ensign, together with a private pennon, contained the letter C in the center. She was at once pronounced to be the *Cambria*.

"A sigh of disappointment swept over America. *Cambria* had sailed from Ireland to Sandy Hook in twenty-three days, five hours and seventeen minutes. It was only an hour and forty-three minutes later that *Dauntless* passed the finish line. Only one hour and forty-three minutes in a race of three thousand miles! It had been a good try, but in the end it had to be conceded that *Cambria,* a slower boat, won the first international yacht race because of faster head work."

Bennett was bitterly disappointed. He lacked two of the gentlemanly graces: when he won, he was inclined to brag; when he lost, he couldn't help griping. *Dauntless* had lost the race because there were too many experts pulling this way and that aboard—yet he had signed on the sailing master and two unnecessary "advisers" himself. The professionals were equally unhappy. Captain Lyons grumbled that "there were too many amateurs aboard," forgetting that yachting was a sport of wealthy amateurs. Captain Samuels recalled that at one point during the race he had again been forced to threaten to clap Bennett in irons if he didn't stop trying to interfere.

A year later Bennett also engaged in acrimonious exchanges with the victorious Ashbury. The Briton had come over with a new schooner, *Livonia,* to race against various entries of the New York Yacht Club, including *Dauntless.* Bennett's yacht beat *Livonia* in a final two-yacht contest.

Ashbury returned to England, fuming that the New York Yacht Club had been guilty of "unfair and unsportsmanlike proceedings."

Bennett responded by returning three cups which Ashbury had donated to his club for presentation to the winners of various races and informing the Britisher that the American clubmen had resolved "that they cannot with any respect compete for the cups deposited with Commodore Bennett by Commodore Ashbury."

Bennett the Younger could no more escape controversy, even as a sporting gentleman, than his father could in the unsporting and ungentlemanly atmosphere of the newspaper business.

4: The New Broom in Printing-House Square

Early in 1867 a handsome carriage began appearing every workday morning among the carts, drays, and wagons that thronged Park Row and carried its product, warm and inky from the clattering presses, to all parts of the city. Behind the smartly liveried coachman sat a young man whose elegance of dress and disdainful manner also seemed out of place in the grubby turmoil of Printing-House Square. He was tall and straight-backed, with an air of authority few of his fellow newspaper editors could manage. His face was long and bony, with a firm jaw, rather suspicious and chilly blue eyes, an imposing nose, and a large tawny mustache. Altogether it was the kind of face one might see among the junior officers of the Coldstream Guards—a combination of boredom, hauteur, and contempt for the rear rankers of the world; the kind of face, settled in a lordly assurance, that usually takes many generations and the expenditure of millions to shape and form. At twenty-six James Gordon Bennett, Jr., had acquired the habit of command, whether merited or not; from then until the end of his life it was the one quality that never changed or weakened.

Young Bennett began showing up regularly at the *Herald* offices immediately after his return from Europe

and the Christmas victory with his yacht *Henrietta*.
Frederic Hudson, long the *Herald's* managing editor and
one of the elder Bennett's earliest collaborators, oblig-
ingly retired to write his long and authoritative *History
of Journalism in the United States*. Young Bennett took
his place as headman of the editorial department and
soon was taking over some of his father's functions as
editor in chief and publisher. Not only had Bennett
Senior decided that his son might be of some use after
all, thanks to his celebrated yachting triumph, but
young Bennett, according to Stephen Fiske, "learned
what good he could do the *Herald* and what good the
Herald could do him."

To the general surprise, Bennett Junior began taking
his duties very seriously. He put in a full day's work,
took a firm hold on the editorial reins, and even interested himself in the mechanical departments of the
newspaper. Unlike his father, who had little interest in
the machines which spewed out editions by the tens
of thousands, the younger Bennett was fascinated by
the mechanics of publishing. He generally treated the
ink-stained artisan with more respect than the most
brilliant editor, perhaps because the latter tended to
make him feel, with some justification, an intellectual
inferiority.

As his father entered his seventy-second year and
grew feebler from the cumulative effects of a strenuous
career, the younger Bennett began taking a stronger
grip on the *Herald's* affairs. Wasn't it about time the
doddering old man had the decency to retire and hand
over complete authority to his son? Perhaps a nudge of
the elbow would help him make up his mind to slip
gracefully into dotage and let the younger generation
carry on.

Young Bennett had been running the editorial department less than six months, but he was already convinced that he could do a better job of publishing the *Herald*, given full authority, than his father with almost a half-century's experience.

One day in the fall of 1867, without consulting his father, he rearranged the masthead. His father's name was dropped completely. The executive roll call now was headed, "James Gordon Bennett, Jr., Editor in Chief and Publisher."

Perhaps he thought the old man's attention had been faltering and the change would be overlooked until it was too late to rescind it without making the family look foolish.

If so, he was quickly and sharply disillusioned.

Bennett Senior's squinting eye had fastened on the presumptuous change in the masthead a few minutes after the *Herald* was delivered to his study. Roaring mad, he drove downtown from upper Manhattan at top speed and hurried into the *Herald* building. In a few minutes, as Stephen Fiske wrote, he managed to "reassert himself," bring the presses to a halt, replate the editorial page with his own name at the top of the masthead, and inform his overeager son that he wasn't dead yet, and had "no mind to retire until I'm damned good and ready."

Aside from that brief essay in usurpation, the young man apparently got along fairly well with his father. It was a relationship based on mutual forbearance, on an agreement not to attempt to "understand" each other or bridge the forty-five years that lay between them. To the elder Bennett, his son must have seemed an undeserving, frivolous fellow who would fall heir to an immensely valuable property without the slightest effort. At the same time he evidently recognized in Bennett Junior a certain toughness of fiber which, properly developed, might stand him well in the journalistic wars. Once he stopped playing the coxcomb, sowed his last wild oat, and really settled down to learning the newspaper business, he would be a worthy successor.

In his last years Bennett Senior was virtually a hermit, secluding himself at his baronial estate on Washington Heights in upper Manhattan, then a rural neighborhood. One of the few visitors that neighbors remembered seeing around the Bennett place was Jefferson Davis, the ex-president of the Confederate States of America, who stayed there incognito and whose presence would hardly have surprised those who suspected that his cantankerous host had never been wholeheartedly pro-Union during the Civil War. Bennett Junior rarely visited there, but established himself in the family town house at Fifth Avenue and Thirty-eighth Street.

The old man appeared at the *Herald* offices several times a week when his health permitted, wrote occasional editorials and, until the day of his death, kept in close touch with affairs downtown. Private telegraph wires connected him with the *Herald* office and with the Bennett town house.

He offered no objections when his son, after only a few months as managing editor of the *Herald,* proposed to start publishing an afternoon edition under the title of the *Evening Telegram.* The *Herald* itself was still a sprightly sheet, compared with most of its competitors, but in recent years it had tended to play down the crime news and theatrical scandal in favor of a more sedate and dignified approach. Bennett Junior's idea was to make use of the juicier and spicier items now neglected in the *Herald* by splashing them all over the new paper, a sound enough idea, since the readers of afternoon papers found sensationalism—gory murder scenes, sexual escapades, spectacular suicides and the like—easier to stomach than those who ingested their news at the family breakfast table, where flaring headlines were likely to seem out of place.

The *Evening Telegram* made its first appearance in July of 1867. It was printed on pink paper, ran to four six-column pages, sold for one cent, and obviously was designed to appeal to readers who tended to move their lips when they read it. Preserved on microfilm, its pages now seem strikingly modern, compared to those of the other New York papers, and present a sort of preview of today's tabloids. FOOTPADS IN THE SUBURBS and EXTRAORDINARY SEDUCTION CASE seemed to be practically standing heads, along with a daily report on the Jefferson Market Police Court news, always slotted on Page One. On a fairly typical day (September 24, 1867), the *Telegram's* top heads on the front page included several murders and suicides described in loving detail, a column of cable news, another of telegraphic bulletins. Sporting news was also brought out on Page One for the first time, and there were lengthy accounts of a prize fight and of the closing of the baseball season with the final game between the New York Actives and the Morrisania Unions. (The Morrisania team won, 15–11, after a tenth-inning rally.) All these stories were topped by large black headlines, startling in their definition by comparison with the spidery type faces, with bank after bank of repetitious subheads, crawling halfway down the pages of the more conservative papers. The *Telegram* was an innovation, gaudy, vulgar, and appealing to the lower intellects, utterly deplorable to all who hoped for finer things in American journalism. It never really caught on as the *Herald* did, but it blazed a path for Hearst, Pulitzer, and all the others who refined and embroidered on its methods. Old Mr. Bennett, in his saturnine way, so totally unconcerned by any further debasement of the public tastes, must have been pleased by it, for the *Telegram* was the *Herald* of his more youthful days.

Perhaps it was his son's bold experiment with the *Evening Telegram* which convinced him it was time to retire, once Bennett Junior was dissuaded from trying to hasten that process by striking the old man's colors on the masthead.

On New Year's Day, 1868, he came down to the *Herald* office for a prearranged meeting with his son. With his Scottish distaste for sentiment, he simply thrust a paper in the young man's hands. The document stated that henceforth his son was to be editor and publisher of the *Herald,* with sole and complete control of the property.

Several months short of his twenty-seventh birthday, Bennett Junior thus became one of the press lords of America and the proprietor of what was then its most widely read newspaper as well as publisher of its most furtively read, the pink-hued *Evening Telegram*. With less than a year's real experience as a newspaper executive, he was taking his inherited place as the professional peer and financial superior of some of the greatest editors in American publishing history.

By now Park Row was not quite so thronged with competing newspapers, but those which had survived the elimination contest of Bennett Senior's day were much stronger and more influential. That short, grubby street, extending northeast from Broadway and Ann to the triangle at Nassau Street known as Printing-House Square, and a few adjacent thoroughfares contained all of the New York newspapers in the post-

Civil War period. The most imposing structure along Newspaper Row was the nine-story, red-stone *Tribune* Building with its 285-foot Clock Tower soaring above lower Manhattan, which faced Printing-House Square. It was then the tallest building in New York City. Also facing the square, at Nassau and Frankfort streets, was the New York *Sun,* with a spiral iron staircase leading up from the basement to its topmost (sixth) story. Its building recently had housed Tammany Hall. The *Herald* was located at Broadway and Ann streets in a stylish, white-marble building vaguely modeled after a French château. The *World,* known as "the white elephant of Park Row," and the *Times* were both issued from buildings in the triangular block between Park Row, Beekman, and Nassau streets. Lesser organs adding their voices to the daily thunder of Park Row's presses included the *Journal,* the *Mail & Express,* the *Commercial Advertiser,* the *Daily News,* the *Evening Post* and the *Press.* Up the street, around Chatham Square, the foreign-language newspapers, mostly German, were clustered in their own enclave.

There was still a tendency toward personal journalism, which the pioneering efforts of Bennett Senior in the direction of reportorial emphasis had not entirely eradicated. To the public as well as to the profession, they were still known as "Bennett's *Herald,*" "Greeley's *Tribune*" and "Dana's *Sun,*" all of the more successful journals speaking in the distinctive tones of their proprietors. A New York editor in those days was a mighty personage, a celebrity with as much glamour as any of the politicians and financiers he publicized, welcome at the White House, courted by everyone from the President down.

Perhaps the outstanding dignitary whose company young Bennett now joined without a moment's trepidation was William Cullen Bryant, "the Nestor of the metropolitan press" and editor of the sober, literate *Evening Post,* whose "purity of tone" was much admired on Murray Hill and other strongholds of respectability. With his patriarchal beard and long white hair, Bryant's presence was required at all momentous municipal ceremonies. Once the nation's most celebrated poet, his output of verse was slowed to a trickle in his last years, but two poems he wrote for the *Ledger,* a weekly that was half newspaper and half magazine and boasted a million readers, brought him $3000. Nobody ever lent more dignity to the journalistic profession than Bryant, and well he knew it. His austerity of manner was so glacial that it was remarked by a contemporary that one would be as likely to take liberties with the Pope as with Bryant.

The muted, temperate, and sometimes equivocal personality of the *Times* was still derived from its founder and editor in chief, Henry J. Raymond, an ex-Greeley disciple. Short, stout, jovial, and popular in all circles —the direct opposite of the lean, dour, and ascetic Bennett Senior, in fact—Raymond enjoyed society and the theater, was fond of driving his sleek span of bays along the winding roads of Central Park. One of his few dislikes was the *Herald's* founder, whom he was said to have threatened with horsewhipping. The provocation must have been intense, because Raymond ordinarily prided himself on a tranquil disposition. His fair-mindedness, he admitted, sometimes caused the *Times'* editorial policy to seem vacillating, if not mealymouthed. "I always try when one side is presented to look at the other, and in turning it around I am instinctively inclined to favor the reverse of the side I first examined." Under Raymond's guidance, the *Times* was foremost in analyzing political and economic trends.

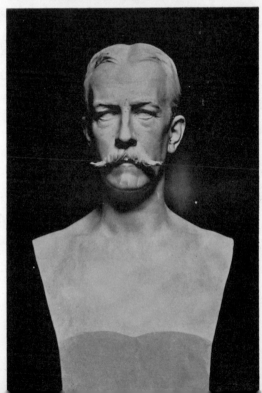

1. & 2. The *Herald's* dynasty. These busts of the Bennetts, Junior and Senior, faced each other across the lobby of their newspaper building.

3. Bennett at eighteen. Already his worldly airs were the envy and despair of his contemporaries. This was his first known portrait.

4. Henrietta Bennett, who married Bennett, Sr., his newspaper, and his social pariahdom. Her contemporaries, belying the photographic evidence above, said she was beautiful.

5. James Gordon Bennett, Sr. He admitted that he was so ugly the inmates of a bordello chased him out on the street.

6. The third lieutenant. Matthew Brady was commissioned to photograph Junior when he joined the Union Navy. Bennett, Sr., was very proud of him. His pride was short-lived.

7. The stone villa at Newport. Bennett built the place in his youth. Soon it was the center of a resistance movement against the dowagers reigning there.

8. Playboy and publisher. Bennett posed for this picture at the age of thirty, not long before his father's death.

9. A coaching party with Bennett at the reins. This gay group was snapped outside the Bennett home on Washington Heights. In mixed company, Bennett generally wore clothes while coaching.

10. In his prime just before a social disaster sent him into permanent exile.

11. Expatriate. Bennett with his guests at La Croma, one of his French estates. The Commodore, as usual, is more interested in his dogs than his human companions.

12. The Yacht *Namouna,* which members of the *Herald* staff, fearing its visitations in New York Harbor, renamed the *Pneumonia.*

13. Ankle deep in dogs. Bennett, second from left, with guests at his home at Versailles.

14. Back from the hunt. One creature safe from his birdshot was the owl. All other birds had to take their chances.

15. A cottage in the country. Bennett himself scrawled, with his ever-ready blue pencil, the notation at the top: "Where I live at St. Germain."

It was also the country's leading Republican organ, having been an ardent supporter of the Lincoln administration, then later of the Radical Republicans who covertly opposed Lincoln, but always of the powerful financial interests whose fortunes were bound up in that party.

The two most potent and individualistic personalities of Park Row, however, were Horace Greeley of the *Tribune* and Charles A. Dana of the *Sun*.

Greeley was hipped on causes—everything from the virtues of graham bread to women's rights. Some people, regarding him simply as an eccentric, refused to take him seriously. They were encouraged in this view by his appearance, which had more than a slight reminiscence of Mr. Pickwick. Tall, stout, and rubicund, he was an easy target for the cartoonists; he had a large pink moon of a face, with blue, myopic eyes behind large spectacles, and a fringe of unkempt white whiskers. He wore baggy frock coats and soiled white vests, and his black cravat was always wrenched to one side. He shuffled around the *Tribune* Building, the very picture of the absent-minded scholar who has just mislaid something important but can't remember what it is, with clippings and galley proofs pinned to his lapels like a walking bulletin board.

"Uncle Horace" talked endlessly—on lecture platforms, at any and all rallies of progressive causes, at social gatherings. William Cullen Bryant may have been journalism's number one dignitary, but Greeley was its torchbearer. Social, political, and economic progress obsessed him, sometimes in the Utopian terms set forth by the communal Brook Farm, by Albert Brisbane's collectivism, by Karl Marx's communism, by Margaret Fuller's feminism, by William Henry Channing's socialism. He devoutly believed that America was destined to be Utopia, if men would only open their minds. Youth never had a more enthusiastic champion, and his advice to "go west . . . and grow up with the country" had a deeper meaning than appeared on the surface. Old as he was, Horace wanted done with hidebound tradition, with the complacency of the established order. Had he been able to channel his enthusiasms into a more disciplined way of thinking, he might have been the greatest American of the nineteenth century—but then he wouldn't have been "Uncle Horace."

Perhaps the greatest newspaperman of the lot was the hard-driving perfectionist Charles A. Dana, editor in chief of the *Sun*. President Lincoln had employed his mercilessly probing mind as an Assistant Secretary of War who roved the battle fronts and acted as the President's incorruptible eyes and ears; he was rightly regarded at various army headquarters as Lincoln's chief spy, and it was on his recommendation, during the long stumbling campaign against Vicksburg, that General Grant was kept in command, and later at Chattanooga that General Rosecrans was sacked. As editor of the *Sun,* Dana was equally the hard taskmaster of his city room. *Sun* reporters worked from twelve to sixteen hours a day every day, six days a week. When they returned from an important assignment, they were cross-examined by the editor himself, who then read their copy and called them on the carpet again if he suspected that some angle had not been explored, some bit of color or human-interest shading had been passed over. As Joseph Pulitzer later commented, Dana was more interested in the news around the news than a mere orderly recital of facts. To Dana, the *Sun's* historian wrote, "Life was not a mere procession of elections, legislatures, theatrical performances, murders and

lectures. Life was everything—a new kind of apple, a
crying child on the curb, a policeman's epigram, the
exact weight of a candidate for President, the latest
style in whiskers, the origin of a new slang expression,
the idiosyncrasies of the City Hall clock, a strange
fourmaster in the harbor, a vendetta in Mulberry Bend
—everything was fish to the great net of Dana's mind."
If Bennett Senior broadened the meaning of news,
Dana labored for reporting in depth, to use a term he
would have deplored. "Be interesting," was his command to the *Sun* city room. He also cautioned against
haste, and *Sun* stories often read like essays composed
by educated gentlemen, which most *Sun* reporters
were. Dana was an exacting connoisseur of grammar,
and men were fired simply for writing "none are" or
using the word "balance" instead of "remainder." He
was probably the toughest editor who ever presided
over a New York newspaper, but as Henry Watterson,
the great Kentucky editor, wrote, Dana was the "most
accomplished of all American journalists . . . what he
did not know about a newspaper was scarcely worth
knowing."

Young Bennett moved into this select and seasoned
company with all the confidence in the world, primed
with a youthful arrogance that allowed him to take his
place among "a batch of reverend seigniors," as a
contemporary wrote, without feeling in the least abashed.

"Many a sidelong glance of amused tolerance they
cast his way as he entered the lists," but he ignored them
with a fine disdain.

If he could not match their years and experience,
Dana's editorial grasp, Greeley's endless enthusiasm,
Bryant's prestige, or Raymond's intellect, he would
outdo them in sheer vigor, enterprise, and originality.

During the four years of the interregnum, while his

father was still alive and exerting considerable influence as his "adviser," he demonstrated an innate capacity for the job he had inherited. He had little or no writing talent, such as had enabled his father to make the *Herald* editorial columns sizzle with invective, and no experience as a working newspaperman. Yet he had several attributes of a great newspaper executive: a nose for news and, better yet, the ability to anticipate or make it himself; a willingness to spend large amounts of money and effort to get what he wanted; a determination to accept responsibility—in fact, to insist upon it. Even in his harum-scarum youth these tendencies were evident; the born editor survived through drinking bouts, amorous escapades, sporting ventures, and brainless antics in high and low society, even though he could easily have abandoned his duties and given himself up to a life of total pleasure.

Early in his career as editor and publisher he made the decision that he would not become one of those lackluster heirs, examples of whom were plentiful all around him, who supinely let the family business slip through their fingers. Bennett Junior, in brief, had a backbone.

"It was the contention of many who worked immediately under Bennett," Albert Stevens Crockett recalled in his memoirs (*When James Gordon Bennett Was Caliph of Bagdad*), "that if he had been born with his own way to make instead of having come into the world with a gold spoon in his mouth, he would have achieved real greatness. But if ever a man was his own worst enemy, that man was James Gordon Bennett the Second. Much of his life he seemed to be a creature of unrestrained desires. If impulse called he obeyed, and no rule existed but to be broken. A habit of never brooking contradiction, the awe, if not fear, which he

inspired in most of those who drew his pay, the possession of an almost unlimited income which made
it possible to pay up, if not in kind, at least in quantity,
for any damage unwittingly or witlessly done to repu-
tations or to property—these seemed to give him
something like assurance that he could indulge his bent
or whim to the utmost . . . damn the consequences!"
Thus, Crockett believed, he "came to be looked upon
as the Czar of a newspaper Russia, or, perhaps, the
Mikado of a journalistic Japan that for comedy rivalled
the mythical domain portrayed by Gilbert and Sullivan."

Mikado-ish was exactly the word for his behavior
on succeeding his father. The elder Bennett, to his
employees, had generally been courteous and consider-
ate, "a man of explosive temper but kindly heart,"
who had been through the mill himself and had a
certain respect for the working newspaperman.

Bennett Junior's attitude, predictably, was considerably less sympathetic. His manner was that of an
aristocrat with a genial contempt for his hirelings. He
considered that their brains were his property, and
whatever they did was merely a reflection of his guiding genius. "I can hire all the brains I want for twenty-
five dollars a week," he frequently proclaimed. He
could be generous, even democratic on occasion, particularly with a few drinks in him, but he was always
the Mikado with a Lord High Executioner waiting to
lop off the heads of any disloyal or incompetent subjects.

With all his lordliness, there could be detected the
defiance, the well-concealed sense of inferiority of a man
who had taken a high place without earning it. Men
of excessive brilliance tended to make him feel uncom-
fortable; thus he named as his successor as managing

editor of the *Herald* not the best available man, but Thomas B. Connery, "a mild and gentle individual, entirely at his master's service." His right-hand man was Edward Townsend Flynn, the ex-office boy whom he had known since his early teens, whose loyalty could not be doubted.

Immediately after assuming control of the property, he established a system of espionage in the *Herald* and *Telegram* offices which introduced the atmosphere of a Byzantine court to the white-marble building at Broadway and Ann. All employees were ordered to write fitness reports on their colleagues. Many refused to do this, but those who complied obviously were willing to spy on their fellows and Bennett made full and contemptuous use of them. The tattletales and office politicians were known around the newspaper as "the White Mice," and their nibblings and squeakings, whether the master was in New York or elsewhere in the world, played an important role in the paper's management from then until its proprietor's death.

It would seem that Bennett lived in eternal fear of a palace revolution, or at least some lesser betrayal. Stephen Fiske, who knew him better than most and was utterly frank in writing about him, said his suspicion of other men's motives verged on the psychotic. "By nature and training," the playwright and critic wrote, "he is too suspicious to trust his friends, and he makes enemies unconsciously of those who would be, and have been, most truly devoted to him, by regarding all mankind as a band of conspirators organized to influence the *Herald* for their own purposes." In this suspicion of men's motives, at least, he had absorbed something of his father's teachings. The *Herald*, as an extremely influential and independent organ, was constantly the focus of attempts at manipulation

by political factions and financial interests. Objectivity
and non-involvement were the guiding principles of
the elder Bennett, who was determined that the *Herald*
would be no one's mouthpiece except his own. He had
built its success on an uninhibited coverage of the
news, favoring no one but the reader. So-called friends
and well-wishers full of advice were a newspaper publisher's worst enemies.

The younger Bennett may have dismayed Fiske and
other friends by his strident refusal to be influenced by
them, but in adopting something of his father's saw-
toothed policy of isolation—except in his editorial attitude toward Fifth Avenue society—he was following a
wise course.

Many of the men working in the *Herald* editorial
department had grown bent and gray in his father's
service, but he showed them scant respect. He would
rake a veteran editor over the coals as readily as the
newest cub on the payroll. Undoubtedly he sensed that
if there was any resentment of his easy ascent to editorship, any snide comment on his missteps, it would come
from the professionally hard-boiled and ostentatiously
cynical men of the city room, rather than the clerks and
mechanics of the other departments. Here was the place
to apply the knout and show who was the boss.

Soon after he assumed full authority, he gathered
the editorial staff together and told them, in a few
hard-bitten words, that he meant to have the final
and decisive word on everything that went into the
papers.

"I want you fellows to remember," he proclaimed,
"that I am the only one to be pleased. If I want the
Herald to be turned upside down, it must be turned
upside down."

For all his roistering, he evidently had devoted

more than a little thought to what he wanted to do as an editor and what he expected of the *Herald* (the function of the *Evening Telegram* being merely to make money) as a newspaper.

He was determined to preserve its eminence in the field of reporting the news and telling it crisply, objectively, with none of the *Sun's* essays at journalistic literature, but he knew it could not simply stand on its merits. The make-up of its pages was revamped to make them more attractive typographically, more readable, catchier and cleaner. The writing, in the issues after he took control, was tighter and more vivid.

Above all, he intended to make the *Herald* a constant surprise to its readers. If he had a motto, it was "Keep them guessing." He aimed to *make* news, rather than wait around to report it. News making can be a costly enterprise, but he was willing to foot the bills. His intention of pioneering in that direction was signified shortly after he assumed the managing editorship of the *Herald*. At his direction a European correspondent cabled the full transcript of the speech made by King William of Prussia in which the Austrian peace terms were first outlined, although the cable tolls mounted to $7000 in gold.

Just as his father made use of the telegraph in its infancy, Bennett Junior began employing the Atlantic cable, whose transmission was perfected only in 1866, to widen his newspaper's horizons and encourage Americans to take an interest in European affairs. He was the first American editor—largely, perhaps, because of his upbringing and education abroad —to explore the international scene in any detail.

The *Herald* was also expensively alert on the domestic scene, paying almost any price to beat its competitors. Thus it scored one of the great beats in journalistic history on the massacre of Custer and his squadron of the Seventh Cavalry on the Little Big Horn. It came about this way: the Dakota Territory correspondent of the *Herald* was Colonel Clement A. Lounsberry, editor of the Bismarck *Tribune,* one of whose reporters, Mark Kellogg, was the only newspaperman to accompany the Custer column. Kellogg thus was an ex-officio correspondent of the *Herald.* He was killed along with Custer and 276 troopers when the Sioux attacked the isolated squadron.

On the night of July 5, 1876, Custer's supply ship, the *Far West,* steamed into Bismarck with several officers who bore news of Custer's ghastly defeat.

Colonel Lounsberry organized his coverage with speed and efficiency. First he established himself at the telegraph office and started writing his account of the battle on the Little Big Horn. One copy was sent to the New York *Herald,* the other was rushed, take by take, to his own office. His reporters rounded up everyone on the *Far West* who could supply news of the Custer tragedy and brought them to the telegraph office to tell their stories.

He worked twenty-four hours straight, filed 50,000 words which filled fourteen columns of the *Herald* in fly-speck type. The War Department denounced the story as a fabrication, but the *Herald* stuck to its guns and beat every other paper in the country by four days. Telegraph tolls amounted to $3000, and Colonel Lounsberry was paid a well-earned $2500, but it would have been a bargain at twice the cost.

Bennett organized a fleet of steam-driven cutters to meet ships "some distance at sea" and outrun his rivals' slower-moving boats back to New York with the news. When the Grand Duke Alexis of Russia came over on the frigate *Svetlana,* a *Herald* cutter intercepted the Russian warship several miles off Sandy Hook shortly after midnight and brought back exclusive interviews. For a time he experimented with balloons to speed news coverage, but abandoned the project when they were found unreliable, likely to drift miles away from their destination. In his first years, wrote Frederic Hudson, the *Herald's* former managing editor, Bennett Junior showed himself to be "as impulsive, energetic and fearless as his father," and eagerly ambitious to expand on Bennett Senior's dictum that the function of a newspaper was "not to educate but to startle."

The *Herald* was said to be making $750,000 a year in net profit, and the younger Bennett intended to plow back a good share of it—while not, of course, skimping on the luxuries and the lordly gestures he afforded himself. But making or anticipating news took imagination and enterprise as well as large amounts of money. Even those who suffered from his autocratic temperament, his eccentric whims, and casual brutalities had to concede that he possessed those qualities. "He knew how to make news," Albert Stevens Crockett said, "not by the simple and unsatisfying process of creating it out of whole cloth, but by starting something that would find an echo in the popular imagination and stimulate a demand for more."

With a dozen rivals snapping at its heels, the *Herald* had to be kept limber and inventive or the pack would bring it down. Its circulation was averaging around 60,000 copies daily, even though it was the highest-priced paper on the street. Once a penny paper, it now sold for five cents, generally running to ten or twelve pages; the *Times* and *Tribune* both sold for four cents and were eight-page papers, while the four-page *Sun* was priced at two cents.

To the men who worked for him, young Bennett was a creature from another world with his bristling dragoon's mustache, his imperious manner, his extravagances and perversities. Rich and powerful as his father had become, Bennett Senior had always been regarded as a fellow newspaperman. The younger Bennett was always the autocrat—benevolent at times, insufferable at others. A *Herald* man checking in for the day's work never knew whether, by the time his long day ended, he might be given a bonus or a raise, fired, denounced by a spying colleague, sent to Brooklyn exile, or told to catch the next steamer for Europe. At least it was never dull around that shop.

Joseph I. C. Clarke, an Irishman who subsequently was promoted to night editor, covered an outing given Grand Duke Alexis at Governor's Island with "all the smart people of New York" attending. Clarke knew that society people under Bennett Junior's regime were to be treated with respect, unlike the satirical treatment ordained by his father, but some Celtic imp squatting on his shoulder when he came back to the office to write his story prompted him to describe the affair in somewhat disrespectful terms. He was particularly amused by the fact that only one carriage was provided to convey the ducal party up a steep hill, while the New York socialites were forced to plod along on foot. Clarke, in describing the scene, quoted a couplet he recalled from his Irish youth:

"Them that's rich can ride in chaises;
 But them that's poor must walk, be Jasus."

Next day Bennett—the Commodore, as he insisted on being addressed by his hirelings—called Clarke on the carpet. He pointed out that the people attending the outing were "all very well off" and "some of them are hopping mad."

Clarke shrugged and said, "I only saw the funny side of it."

Bennett himself suddenly saw the humor of it, laughed uproariously, and said, "Well, don't do it again."

A short time later Clarke was promoted to writing editorials, and one day the Commodore told him that one of his pieces had caught Bennett Senior's eye as "the best editorial that has appeared in the *Herald* in four years." Clarke was given a raise from $40 to $50 a week, a large salary for a newspaperman in those days.

Bennett, he said, was at his best presiding over the editorial "council" held every afternoon just after lunch. "He sat under his father's bust, and the contrast between his staff and himself was striking, often amusing, some of the editors frankly old, others rather faded beaux and bucks, but all anxious to know what he wanted them to think but through one mental defect or another not quite able to grasp it. The day after my promotion I was introduced by him to these elders . . . whereat the editors smiled sadly and looked down their noses.

"It became Mr. Bennett's habit to send for me before the Council meeting, and give me subject after subject for editorials, often indicating the line for treatment. He was bright, resourceful, and generally charming through this period. . . ."

Clarke recalled that Bennett once tried to explain himself by saying, " 'I have two natures. One derives from my Scotch father and the other from my Irish mother—' meaning to justify his turns of cautious calculation with his impulsive outbreaks of action. His hot temper came from both parents. Unstable in many things, in others whimsical to the point of extravagance, close and generous, optimist and pessimist, unrelenting and forgiving, sparkling with joy or deep in the blues, he was a constant puzzle to everyone about him, yet endowed with the perception of great things; prompt, open-handed and broad in their execution, and holding on grimly to the idea that the *Herald* must be kept at the front."

The nighttime Bennett was likely to be a far different creature from the sober, rather strait-laced daytime executive. After a long session of dining and drinking with his friends at Delmonico's, an alcoholic inspiration frequently would seize him and he would descend on the *Herald* city room, silk hat askew, cigar jutting out of his mouth, breezing in on a champagne-scented cloud. Such visitations, Clarke said, were "justly dreaded by those responsible at the time for going to press." Clarke by then had been promoted to night editor, with the task of meeting deadlines according to a schedule laid down with military precision by his employer. "When he swept in with a breeze of good humor as of him who has dined well, and complimented everybody in sight, some strange idea as to the forthcoming issue was apt to develop."

One midnight, when the forms were already locked up, Bennett blew in to make a last-minute correction in an editorial denouncing Tammany Hall and all its works. He told Clarke he wanted to insert the sentence, "This is the last dying kick of the Tammany anaconda."

Clarke tactfully tried to dissuade him by pointing out that a snake couldn't kick.

"That's what my friends uptown say, that an anaconda can't kick—got no legs," the glassy-eyed publisher agreed.

"Suppose you say 'last dying squirm' instead," Clarke suggested.

"No, no, that's the fun of it. Squirm is disagreeable

but I want to give Tammany a kick." Bennett began chanting loudly, "Stick to kick . . . stick to kick . . . stick to kick."

In the *Herald* editorial of that morning, the Tammany anaconda performed the impossible—and kicked.

Red-haired Edward Flynn, as well as night editor Clarke, had to bear up under the young tycoon's wayward impulses, which were almost always induced by alcohol. For all his experience with the bottle, young Bennett was not a hardened toper. He could not handle large amounts of liquor without being knocked galley-west—which was fortunate in a way, since it reduced his alcoholic intake and the consequent toll on his mind and body. Sometimes a half-dozen glasses of champagne or a few snifters of brandy would render him as drunk as a chimney sweep.

One night he was dining at Delmonico's with Edwin Booth, the actor; Jim Fisk, the fat, bejeweled speculator then engaged with Jay Gould in tapping the Erie Railway for all it was worth, and Ed Flynn, who as usual kept a nervous tally of the drinks his friend and employer bolted down. Tonight Bennett was well over the quota that discretion allowed. A fire alarm was sounded nearby, and at Bennett's insistence the whole group galloped down the block and arrived on the blazing scene just as the pumpers were going into action.

In his best executive manner Bennett began shouting orders to the firemen, and when they did not heed his instructions, he ran over to a company struggling with the snakelike contortions of a hose. A fire captain ordered him away from there, but Bennett continued bellowing unheeded orders and interfering with the fire-fighting activities. Flynn, Booth, and Fisk meanwhile stood at a safe distance and watched the fun.

Finally one of the firemen bawled to his comrades, "Let's give that drunken bastard a taste of the hose!"

The hose was turned on Bennett, knocking him flat and drenching his finery.

His companions then hauled the volunteer fireman, soaking and senseless, off to a cab stand and took him home.

Next day Flynn was summoned to his employer's office. Bennett was sneezing and trying to nurse a desperate hangover.

"What the hell did I do last night?" he asked Flynn.

"Made a big fool of yourself."

"How so?"

"You got in the way of the firemen and tried to tell them how to do their job, which they know a great deal more about than you do."

"All right," said Bennett, "order a rubber overcoat for every man in the department and send the bill to me." He gave way to another voluptuous sneeze. "I was never so wet in all my life."

Thanks to his subsidiary career as an international yachtsman, Bennett was often chosen to show the livelier members of the English aristocracy around New York when they came over on visits. There was no better guide, certainly, to the fleshpots and deadfalls, from Delmonico's downtown to the riproaring Tenderloin uptown. Many a visitor went away with an impression of New York as one gigantic blur of gurgling bottles and shapely limbs.

One such visiting notable was A. P. Primrose, the future Earl of Rosebery, a pink-cheeked, fair-haired young fellow about Bennett's age, of whom his tutors at Eton commented, "a portentously wise youth, not, however, deficient in fun." His oft-stated ambitions were to become Prime Minister of Great Britain, win the Derby, and marry an heiress. Everyone thought he must be joking but in due time he married a Rothschild daughter, saw his horses win the Derby three times, and eventually became Her Majesty's chief minister. With Bennett in charge, Primrose trod the primrose paths of New York, and as Don C. Seitz (*The James Gordon Bennetts*) described the hectic explorations of the city's night life, "The two made New York glow together." One night they showed up at the *Herald* city room just as night editor Clarke was putting the paper to bed. Both, of course, were tipsy as lords. After the routine in the editorial department was shattered, Clarke said, "from all over the building I heard of their luminous progress from composing room to press room for an hour or more."

The two young men then adjourned to Sandy Spencer's bar, an all-night place frequented by newspapermen at Fulton and Broadway, where they flipped each other for gold sovereigns, "growing merrier all the time and consuming their winnings."

It was the beginning of a long friendship, which may have put a few hobnails on the Primrose liver but resulted in the constant publicizing of his political career in the *Herald,* which in those years was almost as influential in London as it was in New York.

Lord Houghton, who was Monckton Milnes to the English literary world, was another visitor to the *Herald* editorial rooms, more extinguished than distinguished by the time Bennett towed him into the building. When Bennett appeared, his long-suffering night editor recalled, "he appeared to be lugging or dragging some limp body under his arm. He deposited it on a chair in the room where it sat inert. . . . He seemed scarcely alive."

"A bit winded, that's all," Bennett blithely explained.

His charge came to a short time later, and Clarke, who had read and valued the elderly poet's verses, expressed his appreciation to the brandified Lord Houghton.

Bennett blurted out, "I am glad you know him, who he is, who he was and what he has done and all that, because I don't. Most people keep calling him 'Lord Houston' as if he was the Lord of Houston Street!"

The publisher obviously was ill-equipped for the role of cultural ambassador, but Lord Houghton was so pleased by Clarke's admiration for his writings that "a gleam of life appeared in his faded eyes" and he was able to leave the building under his own power.

Despite this evidence of the collapsibility of literary talent, Bennett kept the *Herald* well stocked with notable writers, who contributed essays or travel pieces to the editorial pages and the Sunday sections. Ill-read as he was, Bennett appreciated the circulation-pulling quality of names like Mark Twain, Walt Whitman, Charles Edward Russell, Charles Nordhoff and Robert Hunt Lyman—all of whom were contributors or staff members at one time or another. Specialists of all kinds, in fact, were sought out and handsomely paid. Lord Beresford, a captain and later an admiral in the British Navy, served as Egyptian correspondent of the *Herald*. To cover the Wagnerian concerts at Bayreuth, Bennett engaged a number of leading German writers.

Mark Twain contributed to the *Herald* from 1868 until his death, the younger Bennett signing him to a contract only a few weeks after he took over as publisher. Twain had just returned from the travels which ultimately produced *Innocents Abroad* when Bennett asked him to come down to the *Herald* offices. Still more the roving journalist than the literary titan he was to become, Twain was highly pleased by the connection and was faithful to the *Herald* to the end of his days. On January 24, 1868, he wrote in his diary, "This is a good week for me. I stopped in the *Herald* office as I came through New York to see the boys on the staff and young James Gordon Bennett asked me to write twice a week, impersonally, for the *Herald,* and said if I would I might have full swing, and about anybody and anything I wanted to. I said I must have the very fullest possible swing, and he said, 'All right.' I said, 'It's a contract—' and that settled the matter."

In the case of another literary genius, neither the *Herald* nor the genius fared so well. A weedy youth of nineteen applied for work at the *Herald* city desk, introducing himself as Stephen Crane. He was told that he could attach himself to the staff on a space-rate basis—that is, he would be given assignments or could dig up his own stuff, but he would be paid only for what the paper published.

It was obvious to the city editor from the start that young Crane wasn't cut out for the newspaper business. Few embryonic novelists, in fact, have found the newspaper business anything but a dull grind, eventually ruinous to the imagination. When sent out on a story, Crane would come back with brilliant descriptions of how fire horses "kicked gray ice out of the gutter into silvery angles"; of how a fat alderman who looked like a "rural soup tureen" would grunt with disgust "whenever ash from his cigar bounced on his vest of blood and black"; of a street cleaner, bowled over by a horse, sending up "a jet of violet, fastidious curses." Generally, though, the butchers on the city desk slashed away such jeweled phrases.

Crane eventually was told to go away, take up some honest trade and forget about being a writer. He disregarded the *Herald* editors' advice, and some years later produced *The Red Badge of Courage*.

Neither of the Bennetts conceived of the *Herald* as a crusader. Both were quite willing that Horace Greeley should pose as the guardian of national morality. The undeniable fact that during the years of the first Grant administration all the "great active forces of society" were "one dirty cesspool of vulgar corruption," as Henry Adams put it, called for little comment or criticism from the *Herald*.

Just at the time Bennett Junior was spending thousands on cable tolls, supervising a brilliant foreign correspondence, and sending intrepid young reporters into the remotest reaches of Asia and Africa, the biggest story of the day was stewing away under his nose. During those first years of his regime, Boss Tweed's Tammany Hall ring was brazenly looting the city of millions of dollars each year, Jim Fisk and Jay Gould were stealing the Erie stockholders blind through the issuance of $53,000,000 in watered stock, and the same two rascals precipitated a nationwide financial panic by cornering the nation's gold supply in September of 1869. The looting operation really went into high gear when the Tweed Ring and the Erie plunderbund combined forces, upon which the combination "wielded the influence of a great corporation with a capital of a hundred millions; it controlled the politics of the first city of the New World; it sent its representatives to the Senate of the state, and numbered among its agents the judges of the courts. Compact, disciplined and reckless, it knew its own power and would not scruple to use it."

All this was going on while the free and supposedly

independent press of New York largely stood by and watched. The only outspoken opposition to the Tweed Ring came from Greeley's *Tribune,* and in those prosperous, amoral times old Horace was regarded as a common scold, a crank and a spoilsport. The *World* was then a Tammany organ, the *Post* was tapping the Tweed payroll for $5000 a month, and even the *Times'* sense of rectitude was kept firmly in check. One of the *Times'* three directors was the partner of Boss Tweed in a printing company, and only after this man died early in 1870 were the *Times* editors permitted to begin digging for the facts which ultimately—but much too late—were published and resulted in Tweed's downfall.

As for the *Herald,* like Dana's *Sun* it preferred to scoff and satirize, to loose its clever barbs and editorial innuendoes, but never to set off the explosion that was needed to destroy Tweed and expose the activities of Fisk and Gould under the judicial protection of Tammany Hall and the curious tolerance of the Grant administration.

A hint as to the reason for the Bennetts' forbearance was provided by Stephen Fiske, who wrote that their *Evening Telegram* "realized a large profit . . . by publishing the municipal advertising, under the Tweed regime." Without that advertising, in fact, the *Telegram* might not have been able to continue publishing without a large deficit. "And here," wrote Fiske, Bennett Junior "first displayed his Scotch instincts for financiering."

For all its dash in covering foreign wars and exploring dark continents, the *Herald* backed away from exposing the machinations leading up to the Fisk-Gould gold corner and the horrendous crash of Black Friday, September 24, 1869.

Jay Gould, a speculative genius if ever there was one, had conceived the plot and carried it out with consummate skill. At the time there was only $15,000,000 worth of gold circulating in the United States, with the United States Treasury holding back another $100,000,000 and controlling the price by releasing certain amounts of it when the quotations at the Gold Room off Wall Street rose too high. Through dubious "certified" checks issued by a bank he controlled, Gould, with Fisk as his chief lieutenant, began buying up large amounts of gold and driving up the price in the summer of 1869. The tricky part of this carefully laid plan, of course, was that the government could bring the price down any time it chose. To guard against this, Gould cultivated the friendship of Abel R. Corbin, who was married to President Grant's sister, and through him the acquaintance of the President himself. Grant was persuaded that the Treasury should withhold its gold, allow the price to shoot up and benefit (so Gould argued) the whole American economy.

Thanks to Grant's never-quite-explained orders not to release the government's gold, the remunerative connivance of Abel Corbin and Assistant United States Treasurer Daniel Butterfield, and the panicky reaction of the Gold Room's speculators, Gould managed to drive up the price to 160 (from 131) before Grant ordered the Treasury to release its bullion and deflate the market on Black Friday. Hundreds of men were ruined in the wild speculation, among them Jim Fisk, whom Gould had kept in ignorance of the essential details of his plot. Gould managed to dump his gold just before the Treasury order, about which he had been tipped in advance, sent the price spiraling down. He emerged from the wreckage with a profit estimated at $11,000,000.

Obviously Gould could not have pulled off his coup without that indispensable pipeline to the White House. Yet no one dared to investigate the extent of the involvement of President Grant and members of his family. Was it plain stupidity or greed which had permitted the Administration to fall in with the gold conspiracy? "Everyone dreaded to press inquiry," Henry Adams wrote, because "they feared finding out too much."

On September 29, five days after Black Friday, the *Herald* was given its chance to dig into the scandal through the soreheadedness of one of its leading figures. Jim Fisk, enraged because he was being blamed for the panic even though he was one of the heavy losers (Gould subsequently showed his partner how to recoup by welshing on his transactions, and reportedly shared his winnings with him), summoned George Crouch, a *Herald* financial reporter, to an interview that night. Fisk told Crouch that he was sick of being blamed and "I can make Rome howl for somebody else besides me." The nub of Fisk's revelations to the *Herald* reporter was contained in these explosive statements:

"Members of the President's family were in with us. The President himself was interested with us in the corner. . . . It was planned by Jay Gould and Abel R. Corbin, President Grant's brother-in-law. Why, damn it! old Corbin married into Grant's family for the purpose of working the thing in that direction. . . . We risked our millions on the assurance that the government would not interfere. Grant got scared, however, when the crisis came, and gave Boutwell [the Secretary of the Treasury] instructions to sell."

When Crouch brought this story back to the office, Bennett and his editors knew they were juggling a very hot potato. Fisk's charges, after all, were unsupported. Apparently Bennett consulted with his father and they decided to hold up on the story. Fisk then gave the same story to the *Sun,* which also refrained from publishing his charges against the President but did venture to assert that Fisk and Gould had used Corbin "as a cat's paw between the bull clique and Washington."

The *Herald,* trying to find some shred of confirmation in Fisk's charges, detailed Crouch to accompany him to Corbin's house. The reporter waited outside while Fisk went in and was closeted with the President's brother-in-law. Crouch then swore out an affidavit that he had seen Fisk enter the Corbin house and stay there for an hour. Another reporter then was dispatched to interview Corbin, who denied everything that was alleged against him. Corbin also declared that "Fisk and Gould have never been to my house since Gould called last summer when the President was here." The *Herald* thus was able to prove him a liar, at least on that score. It also interviewed Gould, who admitted having given Corbin a check for $25,000 to "secure the government's non-intervention."

Finally, on October 8, the *Herald* published the sensational interview with Fisk but, wary of the libel laws, made it plain that it considered the financier's charges of Grant's direct complicity a dastardly lie. "The only thing the President had to do with the 'ring' was to defeat its ends," the *Herald* maintained, and devoted its energies to belaboring Gould as the "great, gold-gobbling gorilla of Wall Street" and Fisk as a "ring-tailed financial orang-utang." In the ensuing congressional investigation, which was notable for its pussy-footing approach to the high personages involved (neither the President nor his wife, for instance, was summoned as a witness), Grant was more or less cleared of everything but a remarkable somnolence, and it developed that his brother-in-law, instead of passing along part of the proceeds, had pocketed them himself.

Through all the incredible follies, the high and low comedy of the several years when Fisk, Gould, Tweed and their associates were looting the city, the *Herald* kept its sense of humor and maintained its reputation for having the best journalistic nose for scandal in the business. If it failed to expose anyone, at least it never hesitated to heap scorn and ridicule on the plunderers. Its weapon was not the scalpel but the comedian's bladder. When Jim Fisk became involved in the fatal triangle with his mistress Josie Mansfield and his ex-protégé Edward S. Stokes, the *Herald* broke the story first, satirically identifying Josie as "Helen of Troy," Fisk as "Menelaus" and Stokes as "Paris" under the headline:

FISKIANA
How Fisk and Stokes Quarreled, Fought
and Did Not Bleed About Lady
Fair with Jet Black Hair
THE WRATH OF ERIE, THE HUMORS OF STOKES
—WAR TO THE KNIFE ALL AROUND

And when Boss Tweed's daughter Mary was showered with presents worth $700,000 by Fisk, Gould, various contractors doing business with the city, and other benevolent parties at her wedding June 1, 1871, Bennett Senior wrote in one of his last editorials: "What a testimony of the loyalty, the royalty, and the abounding East Indian resources of Tammany Hall! Was there a Democracy to compare with 'thy Democracy' in glory, power, and equal rights under the sun? Never!"

But it wasn't the Bennetts' lofty disdain or their most cutting sarcasms and stinging satires which brought the Tweed machine down in ruins. That took a blunter instrument than the *Herald's* rapier. The *Times,* under a new management, secured proof of Tweed's thievery from a pair of the Boss' disgruntled former confederates and published the documents which led to wholesale indictments. Justice was executed on the corpulent person of Jim Fisk by Edward Stokes, who shot him to death. As for Jay Gould—the boldest and brainiest of the lot—he prospered to the end of his days and wound up with a hundred million dollars. In later years he and Bennett Junior became the bitterest of business and personal enemies, and many times the latter must have regretted not having attacked Gould when he was most vulnerable, just after the collapse of the Tweed Ring and his consequent ouster from Erie.

The *Herald,* though it was the most prosperous and widely read paper in New York, simply had no cutting edge. Bennett Senior had designed it as a medium of entertainment, and his son, bold though he was in developing that function, never got around to making it anything else. In the end, perhaps, it was that lack of fundamental purpose of which it sickened unto death . . . newspapers, like people, have to have a reason for living. . . .

Early in 1872, in his seventy-seventh year, the paper's thirty-seventh year, the *Herald's* founder was as fragile as an old stick, with the same grayish color. Bennett Senior had been ailing, fading, for the past four or five years—ever since, in fact, he had given up active management of the *Herald.* That winter Mrs. Bennett and his daughter Jeanette returned to the United States and stayed with him for several months. With the coming of spring, Mrs. Bennett, a generation younger than her husband, yearned for the vernal fragrance of the Paris boulevards. She and her daughter returned to Europe early in May.

Attended only by his servants, his son busy working and playing down in the city, Bennett Senior was stricken with a cerebral hemorrhage just before dawn on the morning of June 1. The stroke was almost instantly fatal.

Only a few days before that—bitter as he had been since youth against Catholicism—he had returned to the Church, apparently having sensed the approach of death. But he had not sent for his son. They were closer in those last years than they had ever been, but it was an affection, a mutual respect that held sentiment and the fashionable nonsense of lachrymose deathbed scenes in contempt. Bennett Senior had been pridefully solitary all his life, and except for that last-minute summons for a father-confessor he was content to meet death alone. He had already provided that his son was to have sole ownership and control of all the Bennett properties, with the provision that he was to take care of whatever needs his sister might have.

A contemporary remembered Bennett Junior "tall and slim, in black, standing beside the casket."

Horace Greeley, along with Dana of the *Sun* and most of the other New York daily newspaper publishers, was among the pallbearers, but his farewell salute in the *Tribune's* editorial columns was characteristically outspoken: "He developed the capacities of journalism in a most wonderful manner, but he did so by degrading its character. He made the newspaper powerful, but he also made it odious." Other colleagues were kindlier. To the *Sunday News,* the elder Bennett was "the greatest journalist the world ever produced." The *Times* cautiously commented that "as a successful journalist and man of business, James Gordon Bennett will be remembered among the representative men of the city of New York." The *Sun* blessed his memory for having liberated the newspaper from the inhibiting influence of "sects, parties, cliques and what is called society."

To the eminent lawyer, moralist, and diarist George Templeton Strong, whose journals provided the most biting commentary yet uncovered on his era, the Bennett funeral was a disgusting exhibition. "Old James Gordon Bennett was buried today under a volley of eulogistic paragraphs and resolutions of dolour and deep affliction," Strong wrote in his diary for June 13, 1872. "Flags at half-mast! This community is devoid of moral sense. It has proclaimed an extra Beatitude of greater influence than all the others together, namely, 'Blessed are the smart.'"

Strong saw little hope for his successor as a standard-bearer of civic morality. Bennett Junior, to him, was simply a young man who "makes money by printing the advertisements of abortionists" and "a leader of fashion in the Belmont Clique."

Less than a year later that worldly young man learned by cable that his mother was dying in Sachsen, Germany, the sudden and hopeless victim of cancer. It was the first her son heard that she had even been ill, the Bennetts being a proudly non-communicative family. Mrs. Bennett, whose "influence upon her son was never very great," as Fiske noted, had asked that neither of her children be told of her condition. Her physicians decided, however, that her son must be informed after she sank into longer and longer periods of unconsciousness.

Perhaps many clues to the instability of her son's character might have been found in her decision to face death in solitude, as her husband had. Wealth often divided American families, largely because of battles over inheritances, but the Bennetts were a special case. Certainly money was not their problem, nor was their

dedication to avoiding each other's company entirely
explained by Mrs. Bennett's decision to live in Europe
while the children were growing up. Bennett Junior
was never "close" to either his father or mother, and in
later years, partly because of his objection to the man
she married, he rarely saw his sister. Somewhere in the
background there were tragic and definitive stresses in
the domestic fabric which might have fascinated an
Ibsen or an O'Neill, or perhaps an Oedipus. If so, the
Bennetts had the decency to keep them well concealed.

Mrs. Bennett, at any rate, died without a last glimpse
of her errant only son. An account of her death was
contained in a letter to the New York *Tribune's* Paris
correspondent from John Bigelow, former editor of
the New York *Times,* who happened to be visiting
Sachsen at the time: "Mrs. J. G. Bennett died here
about three weeks ago, the whole middle part of her
body consumed by a confluent cancer. Like her husband,
she died in the arms of mercenaries; she would not
allow her son to be sent for while she was conscious;
and she had long been unconscious of anything when
he did arrive about two hours before she expired. She
would not allow the doctor to speak of her danger,
seemed unwilling to contemplate death, even when he
was standing in her presence. The daughter, who is at
school at Versailles, arrived the day after her mother's
death."

5: The Bennett Expeditionary Forces

During the years between Bennett Junior's ascendancy to the management of his father's newspaper properties and his self-exile to Europe in 1877, a period of slightly less than ten years, the New York *Herald* was undoubtedly the most brilliantly edited, enterprising, and talked-about newspaper in the world. The liberal English weekly *Westminster Review* did not approve wholeheartedly of the *Herald's* editorial policies, but conceded that its news-gathering capacity was unequaled. "Whatever else might be said of the New York *Herald*, it printed *all* the news; that was not then said of any other New York newspaper." Its make-up was livelier, its style was crisper, its tone was more objective, and it bore the stamp of a freewheeling imagination that made readers open their papers eagerly every morning to see what the *Herald* was up to now.

Oswald Garrison Villard, one of Bryant's successors as editor of the liberal *Evening Post*, said its "international reputation" was "unsurpassed by any journal in the world," grudging though his admiration was.

Concerning the impact of the *Herald* in its best years, Villard wrote: "There were years and years when no rival journalists dared to go to bed before seeing a copy of the early edition of the *Herald*, which they picked up in fear and trembling lest they find in it one of those record-breaking stories which made its name as famous as that of 'The Thunderer' [that is, the *Times* of London] in every capital of the globe. . . .

"The truth is that, if the Bennetts, father and son, were short of some of the ordinary moralities, they were the most remarkable news men this country ever produced. The father revolutionized the whole science of news-getting, and the son outdid him by creating exclusive news. He would invest thousands of dollars in a news story, knowing that it might be two years before he could get any return. There must have been thousands spent without any result, but the younger Bennett had learned in his father's school that nothing pays like news. . . .

"Anyone who has had occasion to test those files of the *Herald* knows that they are remarkable historical material, whereas no historian would care to rely upon the daily journalistic records of today [Mr. Villard was writing in 1923, in *Some Newspapers and Newspapermen*]."

Much of Bennett's fame as a publisher and editor—though not nearly enough to suit him—rested on the brief, rather offhand interview he granted on October 27, 1869, in his suite at the Grand Hotel in Paris, where he was taking a breather from the hectic New York of the Fisk-Gould gold conspiracy. That was the day he handed out the most famous, and commendably terse, assignment in newspaper history.

About three o'clock that afternoon a husky, medium-sized young man with penetrating black eyes, a swarthy, determined face, and a piratical mustache knocked on Bennett's door. He was one of the *Herald's* roving correspondents, who went by the name of Henry M. Stanley.

Stanley found the young publisher—both men were then twenty-eight years old—still in bed.

"Who're you?" Bennett demanded, though they had met before.

"My name is Stanley."

"Sit down," Bennett said, bounding out of bed and pulling a robe on. "I have important business on hand for you." When both men were seated, Bennett continued, "Where do you think Livingstone is?"

Stanley said he didn't know, and in response to a further question replied that he had no idea whether or not the celebrated Scottish missionary-doctor-explorer was still alive. The civilized world had seen the last of him almost three years before.

"Well," said Bennett, "I think he is alive, and that he can be found, and I am going to send you to find him."

Stanley, as he later admitted, was stunned. Sending one man to find another in the unmapped and unexplored heart of Central Africa, at great expense, would be playing a long shot no other publisher could possibly consider. "Do you really think I can find Dr. Livingstone?" he later remembered asking. "Do you mean me to go to Central Africa?"

"Yes," Bennett replied, speaking very deliberately. "I mean that you should go and find him wherever you may hear that he is, and get what news you can of him. . . . Perhaps the old man may be in want. Take enough with you to help him should he require it. Of course you will act according to your own plans, and do what you think best—*but find Livingstone!*"

"Have you considered seriously the great expense you are likely to incur on account of this little journey?"

"What will it cost?"

"Burton and Speke's journey to Central Africa [the expedition of Richard Burton and John H. Speke in 1857 to the shores of Lake Tanganyika] cost between three thousand and five thousand pounds [$15,000 to $25,000 at the time] and I fear it cannot be done under twenty-five hundred."

"Well, I will tell you what you will do. Draw a thousand pounds now; and when you have gone through that, draw another thousand, and when that is spent draw another, and when that is finished, draw another thousand, and so on—*but find Livingstone.*"

Overwhelmed, but all the more wary of such a magnificent gesture, Stanley mentioned that he had heard rumors that if Bennett Senior—who, incidentally, knew nothing of his son's decision to outfit an expedition to the African interior—died, his son intended to sell the *Herald,* which might result in cutting off the search. Certainly no other publisher would be likely to carry out the plan.

Stanley said Bennett's eyes shot off blue sparks of anger and determination when the correspondent mentioned that rumor. "Whoever told you that is wrong," Bennett snapped. "There is not enough money in New York City to buy the New York *Herald.* My father has made it a great paper, but I mean to make it greater. I mean that it shall be a newspaper in the true sense of the word. I mean that it shall publish whatever news will be interesting to the world at no matter what the cost."

Stanley recorded that he "had nothing more to say" on that point; the Bennett presence, "tall, fierce-eyed, imperious," could be most impressive.

Despite the urgency of the mission, Bennett's brief instructions to his explorer-correspondent indicated a rather peripheral approach to the assignment, or more likely they betrayed a lamentable ignorance of geography: "Bagdad will be close on your way to India. Suppose you go there and write up something about the

Euphrates Valley Railroad. Then, when you have come to India, you can go after Livingstone. Probably you will hear by that time that Livingstone is on his way to Zanzibar; but if not, go into the interior and find him, if alive. Get what news of his discoveries you can; and, if you find he is dead, bring all possible proof of his being dead. That is all."

In ultimately carrying out this assignment, Stanley took the rather leisurely approach suggested by his employer and spent fifteen months on various other stories from the day he talked with Bennett in Paris. He wrote travel pieces on Persia and Palestine, covered the splendiferous ceremonies which opened the Suez Canal at Port Said, explored the old battlefields of the Crimean War, and wrote a disapproving account of an orgiastic carnival in Odessa. It wasn't until early in January of 1871 that he finally arrived in Zanzibar to undertake the search for the world's most famous missing person.

That inspired wanderer, Dr. David Livingstone, was the Albert Schweitzer of his age—and perhaps a bit more, to any mind a trifle suspicious of modern saints and the gigantic halo of publicity under which they perform their good works. Livingstone, who was fifty-eight years old in 1871, was a poor Scottish boy who went to work in a textile mill at the age of ten and somehow managed to gain a sufficient education to become a medical missionary. But he was less a doctor ministering to the natives, and much less a mere hymn singer, come to blather at the heathen, than he was an explorer and a scientist. For twenty years he blazed paths through South Africa, crossed the great Kalahari Desert, explored the Zambezi and Lake Ngami, "discovered" and named Victoria Falls. Wherever he went he kept careful geographical, zoological, and botanical records. The great cause that motivated him, however, was the elimination of the traffic in slavery, "the open sore of the world," which he denounced in books, pamphlets, and articles.

In 1865 the Royal Geographical Society persuaded him to undertake the exploration of the watershed between Lakes Tanganyika and Nyasa. Some of his bearers returned to Zanzibar months later with the report that he was dead, and the world mourned prematurely; two years later letters from the missionary-explorer were brought out of the interior. Since then, there had been only silence. Again rumors spread that he was dead. World-wide sympathy for his anti-slavery crusade and the interest he had aroused through his explorations, Africa then being as great an object of curiosity as outer space is today, made him the most fascinating human on earth. Yet no one got around to sending a search party after him until James Gordon Bennett, Jr., whom so many considered a worthless and empty-headed playboy, was seized by his moment of inspiration.

Bennett with his brainstorm and his money, Stanley with his fearlessness and driving determination patently made up, with Livingstone, a trio whose diversity was startling—profligate publisher, ruthless reporter, dedicated humanitarian. The strangeness of this combination was equaled only by the facts surrounding the life of the man who called himself H. M. Stanley, a life that could have occurred, in the picaresque form it took, only in the nineteenth century—and could have been believed only by a generation which wept and suffered through each chapter of a Charles Dickens serial. His youth in particular seemed to have been lifted out of Dickens, with transatlantic contributions by Horatio Alger.

Stanley's life was a struggle almost from the moment of birth. He was the son of Miss Elizabeth Parry, of Denbigh, Wales, and was baptized in the name of John Rowlands, his presumptive father. His mother having fled in shame, he was placed in the care of relatives, who soon wearied of the responsibility and deposited him in the Saint Asaph Union Workhouse, an institution as grim as it sounds. When he was ten years old, his mother visited the workhouse just long enough to drop off a daughter, listed on the records as "a deserted bastard." He would probably have "mildewed in Wales" for the rest of his life, as he later said, except for his reluctance to be beaten. At fifteen he turned on one of the brutes in charge of the workhouse, snatched away his birch rod and beat him senseless, then fled the institution. A short time later he shipped for New Orleans as cabin boy of a sailing packet.

Bullied and abused on the six-week voyage as the lowliest member of the crew, he jumped ship in New Orleans, where he was befriended by a merchant named Henry Morton Stanley. The merchant not only found him a job but informally adopted him after learning the circumstances of his birth. From then on, although the adoption was never registered in the courts, he called himself Henry M. Stanley. He managed a plantation store in Arkansas after his "father's" death. Shortly after the outbreak of the Civil War he enlisted in the Sixth Arkansas Volunteers, which had the great misfortune, eventually, of being thrown into the battle of Shiloh. Stanley was taken prisoner during the last stages of that unscientific grappling in the Mississippi thickets, and was shipped to Camp Douglas, near Chicago, as a guest of the Union Army. The prison camp was one of the North's Andersonvilles, with the prisoners dying by the scores daily in their own filth, ravaged by smallpox and typhoid fever. Union missionaries circulated through the camp persuading the survivors that their only hope was to turn their coats and enlist in the Northern armies. One of those who preferred the label of "galvanized Yankee" to risking death by starvation or disease was the twenty-one-year-old Stanley. He was enrolled in a federal artillery unit, but came down with dysentery and was shipped to a hospital at Harper's Ferry, where he was finally discharged in June of 1862.

Ailing and penniless, he worked for his passage back to England and made his way to his native Denbigh, hoping that he could be reunited with his mother. That poor creature had returned to her family home and was trying to live down her unfortunate past. All she would permit her first-born son was a glimpse through a crack in the door. He was a "disgrace," she hissed at him, and must leave at once. He was never to bother her again.

Somehow, crushed in body and spirit, he survived. The experiences of his youth contributed to the toughness of fiber, the outcast's inner resilience, the determination to get all he could out of the world on his own terms, that eventually carried him to international fame. Having survived this much, he knew the world would never grind him down again.

He worked for his passage back to the United States, and in July of 1864 enlisted in the Union Navy, serving for six months aboard the U.S.S. *Minnesota* while it participated in the blockade of Fort Fisher, North Carolina, the Confederacy's last open port. He attained the rank of "ship's writer," a petty officer charged with keeping the ship's log and other records, and while witnessing the land and sea assaults on Fort Fisher got the idea of describing them in dispatches which various newspapers readily bought for publication. In

January of 1865 the *Minnesota* was sent to Portsmouth, New Hampshire, to be decommissioned. Here Stanley decided to decommission himself also, and severed his connections with the navy. He was now officially a deserter from both the Confederate Army and the Union Navy, a distinction which very few men could claim.

For several years his life was almost incredibly picaresque. He wandered out West, then with two companions undertook an "expedition" to Asia Minor. Near Smyrna one of his friends set fire to and destroyed a native village in a moment of pique. The three men fled into the interior, where thieves robbed them of all of their possessions. The American minister to Turkey supplied them with enough funds to return to the United States.

Now, in 1867, Stanley settled down to the career which was to become, perhaps, the most remarkable in the history of journalism. Signing on as a roving reporter for the St. Louis *Democrat* at fifteen dollars a week, with the usual privilege of selling his stories to other newspapers, he made a name for himself covering General W. S. Hancock's campaign against the Sioux and Cheyenne. He also made a name for a long-haired scout named James Butler (Wild Bill) Hickok, whose career was only slightly less incredible than Stanley's. After a bibulous evening in a post trader's saloon, during which Stanley imbibed much raw whisky and Hickok's tall tales, the correspondent publicized the scout's claim that "I have killed considerably over a hundred" opponents in various gun fights. Before moving on to better things, he helped to establish Hickok's claim to fame as the West's leading gun fighter.

Stanley journeyed to New York in January, 1868, having saved up $3000 from the widespread publication of his western dispatches. The British were outfitting a punitive force under Lord Napier to invade Abyssinia and dethrone King Theodore, who had imprisoned an English missionary and several envoys sent to obtain his release. Stanley wanted to accompany the expedition. When the New York *Tribune* turned him down, he went over to the *Herald* and obtained an interview with Bennett Junior. The latter had just taken over as editor and publisher and was not yet emboldened to speculating large sums on foreign assignments, but it was finally agreed that Stanley would pay his own expenses and the *Herald* would publish whatever it fancied at generous space rates. He followed Napier's long column of English and Irish infantry, Indian Army regiments in red fezzes and green turbans, native cavalry, horse-drawn artillery, and a naval brigade armed with rockets on the march to the Abyssinian capital of Magdala. His vivid descriptions of the capture of Magdala and the sounds of hyenas feasting on the battlefield the night after the victory were the first to be sent from the telegraph station at Suez. And Bennett was so pleased by Stanley's enterprise that he attached him to the *Herald* payroll at $2000 a year.

Subsequently the roving correspondent wrote travel pieces from the Greek islands—then came the summons to Paris and the assignment to find Livingstone.

Stanley apparently was the only man Bennett considered for the job. His coverage of Napier's punitive expedition had made him famous, particularly after the London *Spectator* commented, "Here is the *Times* [the *Times* of London], which for half a century has beaten every journal in Europe in energy and enterprise, actually publishing the latest news of a British expedition through the favor of a London correspondent of the New York *Herald*."

Despite Bennett's instructions to spend money by the

thousand pounds, Stanley, who had learned frugality as a space-rate correspondent, arrived in Zanzibar, the island off the coast of East Africa from which all expeditions to the interior jumped off, with only eighty dollars in his pockets. On the recommendation of the American consul, Zanzibar's bankers extended him enough credit to outfit an expedition of thirty-four men to act as his armed escort against hostile tribesmen, 153 porters and twenty-seven pack animals, with bales of trade goods, provisions, medicines and ammunition. On March 21, 1871, the *Herald* Search Expedition, as it was headlined by its sponsor back in New York, plunged into the interior. The swarthy, superbly confident man at their head, not at all dismayed by the tremendous odds against him, said that in bracing himself mentally for the quest, all he had to do was "free my mind from all else" but "the finding of the man whom I was sent to seek." Before him he kept a far from accurate vision of a frail, elderly missionary waiting to be rescued—and, undoubtedly, a glowing picture of the acclaim that would be his if he succeeded.

For almost eight months Stanley and his men struggled along the Arab caravan route toward Lake Tanganyika, traveling almost twice as fast as the Burton-Speke expedition. Stanley was a merciless driver, undeterred by all the natural and human handicaps which afflicted the expedition. For days on end he was all but delirious with fever. He was beset by a mutiny, desertions, the death and illness of his men and pack animals, the active hostility of the natives through whose territory he passed. When approaching the Arab colony at Ujiji, he learned that a white man had been seen there only a few days before. On November 3 his ragged and weary band unfurled an American flag and marched into the outskirts of Ujiji. A gray-bearded man lifted his cap and smiled. "Dr. Livingstone, I presume?" "Yes." The rescuers were in much worse condition than the man they were sent to succor, living in primitive comfort by the shimmering waters of Lake Tanganyika. Dr. Livingstone, in fact, was astounded that anyone should fancy he needed rescuing. All he really lacked was news of the outside world, and he kept his weary guest up late that night retelling the history of the past five years—the opening of the Suez Canal, the Spanish revolution, the completion of the Atlantic cable, the victories of the Prussian war machine over Denmark, Austria, and France.

It wasn't until the next day, in fact, that Stanley got around to telling Dr. Livingstone who had sent him on what was essentially an unnecessary mission.

"You've heard of the New York *Herald?*" Stanley asked.

"Oh, who hasn't heard of that despicable newspaper?"

Stanley gallantly rose to the defense of his employer. "Without his father's knowledge or consent," he told the missionary, "Mr. James Gordon Bennett commissioned me to find you, to get what news of your discoveries you would like to give, and to assist you, if I can. . . ."

More graciously Dr. Livingstone conceded that he should be grateful to the proprietor of that "despicable newspaper" and allowed that "it makes me feel proud that you Americans think so much of me."

Stanley stayed with Livingstone until mid-March of the following year, once again finding a substitute father. He was a hard and bitter young man, but he was deeply affected by Livingstone's near-saintliness and wrote that "had my soul been of brass and my heart of spelter [zinc], the powers of my head had surely compelled me to recognize, with due honor, the Spirit of Goodness which manifested itself in him."

On May 29, 1872, Stanley arrived back in Zanzibar, shrunken from bouts with malaria and dysentery, his black hair already turning gray. Before returning to Europe and America, he sent back supplies enough to allow Livingstone to continue his explorations for another two years. The two men never met again, Livingstone dying on May 4, 1873 near Lake Bangweolo.

Back in civilization, an ordeal of fame, jealousy, and scandal, harder to endure than the privations of the journey to Lake Tanganyika and back, awaited Stanley. Many times he was to wish himself back in a trail camp, burning with fever, surrounded by treacherous askaris; for with fame came the exposure of his illegitimate birth, his workhouse boyhood, and his peculiar experiences on both sides of the Civil War, which he dreaded more than any poisoned spear. Under all the acclamation that awaited him, there was a murmuring of resentment, of malicious suspicions, and worse yet there was to be the unexpectedly hostile attitude of James Gordon Bennett, Jr., whose reactions were always unpredictable.

At first Bennett had been elated by the cabled dispatches reporting the success of the *Herald* Search Expedition. The *Herald's* circulation rose to a hundred thousand as it began publishing Stanley's accounts of his journey. The *Times* of London wrote of Stanley, "He aimed at the continent of Africa and he hit the bull's-eye." For months the New York *Sun* had been leading a chorus of doubting Thomases, with editor Dana insinuating repeatedly that the Stanley expedition was an elaborate hoax. Now the *Herald* was able to suppress all doubts by publishing a letter which Livingstone had addressed to Bennett:

". . . I am as cold and non-demonstrative as we

islanders are usually reputed to be; but your kindness made my frame thrill. It was, indeed, overwhelming, and I said to my soul, 'Let the richest blessings descend from the Highest on you and yours!' "

Furthermore, he gave the *Herald* the first word of his discoveries in mid-Africa: "The watershed of South Central Africa is over seven hundred miles in length. The fountains thereon are almost innumerable—that is, it would take a man's lifetime to count them. From the watershed they converge into four large rivers, and these again into two mighty streams in the great Nile valley. . . . It was long ere light dawned on the ancient problem and gave me a clear idea of the drainage. I had to feel my way and every step of the way, and was, generally, groping in the dark—for who cared where the waters ran? We drank our fill and let the rest run by. . . ."

In concluding, Livingstone appealed to Bennett to "lend us your powerful aid" in bringing about the "suppression of the East Coast slave trade."

Bennett, of course, was much gratified by the letter and ordered that it be published in facsimile.

As Stanley made his triumphant way from Marseilles to Paris to London, however, Bennett evidenced a growing displeasure. "The fact was," wrote the *Herald's* night editor, Joseph I. C. Clarke, who edited and rewrote Stanley's dispatches as they arrived in New York, "that a certain unfortunate jealousy of his men who had gained great prominence in pursuit of *Herald* work was visible in Bennett from time to time. It was a blot on a bright record of enterprise."

The people cheered Stanley wherever he went in Paris and London, but there was much snide criticism from certain newspapers and much unconcealed annoyance among geographers and other learned men that a mere amateur had invaded the heart of Africa with so little preparation. His triumph, in brief, made light of their work. The Paris Geographical Society denounced him as an impostor. In London the *Standard* and the *Spectator* demanded an investigation of his story, charged that the papers and letters he brought back from Livingstone were forgeries, and insisted that a crude, uneducated American journalist could not possibly have succeeded where the British Government and the Royal Geographical Society, which had made various tentative, halfhearted attempts to locate Livingstone, had failed. Sir Henry Rawlinson, the president of the Royal Geographical Society, remarked that it was not Stanley who found Livingstone, but Livingstone who found Stanley—a slander which that gentle scholar later retracted.

The English newspapers jeered at his unpolished manner and unscientific approach, as he lectured before various learned societies on his African journey. "Grotesque and humorous" was one description of his platform personality in the London *Mail*. Finally Stanley was driven to lash back at his critics and accusers. "Let it be understood," he wrote in a letter published in the *Daily Telegraph,* "that I resent all manner of impertinence, brutal horse-laughs at the mention of Livingstone's name, or his sufferings . . . all statements that I am not what I claim to be—an American; all gratuitous remarks such as 'sensationalism,' as directed at me by that suave gentleman, Mr. Francis Galton [a cousin of Charles Darwin and the president of a scientific society before which Stanley had lectured] . . . and all such nonsense as the *Spectator* has seen fit to attribute to my pen."

Not a word of congratulation had reached him from his employer. Now, while he was the center of controversy, came the first message from James Gordon Bennett. It was a cable reading:

"STOP TALKING. BENNETT."

His subordinates said that by now Bennett was so jealous of all the acclaim given Stanley, with his employer's name only fleetingly mentioned, if at all, that he would fly into a rage whenever his intrepid correspondent's name was brought into a conversation.

"Who was Stanley before I found him?" Bennett would fume. "Who thought of looking for Livingstone? *Who paid the bills?*"

Bennett quite seriously believed that he deserved the major share of the credit because he conceived the idea of the expedition and put up the money to outfit it. His reward was the *Herald's* booming circulation, nothing more. It was Stanley who was summoned to an audience before Queen Victoria (who, incidentally, thought him "a determined, ugly little man—with a strong American twang"), and who received a diamond-studded gold snuffbox with the royal inscription.

So, when Stanley finally arrived in New York on November 20, 1872, it was a cold, inimical welcome he received from the Commodore. A delegation of *Herald* men greeted him on the dock, but Bennett was not among them. A reception was held in the *Herald* library an hour later; Bennett was not present. Finally Thomas Connery, the *Herald's* managing editor, took Stanley into Bennett's office for a ten-minute interview which was not much less formal than the audience granted by Queen Victoria. Icicles hung on the Commodore's every word. Then "Stanley Africanus," the hero of all the ordinary people of the civilized world, was curtly dismissed.

Stanley was scheduled to deliver a series of lectures in America, but his platform manner and his narrative approach fell far short of the eloquence then expected of a lecturer. His first appearance at Steinway Hall was disappointing, Joseph Clarke recalled in *My Life and Memories*. "As a matter of fact the lecture was a mistakenly dry technical endeavor to prove he was truthful and not the villain the *Sun* was painting him. The second lecture was still worse and consisted almost entirely of a string of African names without the expected illumination of the story of the truly wonderful march across Africa to a great triumph."

A member of the *Herald* staff named George O. Seilhamer, who was one of Bennett's leading sycophants and whom Clarke described as "a man of strange malignities," covered the second lecture and termed it "intolerably dull . . . a doleful monotone." He later told Clarke, "I sensed that Bennett was sick of the praise of Stanley. I simply made the truth sound raw, and when Bennett sent for me the next day to reproach me severely, as he did, I could see that he was really gratified."

Stanley's lecture tour was abruptly terminated, even though Mark Twain, introducing him to an assemblage in Boston, said that "When I contrast what I have achieved in my remarkably brief life with what he has achieved in his possibly briefer one, the effect is to sweep utterly away the ten-story edifice of my own self-appreciation and to leave nothing behind but the cellar."

When Stanley's hastily written book, *How I Found Livingstone in Central Africa,* was published, Bennett let him know that "he echoed the slighting attacks of some other papers on its want of literary style."

The *Herald* and its proprietor necessarily stood behind him, however, when the *Sun* and other papers began publishing stories about his background. Having failed to discredit his accounts of finding Livingstone, they chose to attack him on personal grounds. All that Stanley dreaded came to pass: the revelation of his military desertions, his misadventures in Turkey just after the war, worst of all his shameful birth. English newspapers enthusiastically took up the search for grimy little facts, and it was revealed that his mother was then keeping a pub called the Castle Arms in Denbigh, Wales. (That good lady was gratified by a tremendous increase in business, thanks to the son she had twice rejected.) Bennett demanded that Stanley reply to the charges, which he did by denying everything, and assigned Joseph Clarke to write the editorials defending Stanley's reputation. Now Stanley found that even his colleagues on the *Herald,* reflecting the attitude of their employer, were shunning him. He "naturally took the descent from super-hero much to heart," Clarke recalled, and every day would sit by Clarke's desk "with his great fiery dark eyes" and "pour forth the ceaseless stream of his struggles, his triumphs and presently his troubles."

Finally, at Clarke's urgings, Stanley went back to England, now well aware of the bitchy qualities of the fame and success for which he had struggled so long and hard.

Yet he continued and expanded on his great career of exploration, increasingly more at home in the depths of Africa than in the supposedly civilized world. He covered General Wolseley's Gold Coast expedition for the *Herald.* Later he proposed that the *Herald* and the London *Daily Telegraph* finance an expedition to explore the Congo River, and Bennett cabled his usual terse reply: "Yes. Bennett." Stanley then undertook one of the great explorations of all time, tracing the Congo from source to mouth, crossing Africa from east to west, and organizing the Congo Free State—a short-lived political entity that was to give the world much trouble before another century passed. Still unaware of his employer's animosity, he named one of the towering peaks in the Gambaragara country Mount Gordon Bennett (and later Prime Minister Gladstone demanded to know why he had "given it such an absurd name"). But eventually, inevitably, Stanley and Bennett came to a parting of the ways. Bennett simply could not see the wisdom of sponsoring further activities which redounded to his hireling's credit and very little to his own. What should have been a great friendship, a wholehearted collaboration, was soured by Bennett's small-mindedness; yet it was still true that none of Stanley's achievements would have been possible without the wayward Commodore.

There was one sad little postscript to the relationship. In 1891, by which time Stanley had married Dorothy Tennant, the charming and understanding daughter of an English M.P., Bennett sent his star correspondent, Aubrey Stanhope, to interview Stanley at a Tyrolean resort where he was vacationing with his wife.

Stanley thought that Bennett had sent Stanhope to him as a gesture of reconciliation, and talked to the visitor for two whole days, pouring out reminiscences which he believed Stanhope could use in his story. On the third day, somewhat puzzled, Stanley asked the correspondent if something else was on his mind.

Finally Stanhope blurted out, "Do you beat your wife?"

He thoroughly expected that Stanley would assault him, saw the rage flashing in the explorer's dark eyes.

"My God," Stanley said wryly after getting a hold on himself, and thinking back to his own days as a reporter, "I used to have to do that myself."

It developed that Bennett, still resentful of Stanley's fame after all those years, had heard rumors that the explorer was mistreating his wife. Nothing would do but that Stanhope must journey all the way to the Tyrol and ask him that insulting question. And that was the last that Henry M. Stanley ever heard from the man who told him, with magnificent simplicity, to "find Livingstone."

Equally intrepid and enterprising, and far superior as a descriptive writer, was another far-wandering correspondent of the *Herald*, developed under the younger Bennett's tutelage, named Januarius Aloysius MacGahan. If Stanley changed the map of Africa, MacGahan changed that of Europe and brought on a Balkan war through his brilliant reporting. In their day, MacGahan was as famous as Stanley, but his renown, lacking a Livingstone to lend luster to his exploits, has long since faded.

MacGahan was born in Somerset County, Ohio, and was the cousin of General Phil Sheridan, Union Army cavalry commander subsequently given charge of Indian-fighting operations on the western frontier. He went to work early in his teens to help support his widowed mother. In 1868, at the age of twenty-four, he went abroad to further his education. He was in Brussels when the Franco-Prussian War broke out. Through the intervention of his celebrated cousin, who came over to watch the Prussian armies in action as an official American observer, MacGahan was engaged on a space-rate basis by Bennett. His coverage of General Bourbaki's futile campaigning and subsequent interviews with Gambetta, Louis Blanc, and Victor Hugo made a name for MacGahan. One great advantage was that he could move among all kinds of people, it was said, with "the ease and innocence of a child." He had a talent for languages, an even greater facility for winning the respect and affection of every possible type of humanity.

After covering the Commune uprising in the streets of Paris, he journeyed to the Crimea and spent the summer cultivating friendships at the Czar's summer palace. Now a dedicated Russophile, he married Barbara Nicholavna Elagin, a member of the lesser Russian nobility, later that year in Paris.

Partly because of these ties and even more because of his daring and his journalistic brilliance, Bennett chose him the following year to report on the Russian campaign against the dissident Turkomans of Central Asia.

MacGahan arrived in Tashkent to find that General Kauffmann's column, which was to combine with a force under the Grand Duke Nicholas on the Oxus River before attacking the Turkoman stronghold of Khiva, had departed days before. Furthermore, all foreign war correspondents were forbidden to enter the area of operations far across the deserts of Turkestan. Undismayed, he set out on the 900-mile journey to the Oxus, riding in a low-slung wagon called a tarantass and drawn by six horses, accompanied only by a Tartar interpreter, a guide, and a man to care for the horses.

For twenty-nine days he drove across the wastes of Turkestan, pursued by Cossack squadrons charged with intercepting him and menaced by roving bands of Turkomans. In the first dispatch to reach the cable-head at Constantinople, he wrote, "The sands gleam and burn under the scorching heat like glowing cinders; the atmosphere turns to a misty fiery glare that dazzles the eye and burns the brain like the glow from a seven-times-heated furnace; low down on the horizon the mirage plays us fantastic tricks with its spectrum-like reflection of trees and water—shadows perhaps of the far-off gardens of Khiva and the distant Oxus."

On the twenty-ninth day he camped near the Oxus and was awakened at dawn by the roar of cannon across the valley. MacGahan had arrived at his destination. "His ride," said Eugene Schuyler at the American legation in Saint Petersburg, "was spoken of everywhere in Central Asia as by far the most wonderful thing done during the campaign. Even the officer whose scouts had failed to catch MacGahan was delighted at his pluck." The Russian commanders were so impressed by his courage and so taken with his charm that—reluctant as they were to have a foreigner look upon the necessary brutalities of colonial warfare—they allowed him to accompany the forces which stormed into Khiva, the last great stronghold of Islam in Central Asia after the fall of Bokhara, and scattered the Khan's army.

During subsequent campaigning against surviving bands of rebellious Moslems, MacGahan devoted much space in his dispatches to striking descriptions of the endless steppe of Central Asia: "a wide level expanse of plain, cut up here and there by canals and dotted with clumps of brushwood; on the south, extending to the horizon, a sedgy marsh, over which flocks of waterfowl are careering in swiftly moving clouds that sometimes hide the sun; to the west, a caravan with its string of camels, creeping slowly along the horizon's edge, like a mammoth snail; to the east, the walls of a mud-built town, over which, leaning up against the sky like spears, rise the tall slender masts of ships." (Dispatch of April 19, 1873, the scene fifty miles east of the northern shores of the Aral Sea.)

Bennett ordered the MacGahan dispatches played up in the *Herald*, not merely because they described a distant and minor campaign but because he sensed the "American desire for information about distant and little-known regions" and was willing to spend thousands of dollars to satisfy it. The United States by then had largely conquered its own far frontiers, and there was a growing awareness, until now all but nonexistent, of the rest of the world.

In recognizing this new curiosity, which eventually burgeoned into all sorts of national ventures overseas, militant and peaceful alike, Bennett demonstrated the grasp—if not the temperament—of a great editor. Yet he could not suppress less admirable traits in his character and be satisfied with the role of strategist and paymaster. Secretly he wanted to play the dashing correspondent himself; he bitterly envied the men who had the talent and determination of Stanley and MacGahan, but he knew himself well enough to realize that their achievements were beyond him. He could only sponsor them, and sulk in the shadows of their renown.

Thus the more famous MacGahan became as the "Cossack correspondent" and the "will o' the wisp of war writers," the less favorably he was viewed by his employer. Bennett assigned him to cover the Carlist War in Spain (1874) and the voyage of the *Pandora*, which he helped to finance in an attempt to find a Northwest Passage to the Pacific but which foundered amid the ice floes in Peel Strait (1875). In 1876 MacGahan proposed an investigation which was to have historic consequences. There were reports that the Turks had been massacring the Christian inhabitants of their Bulgarian provinces by the thousands. Russia, which regarded herself as the protector of the Christian races of the Balkans, was, as usual, waiting to seize upon any excuse for a march on Constantinople. MacGahan proposed that he be sent to Bulgaria to find out the truth of the reports, and of others that Russia was merely using them as the pretext for an invasion.

Bennett was visiting England that spring, so MacGahan approached him directly at the *Herald's* London office. Exactly what happened during that stormy interview was known only to Bennett and MacGahan, but there were several possible reasons for the quarrel. In the first place, MacGahan was a Russophile while Bennett, for reasons which will be elaborated upon below, regarded himself as a personal friend of Abdul-Hamid, the weird, bloody little man who was Sultan of Turkey. Bennett may have been annoyed, too, because in all the 438 pages of MacGahan's book *Campaigning on the Oxus* his publisher's name was not mentioned once. Also it was not one of Bennett's good years; he was drinking heavily, and the shocking incident which caused him to exile himself from New York was only months in the offing. Anyway the two men quarreled violently, MacGahan stomped up Fleet Street to the London *Daily News,* and before the afternoon was out agreed to investigate the reported atrocities in Bulgaria for that newspaper.

We need not linger over the result, except to see what Bennett lost when he gave way to peevishness. MacGahan journeyed to Bulgaria, found villages with heaps of skulls and bones on their outskirts, and other plentiful evidence of pillage and massacre, and wrote a series of articles which not only roused the conscience of Europe but was credited with starting the Russo-Turkish War of 1877. His dispatches from the Russian forces at the siege of Plevna were among the most brilliant in the annals of war correspondence. A week after that Balkan war ended, MacGahan was informed that a friend, the United States military attaché in Constantinople, had been stricken by typhus. MacGahan hurried there to nurse his friend and himself died of the disease a few days later. An American warship was dispatched to bring his body back to Ohio, and the Bulgarians erected a statue to his memory in Sofia, but he was never again mentioned in the New York *Herald*.

With his unequaled resources for making news, Bennett also interested himself in arctic exploration during this period. While Stanley was tracing the Congo and MacGahan was riding to Khiva, he conceived the idea of outfitting an expedition which would attempt to find the North Pole and also search for the long-lost party headed by Sir John Franklin. He began planning the expedition in the fall of 1873, with Lieutenant George W. DeLong of the United States Navy to lead it, but governmental red tape and other matters delayed the enterprise for several years. The *Pandora*, whose attempt to find the Northwest Passage he had also sponsored, was purchased and rechristened the *Jeanette* for Bennett's sister.

The *Jeanette* finally sailed from San Francisco on July 8, 1879, with provisions for a three-year voyage and a long, heartening farewell cable from Bennett. ". . . Tell him [DeLong] in case he returns next year, unsuccessful, which I don't believe possible, I shall most certainly send another expedition the following year, and continue doing so until successful, but had rather the victory be his than another's. Should DeLong not return next year, or in fact never, the widows of the men belonging to the expedition will be protected by me. Should like him to tell this to his men upon their departure."

DeLong said, "Thank God I have a man at my back to see me through when countries fail."

The *Jeanette* was last sighted steaming off Wrangel Island on September 3—then nothing was heard of her for more than two years.

Two navy ships were sent to search for the DeLong expedition, but could find no traces of her.

When word finally arrived from Siberia, it was apparent that the *Jeanette's* fate was tragic. The ship had been trapped in pack ice off the Lena delta on the northern coast of Siberia; there it stayed for twenty-two months, until on June 13, 1881, it was slowly crushed by the grinding floes. DeLong and his crew dragged their boats over to what was named Bennett Island on July 29. On September 12 they set out for the mouth of the Lena, but that evening a strong gale separated the three boats. Lieutenant George W. Melville, the ship's engineer, led one party safely ashore on the Lena delta. A few days later he organized a search for the other two parties. On March 23, 1882, the bodies of Lieutenant DeLong and two crew members were found in a makeshift camp. A few days afterward three survivors of DeLong's group were located alive in a nearby village. The third party was never found.

Immediately on receiving news of the *Jeanette's* misfortune from Lieutenant Melville, Bennett set about doing everything he could to aid the survivors, who were being cared for by Siberian villagers. John P. Jackson of the *Herald* staff was sent with money and supplies to Irkutsk by rail, then by sled to the Lena delta. Unlike the meeting of Stanley and Livingstone, that of Melville and Jackson was strikingly uncongenial. Jackson, it appears, was regarded as a pushy fellow with an unseemly regard for his own comfort. "He was prepared," Melville wrote (*In the Lena Delta*), "to take me in charge. . . . Very much to his astonishment I was in need of no assistance, and not at all inclined either to surrender myself into his keeping, or to be captured by force." Melville further complained of being "pestered by a popinjay. . . . I have never encountered such a fault-finder. . . . From the wholesale manner in which he grumbled about his eating, drinking, sleeping, about everything that was around him, the sky and earth beneath—I seriously doubt if his halo would fit him should he succeed in edging his way into Paradise, which, I must say, however, is, in my opinion, utterly improbable."

Bickering all the way, the would-be rescuer and his ungrateful subjects made their way to Irkutsk and Saint Petersburg. Jackson eventually returned to Paris, where he was installed as chief correspondent, only to find that he had annoyed Bennett by taking an expensive house in a fashionable section of the capital. The Commodore was firmly convinced that employees of the *Herald* should not try to push their way into the company of their betters—they damn well had to learn their place, which ranked, in all but a few special cases, somewhere below a competent valet. He soon sent Jackson back to New York, successively demoting him from managing editor of the *Evening Telegram* to cable editor of the *Herald*, until Jackson finally quit rather than find himself running copy.

Jackson was a keen disappointment to Bennett, who had been hoping he would turn out to be another Stanley or MacGahan. It was the Commodore's opinion that men like that could be plucked out of obscurity and, given enough guidance and money by their employer, distinguish themselves overnight. All his money, however, could not fabricate another Stanley Africanus or a MacGahan Asiaticus.

6: Pistols at Slaughter's Gap

On New Year's Day of 1877 fashionable New Yorkers tucked themselves under fur lap robes and set out in their sleighs to visit their friends and toast each other with glasses of punch and well-fortified eggnog.

A heavy snow started falling at four o'clock in the afternoon, which only seemed to quicken the holiday mood. To each his own was the rule of the day. A crowd of overstimulated Germans wrecked a brewhouse in One hundred and tenth Street when the proprietor refused to serve free drinks. Seventy-year-old Timothy O'Neill suffered a broken collarbone when he was thrown out of a Second Avenue saloon for grumbling at paying fifteen cents for a glass of hot Scotch whisky. A Waterbury temperance meeting was enlivened by charges that President Grant had gone on a ten-day spree in the White House the previous August, but rejoiced in the fact that he had been succeeded by the teetotaling Rutherford B. Hayes and his wife, who served lemonade at state dinners. One markedly sober household in Manhattan was that of the aged Commodore Vanderbilt, who saw only members of his family and the "equally venerable" Peter Cooper. Two days later the Commodore would be dead.

By nightfall the snow-covered streets would be clangorous with the sound of harness bells, the singing and shouting of merrymakers who had visited at least one too many flowing bowls. "From morning until night-fall," the *Sun* reported the next morning, "the air was one vibration of jingling bells and merry voices." Among young bloods it was the custom to test each other's capacities and the patience of their elders with heroic feats of elbow bending. Tradition, in fact, sanctified the old Knickerbocker custom of New Year's calls, and George Washington himself had spoken well of it.

None was likelier to get tipsy on this occasion than the tall, rawboned man with fiery gray-blue eyes and brandy-flamed cheeks who vaulted out of his sleigh in front of Forty-four West Nineteenth Street, pausing only to instruct his coachman to wait for him before plunging through the snowdrifts toward the door. This was James Gordon Bennett who, as Commodore of the New York Yacht Club and publisher of the New York *Herald*, had proven that the hereditary silver spoon need not necessarily handicap a young man, and who yet had time to carouse with the best of them. He was indisputably the idol of the young bloods who seemed to be trying to re-create Regency London in Gilded Age New York. His dash and style were much envied and hopefully emulated. His defiance of the majestic matrons who, with their mincing viziers, ruled New York and Newport society and presided over the dreary convolutions of the Four Hundred's cotillions was also regarded with awe. People were still talking about how Bennett rode on a polo pony into Newport's Reading Room, the inner sanctum of the matrons, and was henceforth banned from its portals. In reprisal Bennett built his own club, the Casino, opposite his villa on Bellevue Avenue. And who but the Commodore would think of taking his late-evening constitutional by riding a bicycle around the block bounding his Fifth Avenue home while his butler stood at attention on the sidewalk with a silver tray and a decanter of brandy to provide him with a stirrup cup every time he cycled past?

And who but Bennett could have stirred up the city with what had become famous as the *Herald's* "wild-animal hoax" of November 9, 1874? Under such head-lines as "A Shocking Sabbath Carnival of Death" and "Terrible Scenes of Mutilation," the *Herald* carried a horrendous account of how all the wild animals in the Central Park zoo had broken loose, killing forty-nine persons and maiming or trampling 200 others; Governor Dix himself had shot a Bengal tiger, and for hours the whole city had been at the mercy of roving man-eaters and charging elephants. The first extras to hit the streets not only threw the populace into a panic, but caused an uproar in Park Row. Dr. George Hosmer, the journal-istic hero of Gettysburg, tore into the *Herald* office brandishing a revolver and announcing that he was prepared for the worst. George Williams, the excitable city editor of the *Times,* hired a coach, crammed every available reporter into it, and descended on police head-quarters in Mulberry Street at the head of his phalanx, denouncing the police for giving all the facts to the *Herald* and letting the *Times* be scooped. Nobody, as might have been foreseen, had read to the end of the *Herald's* gory account and noted the disclaimer that "the entire story given above is a pure fabrication. Not one word of it is true," and that it was intended to "test the city's preparedness to meet a catastrophe." Night editor Joseph Clarke, who had concocted the story with a reporter named Harry O'Connor, said that "when the *Herald* was brought up to Bennett with his coffee as he lay abed, he was said . . . to lie back and groan." Bennett had approved of the project but had not expected it to have such a realistic impact, which caused the indignant *Times* to comment, "No such carefully prepared story could appear without the consent of the proprietor or editor—always supposing that this strange newspaper has an editor, which seems rather a violent stretch of the imagination."

And who, in the view of his admiring contemporaries, had a better right to wassail on this occasion? In a few days he would be married to the Maryland beauty who decorated the household he was entering in Nineteenth Street. She was the young and lovely Miss Caroline May, whom he had begun courting in the summer of 1875. The previous summer she and members of her family had spent part of the season at Bennett's villa at Newport. Society gossips had noted then that he had given her "the seat of honor on his box" when they went coaching. Since then they had become engaged, and the May family was congratulated on having captured one of the richest men in New York for a son-in-law.

It was generally believed that Bennett had fallen in love for the first time in his life, though he had intimately known many women and had begun his amatory career at an extremely early age. Until now, however, he had always fancied women of a lower social station—actresses, singers, dancers, "females of the demimonde." With the slyness of the satisfied bachelor, he had always replied to questions about marriage with the stock answer that he would be happy to take a wife but no one would have him, a pseudo-gallantry that deceived no one. He had played it safe by associating with women who would not expect and could not demand marriage from the wealthiest young man about town.

And if any of his playmates had presumed to hope that his intentions were honorable, he could always rely upon the services of the exceedingly knowledgeable law firm of William F. Howe and Abe Hummel in their rookery near the Tombs. Howe & Hummel, in their long and profitable partnership, not only defended an all-time record of more than a thousand murder and manslaughter cases, but were the town's leading experts on the breach of promise suit, a field in which they pioneered. Generally they represented (and coached) the young females who claimed to have been wronged by some Gilded Age dandy, but for a few privileged parties—including James Gordon Bennett, Jr., it may be presumed—they acted as protectors of masculine impetuosity. Young Bennett was indeed fortunate in enlisting their sympathies, for as their biographer, Richard H. Rovere, has written, "Howe & Hummel affidavits alleging 'seduction under promise of marriage' troubled the morning-after thoughts of playboys and stage-struck businessmen for a quarter of a century."

In return for their kindly attentions, Bennett always saw to it that Howe & Hummel's activities were favorably publicized in the *Herald,* which unfailingly referred to Howe as "the Nestor of the criminal bar." Amiable little Abe Hummel, a devotee of horse racing, acted as the *Herald's* correspondent during the racing meets at Saratoga. The partners' essays on such burning topics as "Should the Anti-Tights Law Be Repealed?" and "Jack the Ripper Explained" always found a home in the *Herald's* columns. Whenever the firm took on a newsworthy case, the *Herald* would loyally comment that the defendant's hope of acquittal "improved considerably when it became known that he had retained the services of Messrs. Howe & Hummel."

Obviously the *Herald's* proprietor found their services and good offices, rendered in return for the kind of publicity on which a firm practicing criminal law thrives, a highly efficacious means of staying out of trouble. No record can be found of a breach of promise case, seduction charge, or bastardy suit being filed (on this side of the water) against Bennett, despite his notorious explorations of the fleshpots. Most of the young women who might have been tempted to capitalize on any encounter with him when the lights were low and spirits were high were Howe & Hummel clients, and he was safe from scandal so long as he stayed in their good graces. In this, at least, his somewhat variable sense of discretion never failed him. The *Herald* was faithful to Howe & Hummel to the day that the surviving partner, Abe Hummel, was finally disbarred through the tenacious efforts of District Attorney William Travers Jerome in 1907.

Perhaps Bennett's most notorious affair, preceding his engagement to Caroline May, had involved him with a beautiful English girl named Pauline Markham, "supple, dark-eyed and regally statuesque," who had come over with the Lydia Thompson Burlesque Company to disport herself, rather daringly for that day, at Wood's Museum, a new theater far uptown at Broadway and Thirtieth Street. The troupe was the toast of the town in 1868, and Miss Markham was its star attraction with, as one overheated critic wrote, "a voice of velvet and the lost arms of Venus de Milo." In Pauline Markham and her nubile associates, as Lloyd Morris has written, New Yorkers "saw for the first time the 'show girl'—a type that was to make theatrical history and domestic discord." The girls brought the house down when, with pulse-stirring ripples of the torso, they performed "the Grecian bend," a relatively sedate and well-clothed forerunner of burlesque's highest art form, the strip tease.

Every wealthy womanizer in the metropolis took off

in pursuit of the dark-eyed Miss Markham, but Bennett led the pack and won the chase.

He was so enamored of the lithe brunette that there were rumors that he intended to marry her. With possession, however, his interest inevitably faded—and so, eventually, did Miss Markham's charms. She wound up drably as a Harlem housewife, married to a printer.

Now, however, Jimmy Bennett, veteran of fleshpots, terror of polite society, naked coachman, reckless polo player, high-living and free-spending clubman, was about to be tamed by domesticity.

One wonders whether, at thirty-five, he had not suddenly quailed at the thought of settling down, even by the side of the beautiful Caroline; whether subconsciously, in the depths of a drink-muddled mind, he was not desperately seeking an out; whether there was not some half-hidden motive behind the conduct which, in less than an hour, was to horrify Miss May, enrage her family, and scandalize New York society.

Lurching slightly, he was ushered into the drawing room, which was thronged with May and Bennett friends.

He moved around the room, whacking male friends on the back and loudly making bawdy remarks which the ladies present pretended not to hear. Everyone knew his reputation, and most were willing to overlook his unpredictable behavior, particularly when taken by drink. Jimmy Bennett might be a rip, a cutup, a wild man; he might break a chair or two and otherwise affront his hostess, but, by gad, he was never dull and his presence added a certain dash to any occasion.

He grabbed at trays of drinks borne by passing servants and bolted down the steaming punch. Indiscretion was the better part of boozing, and the world would damn well have to take him as he was.

Soon he was lurching from group to group, his eyes bloodshot and unfocused, his tongue thickening, his hair disheveled. He could be somewhat dangerous when overserved, and people were beginning to shrink away from him, remembering his fondness for violent scenes. "He never stifled an impulse," as one long-time associate said of him.

One or two couples, scenting a social disaster, quietly called for their coats and hats and took their leave of their host, Dr. William May, and his wife.

Caroline May, a slender, fair-haired girl with a proud tilt to her chin, tried to ignore the behavior of her fiancé. She knew his reputation, but she had been brought up in a family whose males were all lusty, full-blooded fellows and she was not dismayed by it. And everyone kept telling her how lucky she was to have captured the elusive Jimmy Bennett. If only he could hold his liquor like the Southern gentlemen of her own lineage. . . .

Undismayed she may have been, but she was also quite unprepared for what followed, what was described at the time, with all possible delicacy, as "a breach of the most primitive of good manners."

Jimmy Bennett, happily roaming the crowded drawing room with its cheery fire blazing and everyone in high spirits, suddenly felt the urge to relieve himself. The bathroom was a long, lonely march away, down chill and drafty corridors. It was ridiculous to have to leave such jolly company simply because of what the Nice Nellies described as a "call of nature." Since childhood, though "permissive" methods of child rearing had not yet been formulated, he had always done exactly what he pleased. Right now he had to pump out the bilge, and he damn well wasn't going to walk half a block for the purpose.

So Bennett unbuttoned, unburdened himself.

In the rather confused accounts of the incident, one version was that he urinated into the grand piano, which would seem to be a physical impossibility for anyone less than eight feet tall. Besides, Jimmy Bennett liked music. A more likely version was that he relieved himself in the roaring fireplace, a more hazardous undertaking, perhaps, but certainly not lacking in a picturesque quality.

That brought Dr. and Mrs. May's New Year's party to an abrupt end. Several ladies pretended to faint, others shielded their eyes, still others shrieked and stampeded toward the sliding doors. A number of their menfolk quickly surrounded the preoccupied Bennett until he finished his indelicate task and turned around to inquire where the hell everyone was running off to. He had hardly made himself presentable before a couple of his fellow guests took him firmly by each arm and marched him out of the suddenly inhospitable house. A servant hurried after them with Bennett's hat and coat. Hardly a minute had elapsed before he was deposited in his sleigh and his coachman was ordered to drive him away rapidly—anywhere—preferably to some remote and savage corner of the world where he was always sending other men.

Next day, when he should have been embarking for Pago Pago on his yacht or at least having himself certified as temporarily insane, Bennett stayed in seclusion, nursing his hangover at his town house. Word arrived from Miss Caroline May that she considered their engagement terminated by his unforgivable conduct.

Perhaps a more violent reaction could be expected from the male members of the family. The Mays had a reputation for expressing their resentments in forthright fashion. Dr. May's brother, Colonel Charles May, who had commanded a regiment of dragoons at Buena Vista, once rode his horse up three flights of stairs at Barnum's Hotel in Baltimore to indicate his displeasure with the management. Another brother, Julian, had fought a duel with a man named Cochran in Virginia, with results fatal to his opponent.

Obviously, in dealing with this hot-blooded clan, it would have been sensible, as well as gentlemanly, to have tendered his apologies the moment he was sober enough to express himself on paper. An apology would probably have persuaded Miss Caroline not to break off the engagement; its insulting absence left her no alternative. So it was apparent that Bennett was prepared to risk the wrath of the May family rather than have the engagement not broken off.

On the following day, January 3, Bennett ventured out of his house, going to the Union Club for lunch. If anyone in New York could be expected to shrug off his misbehavior, it was the good fellows who were his drinking, wenching, and sporting companions of the club. His father had spurned membership in the Union Club, demanding in print, "Will it promote principle, taste, philosophy, talent and genius? It may aid cooking, eating, and conversational powers, but one hour of solitary bliss of true genius is worth an eternity of meretricious social happiness." His son, however, had little appreciation for "solitary bliss." The Union Club was his home.

As he approached its portals, he may have been comforted by recollections of its collective talent for tolerance and forgiveness where its members were concerned. The club had refused to expel Judah P. Benjamin, at the height of the war fever in 1861, when he defected to the Confederacy and became a member of Jefferson Davis' cabinet. And one member, who killed a New York policeman during a brawl, was hidden on the premises, then spirited out of the country to South America, where he lived for a year on the club's bounty until it was safe to return to the comradely embrace of his fellows.

True to their tolerant nature, they failed to bar the door against Bennett, although he may have noted a certain coolness when he appeared in the dining room. He was greatly relieved, for it would have been intolerable if his fellow clubmen had turned their backs on him.

Heartened by their display of tolerance, Bennett lunched well and left the club an hour later, bound for the *Herald* office. Just as he was crossing the sidewalk outside, an unfriendly figure loomed before him. It was Fred May, brother of Caroline, ordinarily a hearty, fun-loving type who considered Bennett's prankishness highly amusing. But this latest eccentricity, it seemed to Fred, a strapping fellow of twenty-six, dishonored and insulted his family. To remedy the situation Mr. May had equipped himself with a cowhide whip, the same kind of corrective applied to Bennett's father, though for less discreditable reasons.

Young May rushed at him, lashing him about the chest and shoulders with the heavy thongs of the whip. "Blood stained the snow from the sidewalk to the gutter," one newspaper reported with more enthusiasm than accuracy. At first Bennett made no attempt to defend himself. Bystanders heard him cry out, "Why don't you kill me and get it over with?"

His naturally combative nature quickly rose to the surface, however, particularly since the club windows were lined with spectator sportsmen watching the set-to. He couldn't bear the thought of taking a public beating without offering resistance. So he grappled with his assailant, and the two men toppled into the snow, rolling over and over as they punched away at each other. They might have rolled all the way down to Washington Square in this snarling embrace, had not William P. Douglas and John G. Heckscher come running out of the club to separate them and put an end to the spectacle.

Bennett spent the rest of the afternoon brooding over the incident. Now, he decided, it was *his* honor which demanded satisfaction. Always a trifle medieval in his thinking, he came to the conclusion that the affair could be settled only under terms of the code duello. His sister Jeanette was staying with him at the moment and tearfully tried to dissuade him, without success, then hurried over to the May home to comfort Caroline, who had been one of her best friends.

Bennett Senior had always dusted himself off after such a public assault and then trotted along to the *Herald* office to give his readers a complete account of what had happened. His son, however, decided that the set-to would not be mentioned in the *Herald*.

Next morning the always hostile *Sun* published a full account, giving almost as much space to it as the death of Commodore Vanderbilt, under the heading:

J. G. BENNETT ASSAULTED
A Scene That Startled Members
of the Union Club

The *Sun* reported, in addition, that Bennett "was to have sailed for England yesterday with his bride in the *Russia*," but the marriage had been called off.

Two days later the *Sun* happily gave credence to a rumor that Bennett had "fled to Canada." Other journals, however, were more friendly to Bennett. The Boston *Herald* reported that there was much indignation over May's assault in Newport: "It is a well known fact that Miss May's brothers, cousins and other members of the family spent the past season here, and that they were not backward in accepting of Mr. Bennett's hospitality." And the *Sunday Mercury* of New York pointed out that May "has only himself to blame that the lady's name has become the gossip of not only every drawing room, but in every tavern in the land."

On January 8, the *Sun* came up with a more accurate rumor:

MR. BENNETT AND MR. MAY
Both Out of City, Probably for
a Hostile Meeting

Bennett had sent emissaries several days before to Fred May announcing that he was challenged to a duel. Dueling had long been illegal in the United States, and had even been out of fashion for some years, but May accepted. One of the men who conveyed the challenge to May was Charles Longfellow, the poet's son and Bennett's companion on the *Henrietta's* famous race.

On the morning of January 7 Bennett, May, and their retinue of surgeons, seconds, and interested sports lovers journeyed to the old dueling ground at Slaughter's Gap, which was not only aptly named but conveniently located on the border of Maryland and Delaware, making it possible for duelists to dodge over the line if the authorities of one state or the other proved narrow-minded. There was no interference, however, with the proclaimed plans of Bennett and May to blow each other's brains out in defense of their good names.

The two men met at two o'clock in the afternoon,

having agreed to pistols at twelve paces. Dr. Fred May of Baltimore, a cousin, acted as Fred May's second, while S. Howland Robbins performed in a similar capacity for Bennett.

With due ceremony the two men took twelve paces away from each other, turned, and fired.

Fred May, with an amiable smile, fired harmlessly in the air.

Bennett's shot also went wild, but witnesses could not agree on whether the cause was poor marksmanship or a similar profession of good will. It was probably the latter. Bennett was a first-class shot with any kind of handgun.

According to the *Sun's* account of January 9, both parties spent the night following the duel in a rustic hotel near Dover, Delaware. They immediately "betook themselves to their rooms and ordered beer," the *Sun* said, maliciously adding, "The proprietor of the hotel mistook his guests for pickpockets and consequently sat up all night watching their movements."

In the best continental tradition, the two duelists had been formally "reconciled" with a handshake, and the matter was considered closed. No such reconciliation could be effected, however, between Bennett and polite society. Bennett was still welcome at the Union Club, still spoken to, still on good terms with his old masculine friends, but he was not invited out. Mixed gatherings were closed to him. Fifth Avenue hostesses found that they did not care to entertain a fellow who apparently had not been housebroken. It was simply a polite freeze-out, against which he had no defense, no recourse, no appeal.

His father had endured ostracism most of his life, and welcomed it, because it gave him more time for his work, but Bennett Junior was more of a social animal. He was anything but repentant; outraged at society's ingratitude, he reminded his friends that the world of fashion had been treated with dignity and respect only since he had taken charge of the *Herald*. There was no more of the jeering and satirizing which his father had believed would amuse the bulk of his readership. The Commodore had appointed Nicholas Biddle, whose social credentials were beyond reproach, to act as "social advisor extraordinary" to the *Herald* and see to it that society was tenderly treated. Furthermore, the active editorship of the society page was invested in William Bininger, more gentleman than journalist, the member of a German family which had enriched itself in the grocery business long enough ago to remove the stigma of "trade." One of Bennett's news executives complained that he had to carry around in his head the longest list of "sacred cows" compiled by any New York newspaper proprietor.

One of his few rebellions against the social lionesses of Manhattan occurred under considerable provocation in a dispute with the haughty Mrs. Stuyvesant Fish. A make-up man inadvertently added the list of ringsiders at a prize fight from a sports-page column to the list of guests at a reception given by Mrs. Fish. The lady upbraided Bennett and his editors so caustically that the Commodore ordered that henceforth Mrs. Fish would not be mentioned in the *Herald*. She was reinstated eventually, but only after apologizing in person to young Mr. Bennett. On the whole, however, New York society regarded the *Herald's* columns as its most important and gravely admiring chronicler.

Outraged that he was now being shunned, Bennett decided to live abroad, where his whims would not be regarded with such puritanical horror. It was not so much a case of Bennett banishing himself as of New

York being banished from his cosmos, except as the seat of his lucrative publishing business. Before the year was out, he established himself in Paris, resigning himself to the often feckless life of an expatriate, returning to New York only for brief visits, usually connected with business. He took with him the dubious satisfaction of having engaged in the last recorded duel fought in the United States.

There was a footnote to that affair of honor and the events leading to it, which so drastically altered his life and undoubtedly reduced his potentialities as the most venturesome and imaginative of his generation of editor-publishers. It was supplied by a once close friend, Mlle. Camille Clermont, in her memoir, *Confessions of Gentle Rebecca*, which was published in London several years after Bennett's death.

Camille Clermont recalled that Fred May appeared in Paris some years after the New Year's incident, and rumors sped around the gossipy American colony that he was still determined to avenge the insult and intended to "shoot Bennett on sight." She continued:

"J.G.B. valued his life far too highly to be thus lightly disposed of, so he ordered a magnificent coat of mail to wear under his clothing, and with his long, lanky figure he looked supremely ridiculous. He wore that coat of mail for a month or so, until he tired of carrying the abnormal weight, so he sent two of his friends to Mr. May to ask what his intentions were, preferring the risk of a duel to the constant fatigue imposed by the medieval armour. Mr. May declared that he had no homicidal intentions, so, to his great relief, J.G.B. discarded the cuirass."

Part Two:

Fun and Games Abroad

7: The Crazy American

To the gaslit, neo-Napoleonic Paris still recovering from defeat in the war against Prussia, the excesses and eccentricities of James Gordon Bennett provided a constant supply of entertainment welcomed in that dismal time. So blazing a personality and so extravagant a career had not enlivened the City of Light since the last of the first Bonaparte's flamboyant marshals had faded away. To a capital still blighted by the effects of the Prussian occupation and the Commune's battle of the boulevards, he brought not only a lusty, grand-seigneural style of living, but an income approaching one million dollars a year and a wonderful willingness to spend it. He was "M. Gordon-Bennett" to the Parisians, despite his angry insistence that he should be known as plain Bennett and his name was definitely not to be hyphenated. He was also the first of the "crazy Americans," establishing a standard of behavior that none of his countrymen would ever quite equal, though many would try.

Early in his residence in the French capital he served notice that he was dissociating himself from his compatriots and throwing in his lot with the country of his choice. The gesture also constituted a warning to his fellow Americans that he did not care to be bothered by any friendly advances from them.

For days on end he drove a coach around the city

with a donkey as his only passenger. The bewildered animal was tethered inside the coach with his head sticking out and a sign hung around his neck which read:

"This donkey is the most sensible American in Paris."

Residents in the vicinity of 120 Avenue des Champs Elysées, where one of his several French headquarters was located, were constantly amazed by his capacity for round-the-clock merriment, his escapades, and his unpredictable behavior. Again he had taken to reckless coaching, sometimes in the raw, and always at a pace which suggested that he was being pursued by demons. Once, careening through the streets, he turned his coach over while negotiating a corner near the Arch of Triumph, and he and his passengers narrowly escaped with their lives.

Another time, roaring drunk and alone on the box, he drove his coach-and-four down the Champs Elysées and turned in at his apartment house at No. 120. He cracked his whip and drove his team toward the narrow, arched entrance to the courtyard of the building. A *flic* on point duty nearby shouted a warning that there was not sufficient clearance under the archway for the coach and its driver, that Bennett would dash his brains out, but he paid no attention to the official warning.

The horses plunged toward the archway and somehow cleared it, but Bennett was knocked off the box and landed on the cobbled driveway with a headlong crash that would have shattered any more fragile skull.

Bleeding from mouth, nose and ears, he was carried upstairs by his servants, and his secretary, Charles Christianson, summoned the most expert surgeons in Paris within an hour. His skull was badly fractured, and only an emergency operation relieved the pressure on his brain and saved his life. For weeks he lay near death.

That incident failed, however, to temper his reckless driving or lessen his appetite for speed, which, when the gasoline engine replaced the horse as a means of locomotion, led him to establish the celebrated James Gordon Bennett Cup Races in the early days of the automobile and airplane. A short time after he recovered from his collision with the archway, he was conducting an excursion into the countryside near Pau with his secretary and Lawrence Jerome, "The Prince of Goodfellows," as he was known to headline writers.

Jerome objected to Bennett's reckless handling of the reins, and the latter, with champagne bubbling in his newly repaired skull, ordered him off the box and shoved him inside the coach. Bennett's secretary, the faithful and durable Christianson, was instructed to join Bennett on the box. Off they went, taking the steep Morlaas Hill at the gallop. On the way down, the horses bolted and disaster threatened.

Bennett shoved the leaders into Christianson's hand while he himself hauled mightily on the reins of the wheel horses. The wild, careening struggle with the maddened horses continued for several miles until the coach was finally brought to a stop.

Jerome stumbled out of the tonneau of the coach, angrily demanding, "Whose joke was it, anyway?"

"Not mine," murmured the white-faced Christianson, and fainted dead away.

Even Bennett, Jerome observed, was chalk-white and shaking, and from then on the Commodore was somewhat more subdued in handling his coach-and-four.

During those first years of his forty years of expatriation, the amiable Jerome was Bennett's boon companion and shared many of the escapades which led the

French to believe that either Bennett was a lunatic or all Americans were a trifle moon-struck.

Travelers on the Paris-Bordeaux Express were often startled, and only occasionally amused, by the pair's efforts to relieve the tedium of the rail journey to one of Bennett's country homes. With their impersonations of various bemused travelers, they "created jollity," as Anita Leslie (*The Remarkable Mr. Jerome*) has recorded— at least for themselves. Sometimes both would pretend to be escaped madmen fleeing from imaginary keepers. Or Bennett would impersonate a jilted lover pursuing Jerome, in the role of his successful rival, with a revolver in his hand. Or one of them would pretend to attempt suicide, brandishing weapons or a bottle of "poison," while the other hysterically tried to reason with him. Bennett dearly loved a practical joke, although, as with many of the type, his sense of humor often failed him when anyone else made him the butt of one.

Lawrence Jerome was an admirable playmate, but he had one serious handicap—his strait-laced wife, Carrie, who was not at all amused by alcoholic pranks. She was, in fact, a strict teetotaler. Once at a dinner party her brother-in-law, Leonard Jerome, had the temerity to defend the practice of drinking wine with meals and, as supporting evidence, quoted the biblical passage on Christ's miracle of Cana. Carrie Jerome shook her head and commented, "In that case, our Lord showed poor judgment."

It was quite remarkable that Lawrence Jerome's association with Bennett did not mortally offend his wife and that the marriage endured until Jerome's death of a stroke in 1888, an end predictable enough, considering the vascular stress on an elderly man trying to keep up with the Commodore.

Luckily Carrie Jerome never learned the truth about

the night her husband was summoned from their bed at a melodramatic hour.

A Bennett manservant, his face strained and anxious under lamplight, appeared at the Jerome door to announce that his master had just been involved in a terrible accident and was calling for Lawrence with his last breath. A brougham was waiting at the curb to take him to Bennett's deathbed in a private hospital.

Lawrence dressed hurriedly and accompanied the servant to a house in a quarter in which one would hardly have expected a hospital to be located.

He was led through hallways which seemed to be scented with perfume rather than the expected reek of disinfectants, but he was too distraught to take suspicious note of the surroundings, or to look askance at the voluptuous nudes framed on the walls or the sybaritic furnishings of this curious clinic.

Finally he arrived in a chamber swarming with twenty nurses who filled out their costumes uncommonly well and somehow lacked the severe dedication of their profession. Leave it to Jimmy Bennett to expire amid the naughtiest-looking nurses his friend had ever seen.

Bennett was groaning on the bed, his whole head and shoulders wrapped in bandages.

A rather sinister-looking doctor, who looked as though he would be more familiar with an Apache's dagger than a scalpel, escorted him to the deathbed.

"He has not long to live," Jerome was gravely informed.

"Speak to me, Jimmy boy," Jerome said, bending over his friend.

"You're damn right I'll speak to you, you long-faced old bastard," Bennett roared, leaping out of bed and ripping off his bandages. "Bring on the medicine, girls!"

While Jerome was still struggling to recover his wits,

the hospital staff began carrying in magnums of champagne and other analgesics. Jerome then learned that this "hospital" was one of the more notorious bordellos in Paris, which Bennett had taken over for the evening in devising a way to pry Jerome loose from his wife. Corks popped, the "nurses" slipped into something more decorative, and a good time was had by all. What Lawrence Jerome told his wife when he returned home is, unfortunately, lost to the annals of the matrimonial alibi.

Among the Balkan princes, merry widows, absentee landlords, and South American grandees who frequented the famous Maxim's, "M. Gordon-Bennett," according to H. J. Greenwall, the historian of that place, was easily the "most spectacular" of its clientele. That distinction was earned not only by his lavish hospitality —he was easily the biggest wine buyer Paris had seen since the tarnished glory of the Second Empire, when canal promoters and army contractors were running wild—but also by his somewhat cavalier conduct on entering a restaurant when in his cups. He would march down the aisle, yanking off tablecloths and sending a cascade of china, crystal, and silver crashing to the floor, looking straight ahead and paying not the slightest attention to the distress that marked his passing. Oddly enough few diners seem to have objected to the practice, and in due time it became rather an offhand compliment to have one's repast scattered by the Commodore. The damage, of course, was repaired at once; ruffled tempers were soothed; wads of francs were distributed for any incidental cleaning bills or sauce-stained apparel—and the next day Bennett always paid the tab without question.

Despite this and other peculiar habits, Bennett was always welcomed with low salaams at Maxim's and his other favorite restaurant, Voisin's. Both establishments kept tables reserved for him, even if they were crowded and he failed to appear. Often he would show up late at night, long after the usual closing hour, but he was such a valuable customer that a skeleton staff would be kept on overtime to accommodate him. Sometimes he would arrive at midnight, an orchid in his buttonhole, swacked to the eyebrows, and in his best quarterdeck manner would demand that the staff be paraded for "inspection." Maître d', waiters and captains, wine stewards, chefs, chasseurs and cloakroom attendants— everyone down to the greasiest pot-walloper would line up, brooms, skillets, and other side arms in hand, and submit to examination by a pair of fierce, bloodshot eyes. Finally satisfied, the Commodore would pass down the line again, this time distributing twenty-franc notes in lieu of the *Croix de guerre*. What with ringers hastily summoned from the alley, he would often hand out the equivalent of a hundred dollars before a midnight inspection was concluded.

His tastes, though expensive, were hardly epicurean. A mutton chop was his favorite dish, of which he claimed to be the leading connoisseur. Once, at Voisin's, he found the mutton-chop served for his lunch so exquisitely prepared that he summoned the proprietor, M. Bracquessac, and suggested that the chef be transferred to his own kitchen. Bracquessac was naturally reluctant to lose such a great talent, but was reminded that Bennett not only was the best customer the place had, but bought all the wines for his various establishments and his yacht from Voisin's cellar. So Bracquessac agreed, and the chef was told to report immediately at Bennett's country place just outside Paris.

Later that afternoon Bennett returned to his home at Versailles and immediately repaired to the kitchen to see how the master of grilling mutton chops was getting along.

He found the chef locked in a passionate embrace with one of his upstairs maids, and his rage was towering. Despite his own proclivities, it may be recalled, he looked upon any hanky-panky among persons in his employ, except at odd moments of liberality, with intense disfavor. It almost seemed as though he regarded any form of dissipation as the prerogative of the upper classes. Outraged as any Puritan householder, he set upon the passionate chef, thrashed him, and threw him out the kitchen door.

The chef returned to Voisin's immediately and poured out his tribulations to M. Bracquessac; it was all a misunderstanding—the maid he had been caught embracing happened to be his fiancée.

"Go back and tell M. Gordon-Bennett the truth," Bracquessac advised the chef. "He has a terrible temper, that man, but he is fair."

The chef followed his ex-employer's advice, finding that Bennett had cooled off sufficiently to hear him out.

"Is your story true?" Bennett demanded.

"Quite true, M'sieur."

"All right, I've made a damn fool of myself. Come with me."

The chef followed Bennett into his study, where the latter made out a check for $4000 and handed it to him, saying, "Wedding present." That was all. The chef went back to his kitchen, married the maid, and both worked for Bennett for many years.

Bennett's moods of princely generosity appeared to be freakishly motivated to those who didn't know him very well. Closer observers could detect a pattern, however, in all his outlandish phases, whether he was giving money away, yanking off tablecloths, or providing ad-lib entertainment on the Bordeaux Express. The common denominator in these episodes was alcohol. Sober, he was not only sensible and practical, but glacially aloof from the ruck of humanity. With drink in him he was liable to react in any number of ways: he could be destructive, charming, democratic, autocratic, gay, morose, and sometimes all of these inside an hour; he might be playing the Caliph of Bagdad one moment and lifting a glass with cabbies the next. His impulses, at any rate, were never to be denied—except, on sobering up, by himself.

Late one night an Englishman named Heywood and a party of friends descended on Maxim's. The place was crowded; every table and chair was occupied except the place reserved for Bennett, who sat alone in his corner, obviously sozzled but smiling affably. The maître d'hôtel told Heywood and his friends that he would ask Bennett if he minded sharing his table. The Commodore waved his hand in his peculiarly amiable fashion and said he would be delighted.

There was only one awkward moment as Heywood and his friends joined the Bennett table. In the continental fashion, Heywood addressed him as "Mr. Gordon-Bennett."

"Do you say Mr. Jesus-Christ?" Bennett demanded. "My name is Bennett!"

It turned into a delightful evening for the English tourists. Their host ordered up relays of stewards bearing magnums of champagne. Then, as the hour grew late, he insisted that they all accompany him to his apartment on the Champs Elysées. His exhilaration grew as the night waned. Heywood and his friends were such delightful companions, he proclaimed, that they must all join him at Monte Carlo for a Mediterranean cruise on his yacht. Meanwhile they must have some more champagne. The thought of being parted from his new friends was so unbearable that he summoned his secretary, told him to telephone the Gare de Lyons and order a special train for several hours hence.

Then, satisfied that everything had been arranged, he fell asleep in his chair. His guests politely waited for him to wake up so they could hurry back to their hotel and pack for the cruise.

When dawn peeped through the tall windows of the apartment, Bennett finally roused himself. Sober and disgruntled, he glowered at the litter of champagne bottles, the ash trays overflowing with cigar butts. Then, even less amiably, he eyed his guests; apparently he had forgotten that only an hour or two earlier he could not bear the thought of being parted from them, and worse yet he had forgotten ordering the special train. Without further ado he rang for his butler and instructed him to show his guests the door, then curtly bade them a good morning. Sadder but wiser in the ways of millionaires, the disheveled Englishmen, all attuned to the idea of spending endless days on a sunlit sea, were ushered into the gray drizzle of a winter dawn.

Bennett was violently pro-English in theory, but individual Britons did not always fare well at his hands. Once, boarding the express to Nice, he found all the compartments filled except one, which an Englishman had taken possession of by placing his luggage on the racks and then going out on the platform for a stroll until the train departed. Bennett tossed all the luggage off the racks. To his secretary's amazement, he then climbed up on one of the racks and stretched out, lighting a cigarette and telling his aide what to say when the previous claimant to occupancy showed up.

The Englishman returned to find a demented-looking

American sprawled on the luggage rack and to be advised by Bennett's secretary in hushed and apprehensive tones. "Take care! Don't excite him. He's dangerous. He's a lunatic, sir, and though he seems quite harmless, if provoked to a paroxysm, I fear I might not be able to restrain him."

Bennett "grinned horribly" at that moment, and the Englishmen fled. A few minutes later a guard retrieved his luggage. The rest of the journey from Paris to Nice Bennett and his secretary had the compartment to themselves, although the train was crowded until passengers were standing in the vestibules.

Something about train journeys tended to over-exhilarate him, along with the liquor he consumed en route.

One night on retiring, with some assistance from the sleeping-car attendant, he grandly handed the man 20,000 francs (then about $4000) as a tip.

Next morning his valet, new to the job and his employer's unpredictable humors, recovered 19,000 francs from the attendant and turned them over to Bennett, who immediately flung them back at him as though they were a stack of hot stove lids.

"You infernal idiot," Bennett roared, "do you think I don't know what I'm doing? How dare you interfere with my business? Take the money back at once and if I ever catch you butting in again, out you go!"

The sleeping-car attendant, his whole tip restored, immediately resigned from the *wagon-lit* service and opened a hotel at Boulogne, one more bewildered beneficiary of Bennett in a Harun-al-Rashid humor. . . .

For all his antic moods, the Commodore was regarded as an adornment of European society.

In the first place, he entertained lavishly—in his Paris apartments, at his palatial estate at Versailles, at

Beaulieu on the Mediterranean coast, at his shooting
box in Scotland, all of which he maintained in addition
to his American homes, the Fifth Avenue town house,
the "country" place on Washington Heights, and his
villa at Newport, each establishment fully staffed and
waiting for him to walk in the door.

The European aristocracy, already showing signs of
wear with the encroachments of democracy and political
upheaval, welcomed new sources of hospitality. A de-
posed Balkan king, an exiled or disgraced grand duke,
a marchioness dispossessed by scandal or revolution,
remittance men of all breeds were wandering the watering places in a highly receptive mood. They welcomed
the host who was not only generous but, in the slightly
naïve American fashion, so awed by even the most
shopworn title and the most raddled royalty. It has
been remarked that the rich American's respect for
aristocratic titles was matched only by the titled European's respect for American money.

Anyone listed in the *Almanach de Gotha,* no matter
how shady the reputation, rated the Commodore's
worshipful attention, at least until he was caught filching
the silver.

"Paris and the 'high world' of Europe were always
looking to him," wrote Albert Stevens Crockett (*When
James Gordon Bennett Was Caliph of Bagdad*), "to do
in the most elaborate fashion everything he did in the
way of entertaining. The late King Charles of Portugal
never paid a visit to Paris without going out to shoot with
Mr. Bennett at Versailles; and, of course, only Mr.
Bennett's friends of the highest social distinction were
invited to shoot in company with the King. . . ."

In England, too, Bennett was most acceptable socially,
largely because of his friendship with the Jeromes and
their relationship through marriage with the nobility.

The Amazon queens of New York society may have closed their guest lists to him, but they had to rub elbows with him in England if they wanted to mingle with the best people. He was very much present, along with various Astors, Belmonts, Lorillards, at the wedding of Leonard Jerome's daughter Leonie to Lieutenant John Leslie of the Grenadier Guards in October of 1884. With Lady Constance, the bridegroom's mother, he would have felt quite at home; her eccentricities outnumbered his own, and according to one chronicler she was so willful that when denied her pleasure she would jump "onto the window-sill in Berkeley Square and threaten to dash herself down if not yielded to in every dispute." The *Morning Post's* account of the wedding included a barbed comment on the inclusion of the Commodore at such a lofty occasion: "So you see the Commodore, in spite of his love for yachting, polo and other unholy things, has finally got into good society. Mr. Bennett spends a great deal of money in a lavish, showy, self-indulgent way, but he can't begin to use up his income!"

Mostly, perhaps, for the sake of that unexhaustible income, Bennett was graciously received wherever he went in England and on the continent. His social acquaintance ranged from the Duchesse d'Uzès, who dedicated herself to restoring the French monarchy, to the Sultan of Turkey, whose power was the most absolute on earth. "His movements as well as his conduct were unpredictable," as Al Laney noted in his history of the Paris *Herald,* "and his excesses were subjects for gossip in all the capitals and courts of Europe. . . . Probably every story had some basis in fact even if it were not entirely true, and the character of the man was such that, in any event, elaboration was not only likely but permissible." But a more sophisticated Europe, unlike America, looked on his escapades "with fewer sneers than exclamations of admiring wonder." An American in those days, too, could get away with a lot more abroad, representing a young and much-patronized nation, while boorish or bizarre conduct today is condemned as the natural arrogance of the citizen of a great power.

Not quite all was forgiven him, however, as the super-rich representative of a land widely believed to be all wild frontier a few miles inland from the eastern seaboard. According to his once-intimate friend Camille Clermont, the circles in which he moved never really took him to their hearts, for all his hospitality and his profound respect for any titled nitwit. "Beneath his thin veneer of civilization, J.G.B. was in reality a Barbarian," she wrote, "and education had done little to modify his nature. He had not been tenderly reared, and had never known the gentle culture imparted to most children by their mother. Delicacy and sensitiveness were alike strangers to him, and he had never learnt the precious maxim: 'Never hurt those who love us.'"

If Bennett's nights were filled with revelry, all too often, his days were generally devoted to hard work; he may have been an absentee publisher, but he watched over every phase of his newspapers' operation more attentively than most proprietors who appeared in their offices every day. He never slept more than four hours a night, and shortly after the sun was up plunged into work, no matter how his head ached or his nerves jangled. When in Paris, he would head for the Bois de Boulogne immediately after a frugal breakfast, carrying an armload of the most recently received issues of the *Herald* and the *Evening Telegram*, as well as other New York papers, various reports and balance sheets, and the backbiting intelligence reports of his office spies.

Employees summoned to his Louis XIV estate at Versailles or his villa at Beaulieu, between Nice and Monte Carlo, often were ushered into his bedroom shortly after dawn to find him half hidden by the papers which covered his bed. Generally his working day was from sunrise to sundown. Every story in the *Herald* was compared with the similar account in its competitors, and whenever the *Herald's* coverage was considered inferior, a scorching note would be dispatched to the managing editor in New York. An executive was required to be stationed at all hours of the day and night at the other end of the cable, so that the Commodore's ideas could be translated into action immediately. In addition to that two-way stream of memos and cables, Bennett kept in touch by summoning editors and staff members to his side as though he were no farther from Printing-House Square than Washington Heights. Then, too, once or twice a year, and as secretly as possible, he would cross the Atlantic and descend on the *Herald* building with what one of his editorial writers called a "terrifying suddenness," and shock waves of hirings, firings, promotions and demotions, accusations and recriminations would hit the place like a man-made earthquake.

Although Park Row sneered at him as an expatriate who was simply wringing money out of the *Herald* and had no other interest in the paper, it was literally true that a member of his staff could not get drunk, cheat on his wife, or change the part in his hair without the Commodore's knowing about it instantly. He was not only fantastically jealous of his authority—the surest way for one of his satraps to eliminate another was to waft a rumor overseas that the rival was "getting too big for his boots"—but regarded every word printed by his papers as emanating from himself. If someone else happened to have put those words on paper, they came from what he was pleased to call a "hired brain." His employees simply had to get used to the idea of being treated like so many intellectual zombies. "Every man who worked for the *Herald*," Laney wrote, "no matter how important or lowly his job, had to please Bennett, who was as changeable as a chameleon, domineering, hypersensitive and full of whims."

James L. Ford, a *Herald* editorial writer for many years, said that he was often "asked sneeringly if he [Bennett] paid any attention to the *Herald* and to this I have made answer that once he cabled me from Ceylon ordering an editorial on a local matter, and that on another occasion, just as I had begun to write something about a wealthy New Yorker, a cable message was placed on my desk suggesting that very topic. . . ."

His employees could not complain too much of his minutely detailed orders on how the *Herald* and the *Evening Telegram* were to be written, edited, and managed, but his constant surveillance through the "White Mice," who kept him informed of every rumor that drifted through the shop, was increasingly irksome. A man who had served the Bennett newspapers loyally for years would find himself suddenly under suspicion of treason, his job threatened, his pay arbitrarily cut, all because of the tattling of someone who disliked or envied him.

Cabled summonses to hasten to the Commodore's side were invariably received with dread, because more often than not they meant trouble. Bennett liked to fire a man personally, was not above taking pleasure in making him squirm or beg for another chance. He liked to operate in an atmosphere tremulous with suspense and intrigue, comparable to that of the court of one of the more despotic Levantine emperors. An employee summoned to his presence, Laney has written, "might be kept waiting for weeks and then peremptorily fired. Or he might be showered with gifts and money if the Commodore happened to be in the mood. Bennett preferred to pay small salaries and then give 'presents' to his favorites, but dropped them as suddenly as he picked them up. Every employee lived in fear of incurring his displeasure for some unfathomable reason. He never praised, and if someone outside the paper praised one of his men, that man was doomed."

So many were instructed to "take the first ship for Europe" and a conference with the Commodore that the two-way traffic across the ocean became known as the "Atlantic Shuttle." Sometimes they arrived in Paris, Versailles, Beaulieu, or wherever his new steam yacht *Namouna* might be docked to find that Bennett had forgotten why he sent for them and was extremely irritated by their appearance.

Two editorial executives received the familiar summons once and hastened to one of his Paris offices. The Commodore looked up from his desk in amazement.

"What in hell are you doing here?" he demanded.

"You sent for us."

"Go back to New York."

End of interview.

A *Herald* man, at any rate, was likely to be well traveled before he was fired or quit in search of more stable employment.

Shortly after Charles Henry Meltzer, an eminent music critic, joined the *Herald* staff, he found himself in trouble because of his elaborate hairdo. He was warned that the Commodore had a phobia about his employees' hair—the less of it the better; the ideal employee, it seemed, would have been a hairless albino. He insisted that his men be clean-shaven and have their hair neatly trimmed, although he himself wore his hair long and affected sweeping mustachios any dragoon would have envied. Meltzer, however, dressed his hair like a musician, with long bangs in front and a fringe overlapping his collar in the rear. The "White Mice," of course, informed Bennett immediately of Meltzer's luxurious mane.

"TELL MELTZER TO CUT HIS HAIR," the Commodore cabled New York at once.

The music critic was given the message but refused to comply, holding that a man's relations with his barber were sacred and confidential.

On being informed that Meltzer was holding out, Bennett cabled his managing editor in New York: "SEND MELTZER TO ST. PETERSBURG."

Meltzer, somewhat puzzled, obeyed. When he showed up at the Russian capital, the *Herald* correspondent there was queried as to whether the critic had trimmed his hair. The answer was no. "SEND MELTZER TO BERLIN," Bennett telegraphed Saint Petersburg. Even the brush-cut Prussian hair styling made no impression on Meltzer. In similar fashion, Meltzer was sent to London, Copenhagen, and Stockholm. It may well have been the only Grand Tour undertaken for tonsorial reasons. But Meltzer continued to flaunt his mane. Finally he was ordered back to New York, where Bennett ordered that he be shorn of his job. Meltzer brought a successful lawsuit against his former employer, and the Commodore subsequently was shorn of damages.

Bennett was even less pleased with the result of his summons to Daniel McCarthy, who had been a New York Central engineer until his talent for drawing earned him a place on the *Herald* staff. The Commodore was then touring France in a tallyho loaded with his aristocratic friends, and wanted McCarthy to execute sketches of him in this lordly company. McCarthy was to proceed to Trouville and wait until his employer's party arrived at the resort. Days passed, and McCarthy amused himself by drawing some of the local washerwomen pounding their linen on the banks of a nearby scene. He sent these sketches to Bennett's Paris headquarters, which rebuked him for warming up on such lowly subjects.

Bored and resentful, McCarthy took to hanging around the local bistros and absorbing large quantities of brandy to relieve the tedium. He was soon embarked on an epic bender.

Finally one day, with a great clatter, Bennett's equipage rolled into Trouville, "well laden with fast specimens of European nobility, male and female." Bennett, at the reins, began shouting for his artist the moment he brought the conveyance to a halt.

McCarthy staggered out of a nearby bar, full of cognac and indignation at being kept waiting so long.

He eyed the Commodore on the box, then the gorgeously dressed patricians hanging from every window of the coach.

"Say, Bennett," he yelled, "how much do you pay these kings for riding around with you?"

McCarthy was coldly instructed to return to Paris, where orders awaited him to sail for New York, and there he was fired. His talents were quickly enlisted by the New York *World*, whose editorial page took on a particularly malicious sparkle when he was called upon to lampoon Bennett.

Another Irishman employed in the London bureau of the *Herald* was ordered to Paris for some misdemeanor of which Bennett had been informed. Fortunately the culprit had heard of Bennett's extreme fondness for dogs of the smaller species. The Commodore surrounded himself with a pack of thirty or forty Pomeranians, Pekingese, cocker spaniels, Chihuahuas, and Yorkshire terriers, who accompanied him wherever he went. Whenever a job applicant was interviewed, Bennett always had him inspected by several of his dogs. If they liked him, the applicant was accepted; if they bristled, he was quickly ushered out. So when the Irishman was summoned to Bennett's Paris apartment, he lined the cuffs of his trousers and the band of his silk hat with tiny strips of raw liver. He made his way toward the Commodore amid a yapping mass of little dogs, who swarmed all over him with affection. Bennett was delighted. "You must be a good fellow," he said, "or my dogs would find you out." He forgot all about dressing down his caller, and was even more impressed when the Irishman took his departure and the dogs could hardly bear to be separated from him. From then on, the Irishman could do no wrong and held down a good job in London for years.

Managing editor Connery and some of the other New York executives were disturbed at the attrition of their staff because of the "Atlantic Shuttle." Some of their best men quit rather than face a wigging overseas, and the editorial department constantly was short-staffed because of reporters or editors detached from duty to answer their publisher's summonses. The executives therefore were emboldened to protest when Bennett sent for a certain valuable feature writer. They cabled that the man was "indispensable" and could not be spared from his tasks. Back came a cable from the Commodore: "SEND LIST INDISPENSABLE MEN." The editors complied with the names of a dozen of their best men. Bennett immediately ordered that every one of the men be fired. "I will have no indispensable men in my employ," he told his secretary, Charles Christianson.

The quietly able Connery himself was ordered to retire on pension at the end of 1882, although he was only forty-seven years old. The "White Mice" had planted the suspicion in Bennett's mind that Connery was "getting too big." Connery's replacement was Bennett's boyhood friend, Edward T. Flynn, who was heartily disliked by many other *Herald* employees because of his preferred status. But even Flynn was not sure of his standing, and when Joseph Clarke wanted to quit rather than be promoted to assistant managing editor, he said, "Hold on, old boy, I don't know how long I'm going to last."

Flynn had performed competently as managing editor of the *Evening Telegram,* but he was soon receiving a constant flow of instruction and advice from Paris. Several samples of Bennett's views on how to manage a newspaper have been preserved:

"Try to carry out in the *Herald* the same principles of economic management combined with enterprise and thorough condensation of the news that you practised so successfully with the *Telegram.* . . .

"Have particular attention paid to Wall St. so as to have good local articles whenever there is a chance, but take care not to let the paper be used either by the writers themselves [financial reporters were believed unusually susceptible to bribery by brokers and speculators interested in booming certain issues] or by outsiders who may influence them for this purpose. Let there be a local feature of some sort every day, not a mere flimsy sensation worked up out of whole cloth, but the chief topic of the town, whatever it may happen to be, thoroughly well written and edited so as to make it fresh, lively and readable. . . .

"Avoid the habit correspondents are apt to get into of sending dribbing, unimportant dispatches which only increase the bills for telegraphing and cumber up the paper. I want you to treat the *Herald* exactly as if space were as much an object to it as it is to the *Telegram*. Use the same judgment and economy with the *Herald*. Don't consider that because the *Herald* is larger it has any more waste room than the *Telegram*. . . . Never, however, spare expense or space when the news justifies it. Whenever there is an important piece of news I want the *Herald* to have the fullest and best account of it. . . . The instant you see a sensation is dead, drop it and start in on something new. . . .

"The Ship news is never to be left out, or rather should be the last thing to leave out . . . though that *has* been done. . . .

"I want the notices of theatres to be brief, lively and always frank and fearless."

He also cautioned his papers against "Americanisms," such as using "stack" for "funnel" in describing a ship, as though Anglicisms were somehow more beneficial to an American readership.

Furthermore Flynn was to see to it that his staff kept their noses dry during their long working days. "Any reporter found to be drunk or under the influence of wine while on duty should be suspended three months without pay. How are O'Connor's habits now? I see he is at Albany—sent there by Mr. Connery, I suppose. Find out from Cummings, and if bad suspend or remove him."

Bennett's presence in the *Herald* building was almost palpable, and that was just the way he wanted it, to make every last hireling feel that his eye was upon him and his fiery breath was singeing the short hairs of every expendable neck. To carry out this illusion and dreadfully enhance his figurative totem, the Commodore's office was maintained in perfect order, as though he had just stepped out for a moment—a fire was kept burning on its hearth; each edition of the *Herald* and the *Telegram* was placed on his desk, and every day the head copy boy was required to sharpen two dozen new pencils and place them on his writing pad. (And every night that same copy boy sold those same pencils to a friend, who put on dark glasses and a sign reading "I Am Blind" until they were disposed of along Park Row.)

Nowhere was the Commodore's unseen hand heavier than on the city room, where his reporters' respect for the English language was enforced by ironclad rules. Bennett was an inept writer and a wretched rhetorician, as surviving samples of his editorial writings amply demonstrate ("kicking" anacondas and all), but he was resolved that his henchmen would make up for his deficiencies. The Commodore was hard put to compose one lucid, let alone felicitous sentence, but he was a stickler for style, a foe of the cliché, an ardent crusader for proper usage. When the brilliant Texan Stanley Walker became city editor of the New York *Herald Tribune*—half of which was Bennett's old *Herald,* if such things can be fragmented—he uncovered Bennett's style sheet with the "red rags waved by careless writers" which he abominated. Some of his strictures were:

"Don't call a theatrical performance a 'show.'

"Don't apply 'schedule' to the movement of persons, as: 'Ambassador Bacon was scheduled to leave Vienna.'

"Don't use 'New Yorker.'

"Don't use 'week-end' or 'over Saturday.'

"Don't use 'guest of honor' or 'maid of honor.'

"Don't use 'gang' or 'gangster.'

"Don't use 'diplomat'; use 'diplomatist.'

"Don't use 'minister' except for diplomatists.

"Don't use 'plan' except in connection with drawn architectural or engineering plans. Do not use it as a verb. 'Planned' and 'planning' are taboo.

"Don't use 'house guest,' 'house party' or 'reception guest.' "

No style book in existence, however, could guide his anxious, dyspeptic editors in trying to anticipate or deal with his whims. Once when that nervous council was awaiting Bennett's answer to an important proposal, they received, instead, a cabled command to "send two mocking-birds by special messenger." The editorial board, in consultation with the dog-and-bird editor, located the birds and sent them off. That still didn't answer their question, and they were even more perplexed by the next message from the Commodore, "Send mocking-bird food." Weeks later they learned that Bennett had forgotten all about the policy matter awaiting his decision when he got involved in a dinner-table debate over the merits of the American mockingbird, which he declared was the finest warbler in the world. An English lady present insisted that the British species was much superior. Bennett had sent for the birds to prove his point, since he could not bear to lose an argument. Then he learned that his birds wouldn't vocalize without their native seed for nourishment; hence the second cable. In pressing his side of the mocking-bird controversy, which aroused all his latent patriotism, Bennett could spare no thought for his editors' problem: he was loud in condemning everything American, on occasion, but was enraged when any "foreigner" ventured on the same tack.

If a man can be judged by the enemies he makes as well as the company he keeps, Bennett, more by accident than design, perhaps, was sometimes to be found on the side of the angels. He had a thousand dislikes but very few hatreds. Only three men drew his unreserved contempt and ill will: William Randolph Hearst, Kaiser Wilhelm of Germany, and Jay Gould, although he had little or no personal contact with any of them. Each of them he fought to the last ditch, with varying success but unremitting energy.

His collaboration in the fight against Gould's dictatorship of the American telegraph and cable system was, in fact, one of the brightest spots of his career.

So far as can be determined, Bennett and Gould never met in person, since even while the former was living in New York he traveled in entirely different circles from the home-loving Gould. Even before their all-out clash of the 1880s, however, Bennett had conceived a strong distaste for the undersized but venturesome financier who, ever since the close of the Civil War, had been creating havoc with the American economy. The *Herald* had commented bitterly on Gould's seizure of the Erie Railway and his coup in the gold market of 1869, had categorized him the "skunk" rather than the "wolf" of Wall Street, and had opposed all his subsequent maneuvers, all to no avail. During the seventies Gould had captured control of a large share of the American railroads, among them the Wabash, the Union Pacific, the Missouri Pacific, the Texas & Pacific, and lesser carriers. In 1881, in two lightning forays of unparalleled audacity and speculative skill, Gould had added Western Union and the whole elevated railway system in New York to his domain. In addition to shouldering the house of Vanderbilt out of Western Union, he had obtained control of the transatlantic cable facilities. And here, in particular, the Gould interests collided with Bennett's. Cable rates were raised to exorbitant levels, which greatly increased the cost of the *Herald's* extensive foreign correspondence.

While Bennett was snarling over his cable bills, one day in autumn of 1883 he was approached by a visiting American likewise concerned by the Gould monopoly. His name was John W. Mackay, one of the four kings of the Comstock Lode.

Mackay's particular gripe was that his wife, like Bennett, was an expatriate, living in England and France, and the cost of communicating with her was becoming irksome even for a multimillionaire.

The two men decided to break Gould's cable monopoly, although Bennett never had and never would again concern himself financially with any enterprise outside of the newspaper business.

A firmly devoted alliance was formed by the two men, disparate as they were in character, background, and personality. Mackay, in the first place, was a self-made man, and until he struck it rich in Nevada silver his life had been an arduous one. Born in Dublin ten years before Bennett, he had migrated to the United States in his youth, worked in saloons and shipyards, and unsuccessfully sought his fortune in the placer workings on California creeks. Mackay was in his early thirties by the time he joined the stampede to Virginia City and finally carved the $100,000,000 fortune out of the silver mines in partnership with three other Irishmen. While raking in his share of the bonanza, Mackay heard of the plight of a pretty young Canadian girl, Marie Hungerford Bryant, a barber's daughter whose husband had died and left her penniless in the mining camp. Instead of contributing to the fund being raised to send her and her infant daughter home—the latter would become Princess of Colonna, thanks to her indulgent stepfather's fortune—Mackay married the young widow. Aside from the fact that his granddaughter married Irving Berlin, the name of John W. Mackay should be fondly remembered today as one of the very few nineteenth-century capitalists who did not yearn to gobble up the whole country. Under the impact of sudden wealth, he remained modest, unassuming, and sensible; "of all the bonanza millionaires," it was said, "he was the only one who could be called popular."

Even before they met, according to one of Mackay's biographers (Oscar Lewis, *Silver Kings*), the silver magnate had conceived an admiration for Bennett "second only to that he entertained for General Grant." The reason for it, since self-made men rarely have much use for the silver-spoon generation, has never been made clear. Mackay did have a large respect for the New York *Herald,* its policies and attitudes, however, and perhaps that admiration was extended to its publisher. The two men, at any rate, hit it off well, and unlike many such financial combinations, theirs was never shadowed by even the most fleeting disagreement or suspicion of betrayal. Bennett was not easy to get along with, but he so respected Mackay's judgment and integrity that, while putting up twenty per cent of the capital for their struggle against Gould, he left the tactics of financial campaigning entirely to his partner.

A predictably long and bitter contest ensued, with the terms about equal. The Mackay-Bennett resources totaled about the same as Gould's. In the latter's favor, of course, was his genius as a manipulator, a monopolist, and an infighter. On the other hand Gould was handicapped by the fact that he was overextended, with the necessity of raking up dividends for the many issues of watered stock for which he was responsible. The

Mackay-Bennett money was solid, unencumbered, and they were able to conduct their fight without enlisting other investors and submitting to outside interference.

They formed the Commercial Cable Company, and within a year a specially equipped steamer, the *Mackay-Bennett,* was laying the first of two cables from New York to London. Until now Gould's Western Union had maintained a monopoly on the traffic between Heart's Content, Newfoundland, to Ireland, where his system hooked up with that of an English combine's. By late 1884 the new company was joining in vigorous competition with Gould's, which up to now had been charging seventy-five cents a word on its transatlantic messages. Much of Gould's success in railroading had been derived from his practice of ruthlessly slashing rates and ruining his competition. So now a rate war developed: Gould cut to fifty cents a word, Commercial Cables to forty, then Gould also to forty. By now Gould was complaining, "There's no beating John Mackay. If he needs another million or two he goes to his silver mine and digs it up." Meanwhile Bennett's newspapers were benefiting from the reduced rates, with what a *Herald* editor, Joseph Clarke, called "an increase in the volume and value of its foreign service."

Mackay and Bennett soon learned, however, that they would have to widen the front of their attack on Gould. The latter's Western Union, holding a near-monopoly on the American telegraph system, refused to relay any messages to be transmitted over the Mackay-Bennett cables. Thus it became necessary for them to buy control of the Postal Telegraph and patch together a competitive system by combining with a number of smaller companies. Gould fought back with all his resources, cutting domestic rates, attacking the financial position of the Postal Telegraph combine. One of Mackay's

Comstock partners, Jim Fair, was predicting that Mackay would "sink his last dollar to the bottom of the Atlantic," and Bennett, though not so deeply involved financially, was also feeling the strain. By now the cable rates of both companies had been slashed to twenty-five cents a word, a cut deeper than even Mackay and Bennett had bargained for.

Meanwhile, always vulnerable on personal grounds, Bennett was being attacked unremittingly in several Gould-influenced New York journals. Gould held a mortgage on the *Tribune,* now being published by Whitelaw Reid, and naturally it parrotted his opinions; likewise the *Evening Mail & Express,* owned by his close collaborator, Cyrus Field, until the latter tried to outmaneuver Gould and was ruined in the process. Field had built the first Atlantic cable, and was jealous of his successors. Until 1883 Gould himself had published the New York *World* and proved himself a master at adapting journalism to service as a propaganda weapon in his financial wars.

In the midst of their battle over the cable monopoly, Bennett exposed a Gould scheme in the *Herald*. The financier, as the *Herald* revealed, was engaged in a plot to wreck the Kansas Pacific Railroad, which only a few years ago he had sold to the Union Pacific at a grossly inflated price. The *Herald's* revelations not only derailed his scheme but caused Gould to lose his temper, an extremely rare occurrence for that cool and canny operator.

In retaliation, Gould composed an open letter addressed to Bennett but sent to all the New York papers except the *Herald* and the *Telegram*. It recited Bennett's missteps at length and denounced him as a disloyal expatriate, a duelist, a social leper. "Let me see," Gould wrote, "I have known you about thirty years, and during all that time your life has been one of shame. Your private life has been a succession of debauches and scandal, so that your name is on every tongue as Bennett the libertine. And however gentlemen might meet you in their clubs or hotels, not a gentleman in New York, as you well know, would allow you to cross the threshold of his residence where virtue and family honor are held sacred."

Nothing could be kept secret long on Park Row, and the *Herald* editors got wind of the letter before it could be published in the other papers. A galley proof of the letter was somehow smuggled out of the New York *Press*' composing room and brought to the *Herald,* which published it at the same time as the other morning papers, thus poulticing much of the sting in Gould's denunciation.

A *Herald* editorial commented, "Gould the corsair has been hit hard by the *Herald,* which has told the truth about the methods he has pursued to gather a fortune from wrecked railroads and the bankruptcies of scores of honest men."

Bennett was so pleased by the way his editors had boldly taken the wind out of Gould's sails that his own reply, in an editorial footnote, was uncharacteristically mild:

"The proprietor of the *Herald* lost his reputation long before Mr. Gould was ever heard of."

Unshaken, Mackay and Bennett held on grimly as Gould continued to cut domestic rates and reduced the cable toll to twelve cents a word. Public opinion was largely on the side of the partners, Gould then being the leading contender for the title of the most hated man in America—the target of the labor unions, liberals of all shapes and hues, and the burgeoning anti-monopoly movement. But it would take more than sympathy to prevail against Jay Gould. His bag of tricks was all but bottomless.

One of the main links in the Postal Telegraph system was the Bankers & Merchants Telegraph, which under a contract signed in 1883 had combined certain of its properties with the American Rapid Telegraph, a circumstance which Gould, with his keen scent for the possibilities of corporate troublemaking, saw as his opportunity to strike at the Postal Telegraph. In this enterprise he was joined by Fred May, who had fought the duel with Bennett in 1877 and apparently was not averse to increasing his present difficulties. May was a friend of the receiver for the Rapid Telegraph, whom he brought aboard Gould's yacht and who was induced to authorize Western Union to act as his agent.

Through various legal proceedings Gould, as the representative of the Rapid Telegraph, was given the right to reclaim that company's lines and other assets which had been mingled with the Bankers & Merchants Telegraph, facilities which were now being used by Postal Telegraph. At Gould's orders all of the Bankers & Merchants' lines except those leading into Washington were cut down on the pretext that they were part of the Rapid Telegraph's property. This highly illegal action all but ruined the Bankers & Merchants and seriously crippled Postal Telegraph, but Gould fought a successful delaying campaign in the courts for years.

Mackay was so disheartened that he wrote Edward S. Stokes, the largest bondholder in Bankers & Merchants, that "I don't give a damn about the money I've put in. I just want to get out. . . . The best thing to do is to sell out the whole plant to the Western Union, ticker and all."

Bennett, however, would not hear of surrendering to Gould, of whom the *Herald* was to editorialize, "He reckoned the possible ruin of thousands as a matter in which he had no concern." Faraway from the arena of financial combat, he urged Mackay to hold out against Gould's constant harassments, and wait for better times. Eventually Gould would damage himself as much as his competitors through his ruthless tactics.

Bennett's hunch proved correct. Gould, by the summer of 1887, had grown as weary of the battle as Mackay. That fall an agreement was reached whereby both sides would cease their rate cutting in the continental United States, and a short time later the cable tolls were also stabilized. Western Union was forced to recognize Postal Telegraph as having codominion status. For once Jay Gould had been fought to a standstill, and for at least a junior partner's share in that victory the public could thank James Gordon Bennett, Jr.

Even before Bennett joined forces with Mackay for the battle with Gould, the latter unwittingly, and for once without malice aforethought, brought about the greatest threat to Bennett's position as the foremost American newspaper publisher. That threat was embodied in and fulfilled by a myopic Hungarian immigrant named Joseph Pulitzer. On May 8, 1883, some months before Bennett allied himself with Mackay, Gould sold the New York *World* to Pulitzer, whose brother Albert published the *Morning Journal* and who himself was the publisher of the St. Louis *Post-Dispatch,* for $346,000. Gould had casually acquired the *World* in a package deal with the Texas & Pacific Railroad, had used it as a bludgeon in his stock-market raids, and finally had wearied of making up its annual deficit. He sold it to the first man who was foolhardy enough to take over a losing venture, and who just happened to be the one man who could challenge the preeminence of the *Herald*.

Within three days of taking over the *World*, Pulitzer revamped its stodgy make-up, shook some life into its somnolent staff, and served notice that personal journalism was making a comeback on Park Row. If the other papers were stanch defenders of the status quo, the *World* would take up the cause of New York's swarming millions, the hordes who shuttled between sweatshops and slum tenements. "There is room in this great and growing city for a journal that is not only cheap but bright, not only bright but large, not only large but truly democratic—dedicated to the cause of the people rather than that of the purse potentates—devoted more to the news of the new than the old world, that will expose all fraud and sham, fight all public evils and abuses—that will serve and battle for the people with earnest sincerity." Like Bennett the elder, he lashed out at "High Society," at the "sordid aristocracy of the ambitious match-makers who are ready to sell their daughters for barren titles to worthless foreign paupers." He would promote the "aristocracy of labor." His scheme was simple enough: to appeal to the readers who once had been wooed by the *Herald*, the *Sun*, the *Times* and other successful papers, then dropped once they had attracted a wide audience.

Well aware of the seriousness of the threat posed by Pulitzer, Bennett responded by dropping the price of the *Herald* from three to two cents in the following September. Unfortunately this measure only involved the *Herald* in difficulties with the newsdealers, who had to take a corresponding cut in their share of the proceeds. The dealers organized themselves, promoted a boycott of the *Herald*, held parades and demonstrations, all aimed at forcing Bennett to restore their original commission. Bennett, of course, fought back with counterdemonstrations and an ill-tempered propaganda campaign, but the only winner in this contest was the *World*, which kept taking circulation away from the *Herald*, not only because of the bad public relations arising from the dispute with the newsdealers but by making the *World* the liveliest sheet in town, crackling with enterprise, pouring on the "crusades," looking on the metropolitan scene with the breezy irreverence that almost half a century before had boosted the *Herald* to the top of the heap. Bennett finally was forced to settle the newsdealers' strike on their terms, but by then Pulitzer was off to a flying start.

By then, too, Bennett was engaged in the classic folly of a war on two fronts. He was sinking all his available resources—while not, of course, stinting on his extravagant style of living—in the fight against Western Union and the man who, inadvertently, had recruited Pulitzer for the New York circulation war. (Pulitzer, incidentally, attacked Gould far more vigorously than he lashed back at his journalistic rivals.) Just when Bennett should have been expending all his cash reserves and his mental energies on dealing with the *World*, he was battling the cable and telegraph monopoly. The result was that he achieved cheaper cable rates for a newspaper which was being beaten daily on the handling of local and national news by a rival which boasted that it would devote itself "more to the news of the new than the old world." A newspaper, Bennett was soon to learn, could not live by prestige alone.

He wryly acknowledged this in an editorial he wrote for the *Herald* in October of 1890, when Pulitzer was forced to retire from active editorship of the *World* by blindness. "What the Greeleys and the Raymonds and the Bennetts did for journalism thirty years ago, Pulitzer has done today. It is true his methods have been queer and peculiar, but after all they have suited the present American public. . . .

"We have not always agreed with the spirit which has made his ideas a journalistic success, and we cannot refrain from regretting that he did not encourage us in the new departure which he made, instead of merely astonishing us, frightening us, and, we may add, now that it is past, perhaps a little bit disgusting us."

By the time he wrote that reluctant salute to his rival, a young man named William Randolph Hearst was already lighting up the San Francisco journalistic scene with his first newspaper and meditating an invasion of New York with even more "queer and peculiar" ideas than Pulitzer had generated.

Between Pulitzer's *World* and Hearst's *Journal*, his now staid and respectable *Herald*, once the guidon bearer of the "new journalism," would soon be placed in the lamentable position of an elderly reporter chasing the fire engines on the heels of springier-legged young colleagues.

But the Commodore was essentially undismayed.

"Nothing," he was very fond of saying, "can hurt the *Herald*."

8: Childe *Herald* in Paris

Instead of consolidating his position, Bennett decided to expand his newspaper properties in 1887, when the costly victory over Gould and Western Union had been achieved. He was forty-six years old and crustily confirmed in bachelorhood; the thought of sharing his time, his thoughts, his possessions and indulgences with a woman who would have a legal right to them was still unbearable, and Paris, after all, was a bachelor's paradise.

Since there was small chance that he would have to provide for any children, he could spend his million-dollar income as he pleased, and there was no possession more satisfying than a newspaper. He was still nominally responsible for his sister Jeanette, but she had greatly annoyed him by marrying Isaac Bell without his permission. (Bell was United States minister to The Hague for a time, but died in 1889 at the age of forty-two. Bennett's papers, undoubtedly on his orders, found room for only one paragraph to report the death, and the fact that Bell was Bennett's brother-in-law was not mentioned.) This estrangement naturally was extended to his sister's son, Isaac Bell, Jr., whom Bennett had seen just once.

The Commodore had stood at the foot of the infant's cradle, staring down at his nephew. Then, without a word, he reached into his pocket and drew out a check for $100,000, tossed it at the infant's feet and stalked away. It was typical of the Commodore that, having announced he would have nothing more to do with his nephew, he kept a sort of distant watch over him. When the Irish peasantry rose up against the landed gentry late in the century, young Bell was living on a Galway estate and was master of the noted hunt, the Galway Blazers. Fearful of what might happen to the young man but unwilling to make any direct inquiries as to his safety, Bennett sent a correspondent from London, ostensibly to cover the outbreaks but actually to make sure Bell was unharmed. "While the Commodore would never have anything to do with his nephew," wrote the correspondent, Albert Stevens Crockett, "he was undoubtedly very fond of him, and very proud that the young man was maintaining some sort of position among the Irish gentry."

Crockett found Bell quite unharmed and eager to talk about the Commodore. "Of course I never see my uncle," Bell told Crockett, "but I am deeply grateful to him, for it is to him that I owe everything I have. When I was a baby, lying in my crib, he came into the room and threw a check for $100,000 upon the foot of the cradle, and that has been my main reliance ever since."

With no real family ties and no very substantial friendships to occupy him, Bennett decided to publish his own English-language paper in Paris. Everyone called it the Paris *Herald,* although Bennett angrily insisted that it was the European edition of the New York *Herald.* Under any name, it became an enduring American outpost in Europe. It kept publishing throughout World War I and resumed publication after the German occupation of Paris in World War II, and for almost seventy-five years it has provided the American abroad a steadfast contact with his homeland. No newspaper of its size has ever given birth to more legends, surrounded itself with more glamour, or produced a livelier effect on European journalism. The *Herald* in Paris, in addition, constituted the one lasting monument to its founder.

His primary reason for establishing the first American newspaper on the continent was to keep himself busy, to have a property near at hand which he could descend upon, as he did the *Herald* in New York, whenever the whim seized him, galvanizing the place with his terrifying presence, turning the paper upside down, ripping out stories and advertisements which annoyed him, rampaging from press room to editorial department to composing room, promoting and demoting on a momentary inspiration. The *Herald* in Paris was, first of all, his plaything. The atmosphere of a newspaper office, which to an outsider might seem to be compounded largely of musty smells, the reek of ink and newsprint in every corner, the incessant clatter of telegraph keys and linotypes, the occasional quaking of presses beginning a run, was the breath of life to him. It was one of the world's nerve ends. In those days, too, the power of the printed word and the influence of the newspaper were so much greater than today. A newspaper proprietor could feel, even if he lacked Bennett's touch of megalomania, that he was one of the movers and shakers.

Furthermore he intended to make himself the voice of America on the continent. From his earliest days as a publisher, he had promoted the idea that each nation should know more about all the others. More than any other publisher he had made America aware of Europe, as well as Asia and Africa. Now he was determined

that Europe would, in turn, learn more about the
United States. He was one of the first of the inter-
nationalists, although it was not true, as his enemies
charged, that he hated his native land. He defined his
attitude very precisely once to Albert Jaurett, one of
his executives on the Paris *Herald*: "I love America,
but I hate most Americans." One of his strongest be-
liefs, with World War I still almost three decades in the
offing, was that a firm understanding must link France,
Great Britain, and the United States. Though both an
Anglophile and a Francophile (and a Germanophobe
long before suspicion of Imperial Germany was fashionable) he remained intensely—almost ludicrously, in
some eyes—American.

In a note to one of the Paris *Herald* editors, he once
declared that he regarded himself as a watchdog of
American foreign policy, and he himself would take
action if the State Department proved to be too timorous
in some matter.

"My foreign policy," he once said, "is simply this:
If a nation is friendly to America, I wish the *Herald* to
be friendly to that nation, but if a nation shows an unfriendly policy, I wish the *Herald* to adopt an unfriendly tone. This may not be patriotism, but it is the
course I wish the *Herald* to follow."

Always bumptious, Bennett, in fact, considered himself a sort of ex-officio, one-man State Department, with
his correspondents as his ambassadors. During a political
crisis in Venezuela, for instance, Bennett suddenly
decided that it was his duty to support Washington in
its expressed intention of upholding the Monroe Doc-
trine. What better way to defend American principles
than to establish a *Herald* in Caracas? He made elaborate
plans to send Albert Jaurett to Venezuela for that

purpose, but "the whole affair finally boiled down to sending a reporter to find out what was going on down there." It was finally determined that South America would be able to struggle along without direct guidance from Bennett and his ambassadorial *Heralds*.

Two years after the Paris *Herald* was established, Bennett began publishing a London edition and continued it for slightly less than two years, taking even larger losses than the Paris edition's estimated annual deficit of $100,000. The English preferred their own newspapers, and there were not enough Americans visiting or resident in London to support a daily paper. In its brief life, however, the London *Herald* produced a revolutionary effect on the appearance of the British newspapers, introducing such innovations as livelier headlines and make-up, brisker writing, photoengraving, the special supplement, and the comic section. Alfred Harmsworth (later Lord Northcliffe) was especially quick to adopt the style and methods of presentation imported by the London edition of the *Herald* for his *Daily Mail*. Harmsworth, in fact, became the leading exponent of what was then called "yellow journalism," the sort of sensationalism which Pulitzer and Hearst, in their white-hot competition for circulation, were to perfect in the last years of the century.

The Paris edition, then, was the only overseas *Herald* to survive, although its circulation and advertising were only briefly sufficient to gladden the heart of a business-minded publisher. It was Bennett's toy, and some of his experiments with it fully expressed the freakish elements in Bennett's temperament. At one period he dazzled his readers by printing the Paris edition in colored inks, running through the spectrum until he finally returned to black. Only a few days before the first issue came off the press, he told his staff at a luncheon in his apartment on the Champs Elysées that they were to obey every instruction that came from him, no matter how odd it might seem, and continued:

"I consider a dead dog in the Rue du Louvre more interesting for the *Herald* than a devastating flood in China. I want one feature article a day. If I say the feature is to be black beetles, black beetles it's going to be."

The Paris *Herald*, to use the title he abhorred but which was its designation to generations of visiting Americans, was published at 38 Rue du Louvre, where its editorial, press and composing rooms were located, while the business office was at 49 Avenue de l'Opéra, a few doors below the Café de la Paix. In this latter office was located the huge registry in which touring Americans signed their names. The real headquarters of the operation, however, were at Bennett's Paris apartment, or wherever he happened to be living, on land or sea.

On October 4, 1887, the first issue rolled off the presses. It consisted of four six-column pages, with the first three largely given over to news and the fourth to advertising. In that first issue the top display was given to a column of dispatches cabled from New York; also prominently played up were a column each devoted to news of the London and New York stock exchanges, in which the most important item was a report that Jay Gould, in collaboration with Collis P. Huntington of the Southern Pacific, had recaptured control of the Pacific Mail Steamship Company.

Much of Page Two was given over to the "Personal Intelligence" column, which reported the movements of prominent Americans on the continent and carried various gossipy tidbits about persons famous or notorious in international society:

"Mr. William K. Vanderbilt will return from London to the Bristol on Wednesday.

"Mr. James G. Blaine and family arrived at the Hotel Vendôme Sunday from Geneva.

"The Empress Eugénie still possesses an umbrella which cost $2,000. The handle is a mass of splendid gems.

"Joe Andrews, the San Francisco diamond collector, wears a $15,000 cluster of diamonds on his necktie. . . .

"Prof. John L. Sullivan's new book is almost ready for publication. It is expected to make a great hit.

"Mr. and Mrs. Henry Watrous of New York are coming abroad to study art together and think of opening a charming little studio in the artists' quarter."

The rest of the paper was given over to editorials, a dispatch from England detailing how the Vicar of Cretingham had been shot to death by his curate, and the letters to the editor—frequently, and sulphurously, answered by the editor—through which Bennett "established that personal relationship with his readers," as Al Laney (Paris *Herald*) has written, "which, continued and expanded, was to be of such value to the paper in its later years." The names of all the Americans who signed the registry at the *Herald* business office also were listed.

In those first issues, Bennett set the pattern for his Paris paper, eccentric and informal as it was, which was to make it one of the more remarkable American institutions abroad. In the third issue, a reader complained in the letters column that he missed seeing the customary "greeting article" which heralded a new publication and set forth its high-minded aims. Bennett himself replied to this letter in an editor's note in his usual peppery style:

"This is not a new paper. The *Herald* is over half a century old. The fact that we have chosen to publish a European edition is a detail. We do not, moreover, believe in buncombe articles about 'long felt needs' and telling what one intends to do, and what not to do. A good newspaper speaks for itself."

In the first several weeks of publication the Paris edition of the *Herald* accurately reflected the determination of its creator to provide a tourists' newspaper, an expatriates' organ and an international society sheet that would entertainingly bridge the sometimes dismaying gap between home and abroad. The homesick grain-elevator owner from Iowa, the Philadelphia spinster living off her income, the New York yachtsman, the society lady flitting from spa to spa with her children, even the sojourning Englishman and the odd Frenchman who wanted to understand America, all found sustenance in the Paris *Herald;* it told him where his friends were, where the best places to eat and stay were, how to adjust oneself to the strangeness of European customs, and it remained intensely American.

Among the titillations offered in those first issues were a report on the recent successes of a fast-moving American jewel thief known as "Mr. Van Dyke," who had been reaping a glittering harvest in Berlin, Vienna, Rome, and Budapest; an account of a Russian lady whose death at a Saint Petersburg ball was attributed to a tight corset; a story on the three Boston society girls caught in an opium den with three Harvard juniors, "sitting with pipes in hand," and a Page One column considering the moral problem posed under this headline:

IS WALTZING REALLY
SO VERY WICKED?
Is There Any Harm in Our Girls
Fluttering About Inside
of a Glad Man's Arm?
—The Cynic Says
There Is—The
Girls Say No

Editorial comment in a news column was strictly forbidden in the New York edition, but Bennett relaxed the rule for the Paris *Herald* when it came to reporting a move by Jay Gould and Western Union to abrogate the truce with Mackay and Bennett on juggling the cable rates. "Jay Gould and his partners in the cable pool have decided to make war to the knife on Messrs. Mackay and Bennett. By this war they hope to force their competitors to either sell out the Commercial Cables or consent to join the pool in advancing rates to sixty cents a word. Messrs. Mackay and Bennett would rather lose the millions they have put into the enterprise than to submit to the dishonor of promising the public one thing at the start and in the end doing another. The war measure of the pool is to reduce cable rates to six cents a word, and they expect in this way to cripple the Commercial company. Gould and company has united with the English cable magnates in this fight for the restoration of an arrogant and oppressive monopoly." The Paris *Herald* signified its intention of keeping a close watch on the tricky Mr. Gould for the benefit of traveling investors whose interests might be endangered by his maneuvers. It cited rumors that the "Little Wizard" was trying to snatch control of the Atchison, Topeka & Santa Fe Railroad, much of its stock owned in Boston, and predicted that "straitlaced Bostonians will wash their tapering hands of the whole business if Gould is to have any sway in Atchison affairs."

Almost immediately the Paris edition's clever mixture of news and gossip caught on with its rather limited but well-heeled potential readership. The society columns gave European royalty and its hangers-on a new sense of importance in a world which was increasingly repelled by aristocratic pretensions. There were literally hundreds of princes, dukes, counts, barons, marquises, even an unemployed king or two, and their feminine counterparts, wandering around the resorts and watering places of Europe. And wherever these somewhat disenchanted personages gathered with their retinues, eyes peeled for American heiresses and their ambitious mamas—in Carlsbad and Marienbad, where royal innards were purged and reorganized, at Aix-les-Bains, Saint-Moritz, on the Riviera—there were *Herald* correspondents recording everything that was happening. Soon the Paris *Herald* acquired the highest social rating of any periodical in existence. All the courts of Europe subscribed to it, and 200 copies went daily to the Czar's entourage in Saint Petersburg. Within a few years, Laney noted in his history of the paper, "Bennett's personal prestige on the continent was enormous. . . . He himself was of this world when he chose to be, and there is no doubt that he was feared in these circles too because of the well-known violence of his temperament."

Bennett's thoroughly American idiosyncrasy of adoring royalty, even in its shabbiest and most discredited forms, involved him in the deepest embarrassment of his publishing career, leading him into a reckless collision with democratic institutions that utterly abashed him. The consequences of his sympathy for monarchial aspirations, in fact, almost wrecked the *Herald* a little more than a year after it started publication.

The Commodore, heedless of the warnings of some of his friends and advisers, decided to support the grandiose ambitions of the original Man on a White Horse, General Georges Ernest Jean Marie Boulanger, whose demagogic talents and dashing manner persuaded many Frenchmen that he was destined to be the savior of a nation still humbled by its memories of Metz and Sedan and the loss of Alsace-Lorraine to the victorious Prussians. A veteran of that war, General Boulanger had risen to command of the army of occupation in Tunisia by 1884, but a dispute with the political resident resulted in his recall and his determination to plunge into politics. Aligning himself briefly with Clemenceau's Radicals, he was appointed Minister of War in January, 1886, and made himself highly popular with his army reforms and his intimations that a resurgent France could avenge the humiliation of 1871. Every time he appeared on the boulevards, a magnificent figure on horseback, cheers went up for the "brave general." To the masses he represented a hope of revenge, to the always watchful anti-republican forces a popular hero who might be used to bring about a dictatorship or restore the monarchy. A Boulangist movement was soon born, its midwives some of the most sinister and ridiculous people in France.

Boulangism suffered a temporary setback in 1887 when a new government came to power, disregarded the clamor of the general's followers, and excluded him from the cabinet. Perhaps if he were removed from the worshipful mobs on the boulevards and from the aristocratic schemers behind them in the Fauborg Saint-Germain, the new government believed, the movement would collapse and the hardheaded political sense of the people would reassert itself. Boulanger was ordered back on the active list and given command of a corps headquartered in the provincial backwater of Clermont-Ferrand. Further, he was sternly directed by the war ministry to stay away from the capital. But the general, drunk on applause and flattery, could no more keep out of Paris than Napoleon could find contentment on Elba. Twice he defied his superiors by slipping back to the capital, and was summarily removed from command and dismissed from the army.

In the fall of 1888 he was encouraged to stand for election to the Chamber of Deputies, from which forum it was expected that he would launch his final campaign against the Republic and lead a more glorious France to victory against Prussia. Now the anti-republican forces came out in the open. The Comte de Paris, the perennially hopeful pretender to the throne, offered Boulanger his blessings in the election of January, 1889, and every reactionary, super-patriot, militarist, and mossback still entranced by memories of the Bonapartes or the Bourbons joined in attempting to turn the clock back.

Among those bereft of their senses by Boulangism was Bennett himself, though only a dozen years before he had strongly opposed suggestions of a third term for President Grant because it would be a threat to democratic government. His line of reasoning was hard to trace. As an American citizen, certainly, he had no business meddling in the affairs of the French Republic, particularly to help overthrow it. Perhaps, at the moment, he was merely thinking more like a misguided French patriot, eager to do in the Germans, than a U.S. citizen. In any case, he was utterly indiscreet. As a member of the elegant but subversive salon of the Duchesse d'Uzès, a center of royalist intrigue, he pledged his support of the papier-mâché hero. The duchess gave hundreds of thousands of francs to the campaign and Bennett, flattered by her friendship, not only made financial contributions but threw the *Herald's* influence into the cause.

He could not be persuaded by his more sensible friends that he was pursuing a dangerous course, that the real political strength of France was still weighted in favor of the Republic. Nor would he take heed of the editorial opinions expressed in the solider Parisian journals as the election campaign grew hotter. *Temps* commented that "General Boulanger denounces dictatorship—not his own dictatorship, but the dictatorship of anyone else." "Voters," pleaded *Evénement*, "don't allow France to be torn apart by the old and worn out political parties who push General Boulanger forward."

A survey of the Paris edition of the *Herald* during the January weeks when Boulanger was campaigning for the deputy's seat in the Department of the Seine shows its coverage betrayed a strong bias in favor of the general.

On January 5, 1889, the *Herald* reported that "Paris is already vivid with General Boulanger's pink, green, red or yellow posters. . . . The 'Brav' General's flaming creeds and signatures now extend from the Moulin de la Galette to the Catacombs, and everybody from the Buttes Chaumont to the Arc de Triomphe asks, 'Will he be elected?' All the Boulangists are in high glee." A few days later the *Herald* congratulated the Royalist factions of the Twentieth Arrondissement for agreeing at a caucus not to enter a candidate against Boulanger. On January 11 the *Herald* described how "the people of Paris worship the hero of the moment" at one of the thrice-weekly receptions held by the posturing Boulanger in a tapestried salon of a hotel in

Rue Dumont d'Urville. "An atmosphere of awe seemed to penetrate the place." The less awed, as other journals reported, took note of the fact that the eupeptic general never quite got around to spelling out how he was going to "save France." Yet he had become "an open menace to the parliamentary republic," on the vague understanding that once he was given the power he would sweep away the inefficient machinery of democracy.

All of a sudden the *Herald* changed its mind about Boulanger. On January 24 an editorial warned that "Boulangism means revolution. If General Boulanger had made a canvass like the present against the Emperor, it would have ended in his summary exile to Cayenne." The next day the *Herald* pointed out that "Boulanger's canvass either means revolution or an impertinent waste of time," and recalled that the two previous revolutions had played out their final scenes at Waterloo and Sedan. On January 27, the eve of the election: "Boulangism is a weapon, an expedient to break down the Republic. . . . It represents every element of Bonapartism but the genius of Napoleon."

What had changed the Commodore's generally unchangeable mind on the issue of Boulangism? On January 20 he had been summoned to the Ministry of the Interior, and the first man since the roaring days of Bully Samuels had dressed him down and put him in his place. Bennett never revealed what caused him to abandon "the brave general" less than ten days before the election until one day in the early 1900s when French workers called a strike to protest the actions of the Paris prefect of police. Editorial employees of the *Herald* had decided to join in the one-day work stoppage. When Bennett got wind of this, he rushed over to the *Herald* office and called a meeting of the staff.

"Gentlemen," he told his reporters and editors, "I am informed that you are planning to declare a one-day strike as a protest against something for which the police department of this city is responsible, and I am wondering whether you would like to know what happened to me in somewhat similar circumstances.

"A few years ago, a lady who stands very high in French society undertook to finance and support a movement intended to change the government of France. General Boulanger, whom some of you remember, was led to believe that he could be instrumental in restoring some form of monarchy to take the place of the republic, and the Duchess gave him her support. Foolishly enough, I thought at the time that anything so noble a lady approved could only be for the good of France, and I therefore arranged to give her and her Boulanger movement the full support of this paper.

"This went on for a while until the men who were then at the head of the French government decided to take cognizance of the movement and put an energetic stop to it. One of the first steps was directed at me, and I received a polite, but quite strongly worded invitation to call at the Ministry of the Interior, which, as you know, has charge of all police work and measures, for a talk with Monsieur Constans.

"His Excellency, the Minister, greeted me coldly and addressed me in no uncertain terms. 'Mr. Bennett,' he said, 'I understand that you have a fondness for France and that you enjoy making your home in Paris. We, too, enjoy having you with us and respect and admire you for the part you play in our capital city by publishing there a European edition of your great American newspaper. But, however great your paper is, we cannot overlook the fact, of which we are now compelled to remind you, that you are publishing here a foreign newspaper to which we have granted the fullest degree of hospitality.

"'Now, Mr. Bennett, you have chosen to take sides with an element which is attempting to undermine and even overthrow our system of government, and that, we cannot, under any conditions, countenance. We must therefore ask you to refrain from giving aid to those who are opposing us, or this government shall find itself compelled to ask you to leave the country and take your paper along with you.'

"That is what I was told by the government of France, and I need hardly tell you that when I thought it over later I fully agreed and immediately ordered my staff never again to take sides in French politics.

"Now you, my friends, are planning to strike as a protest, not at all against anything connected with this paper, but against some action taken by the government of this country of which you are all enjoying, as foreigners, the hospitality. Go ahead, if you wish, but I must warn that the names of those who take this step today will be sent up tomorrow to the Ministry of the Interior in order that you may receive some of the medicine which was given to me."

The *Herald* staff, of course, immediately voted against participating in the strike.

As for the Boulanger affair, it had been handled with great finesse by the French Republic. The general won his election with 244,000 votes to 162,000 for his opponent, but the government realized that sympathy for his "cause" was confined largely to the impressionable boulevards of Paris, where Royalist propaganda funds were largely expended. A few months after his election M. Constans issued a warrant for his arrest, charging treason, but Boulanger had fled to Belgium a few steps ahead of the police. He committed suicide in Brussels less than two years later.

Three days after the Boulanger election the *Herald* in Paris turned with great relief to another and less explosive sensation with which to divert the minds of its readers.

The date line was "Meierling"—now spelled Mayerling.

For days the mysterious deaths of Austrian Crown Prince Rudolf and the teen-aged Baroness Maria Vetsera, whose bodies were found in his hunting lodge at Mayerling, were the subject of fantastic speculation hardly lessened by the conflicting versions released by the Austrian authorities. An early headline in the Paris *Herald* read:

PRINCE RUDOLF'S GHASTLY SECRET
The Cloud of Mystery Surrounding His Tragic
Death Growing Darker Than Ever
A BEAUTIFUL BARONESS INVOLVED

The *Herald* reaped the full crop of rumors, variously reporting that the Crown Prince had died of a stroke, that he had been assassinated, that he had been killed in a duel with a "Prince X," that a gamekeeper had caught him with the former's wife and shot him after a chase through the woods. It wasn't until February 8, in fact, that the *Herald* finally was able to publish what is now accepted as the truth of what happened at Mayerling, that the prince had shot his young mistress and then himself. This romantic tragedy caused such a sensation that the *Herald* had to keep its presses running twelve hours a day to supply the demand for the latest rumor issuing from the Austrian capital; no other story until the beginning of World War I provided such

a circulation booster. It also served admirably to conceal
the Paris *Herald's* embarrassment over its short-lived
and never-repeated trespass on the domestic politics of
France.

Although warned off the subject of French politics
when they involved overthrowing the government,
Bennett's behavior as publisher of the Paris *Herald* was
unchastened and generally uninhibited. The *Herald* was
a lively, highly personal sheet mirroring the crochets,
phobias, prejudices, good and ill humors, and extravagant ideas which flitted through the mind of its mercurial publisher. Features in praise of small dogs and
owls, for instance, had to be run frequently and
prominently displayed, though the general interest in
these subjects was limited.

Bennett's passion for the smaller canine species has
already been described, but it was almost exceeded by
his superstitious, near-pagan worship of the owl. That
bird was his talisman, his all-powerful medicine against
ill fortune—so much an obsession with him that only a
psychiatrist could come up with reasons for its en-
chantment for him. Live owls flitted around his various
estates, as privileged as any sacred monkeys around an
Asiatic temple. Stuffed owls, owl statuettes, paintings of
owls stared at one from every vantage point of his
various homes. The bird was plastered on his yacht,
his carriages and coaches, the masthead of his papers,
his stationery and, according to a Park Row rumor
told Gene Fowler (*Skyline*) by Damon Runyon, "one
of his girl friends had owls tattooed on both her knees."
Bennett himself gave as the reason for all this owl
worship the fact that, when he was commanding the
Henrietta on patrol off Port Royal during the Civil
War, he fell asleep on watch one night, and his vessel

was about to run aground on a reef when the hooting of an owl awakened him and saved the ship.

All his passions and prejudices were given full vent in the Paris *Herald* (and, of course, to a lesser extent in the New York *Herald*) regardless of how much they offended his readers or affronted the good taste and good sense of his editors. Some of the stuff that Bennett inflicted on his papers could have been published nowhere else in the world. A case in point was the journalistic *cause célèbre* represented by the "Old Philadelphia Lady." One day a letter under that signature was received by the Paris *Herald* and published in the "Letters to the Editor" column, on which Bennett maintained an unusually close watch. It read:

"I am anxious to find out the way to figure the temperature from centigrade to Fahrenheit and vice versa. In other words, I want to know, whenever I see the temperature designated on the centigrade thermometer, how to find out what it would be on Fahrenheit's thermometer."

This utterly commonplace communication, which in any other publication would have been briskly answered and promptly forgotten, achieved a fame in newspaper correspondence equaled only by Virginia O'Hanlon's plea to the editor of the New York *Sun* for convincing evidence of the reality of Santa Claus. For some obscure reason it tickled Bennett's odd sense of humor; he ordered it be run every day, without answer or explanation. Days of repetition finally irked many of the *Herald's* readers, and they wrote in demanding that "Old Philadelphia Lady's" plaintive query be stilled, even canceling their subscriptions. Bennett, in his autocratic way, refused to state why it should be printed every day, but he was pleased by the commotion it caused. It was a mystery, concealed under the countless wrappings of the Bennett psyche, which was never to be cleared up. "Old Philadelphia Lady" became a *Herald* institution. Her letter appeared every day in the letters column until several days after the Commodore's death, when his editors took great pleasure in finally quieting the old dear. Her identity was never revealed.

A stop-off at the Paris *Herald* was a must on the itinerary of every roving newspaperman. Usually it was an experience of brief duration, terminated either by one of the Commodore's temperamental house cleanings of the small, cramped city room or disgust at the way he treated his editorial serfs, especially when in drink. On occasion he would swoop down and fire everyone in the office. One of the quickest ways to get fired was to mention in print one of the persons whose names were to be found on black lists pasted on the walls of the city room. Sometimes the whole staff would be sent scampering into the night on some weird assignment he had dreamed up over the magnums at Maxim's. In living memory, his reputation as a mercurial employer is equaled only by that of an eastern publisher for whom the author and many hapless fellow waifs briefly labored some years ago. This gentleman occupied a penthouse on the roof of his newspaper building. When the moon was full or something else disturbed the balance of his mind, he would come romping into the editorial department in flaming red pajamas and fire everyone on the right side of the room, or everyone with blue eyes, or everyone with his tie at half-mast. His behavior, however, was never mitigated by anything like Bennett's equally whimsical generosity.

His severity toward employees who drank on the *Herald's* time was a variable quality, depending on his mood and which way the psychic wind was blowing. One day he appeared in the city room looking disgruntled, at loose ends, poking around the dingy chamber, peering at proofs and wire copy. It looked like a good time to stay away from the Commodore, but a robust and rollicking fellow named George Cooper disregarded all the danger signals. He sailed into the room with a fine brandy glow, the kind that makes all men brothers, and it distressed him to see his employer looking out of sorts.

Cooper went over to Bennett and slapped him heartily on the back.

"Bennett," he roared, "you come along with me— I'm going to show you Paris."

Everyone waited for Cooper to be summarily detached from the payroll and possibly flung down the stairs.

Instead the Commodore grinned and said, "All right, laddy, lead the way!"

He linked his arm in his reporter's, and the two men sallied forth on a binge that lit up the more raffish sections of Paris for several days.

When Cooper finally returned to work, he found that Bennett had ordered the business office to double his salary.

Generally, however, the Commodore's appearances caused nothing but terror and confusion. One of the few *Herald* employees whom the Commodore never bothered was Frank Cohick, the mechanical superintendent. One night Bennett fired all his editors, went to the stairs leading to the composing room, and shouted down to Cohick, "Come on up here, Cohick. You're all through downstairs. I've just fired all these men. You're the boss up here now, the editor in charge. Now go out and hire yourself a staff—I'm going to fire all the reporters too!" Then the Commodore stomped out of the building, Cohick returned to his own job of getting out the paper, and everybody else stayed put. Next day, his head cleared, he'd forgotten all about discharging the entire editorial staff and no one bothered to remind him. As a matter of fact, according to Laney, the Commodore had some cause for periodically cleaning out his editorial department. "The staff usually consisted of a few competent men, a few others who, though well educated, had seen better days, and derelicts of the type which seemed to cling to the Paris *Herald* through all the years of its life. . . . In addition, Bennett always had on his paper as special writers a number of characters who seemed to be out of books."

His harried staff finally rigged up an alarm system to put them on guard against the Commodore's sudden manifestations. They bribed his butler to give them a ring whenever he left his apartment breathing fire and heading for the Rue du Louvre. The doorman downstairs was similarly alerted to warn them when he entered the premises.

One night the warning system failed, somehow, and the Commodore came into the building the back way, through the composing room.

All of a sudden the staff heard his heavy tread in the corridor outside and the terrible man was surveying his editorial department with blood and brandy in his eye. Earlier that evening, as a joke, some of his fellow workers had dumped a dozen empty beer bottles on the desk at which Billy Bishop, the sports editor, was working. Bishop had been a copy boy until one day Bennett came down to the office with two of his Pekingese at his heels. The Pekingese took a liking to Bishop, and Bennett promoted him to sports editor on the spot.

Everyone busied himself as the Commodore slowly walked over to Bishop's desk, glowering at the hedge of bottles behind which his sports editor was working away, hoping to escape his employer's notice.

But Bennett stalked over to him and bellowed, "You're Bishop, aren't you?"

"Yes, sir," young Bishop said.

"What's your salary?"

"A hundred francs a week, sir."

"Those your bottles?"

Bishop gulped, gallantly lied, and said they were.

"On your salary," Bennett said, "you can't afford a thirst like that." He turned to the city editor, whose name he had forgotten, such functionaries coming and going with great rapidity, and snapped, "City editor, come over here. I want you to raise Mr. Bishop's salary fifty francs a week. He needs it to pay his beer bills."

The Commodore then took his departure, so pleased with having created a new Bennett legend, perhaps, that he clean forgot whatever raging concern had brought him down to the office in the middle of the night.

Bennett's preoccupation with the Paris *Herald* naturally took a lot of pressure off his underlings on the New York papers, but at least once a year, and with all the suddenness of a cavalry raid, he would disembark in New York to spread confusion and dismay in the *Herald* building, which, as Ralph D. Blumenfeld, one of his executives, wrote, he always left in a "whirl of disorder." His associates could never decide whether those visits were an outcropping of sadism, an indication of lunacy, or served some purpose obscure to everyone but the Commodore. All they knew was that before his annual stay was over, the operation would be a shambles, with key men fired or demoted and new men in posts for which they were not trained. There was only one way of telling that he might be New York-bound, according to Blumenfeld. "Whenever he failed to keep the cables busy with orders, suggestions and criticisms, mostly the latter, the office executives knew he was either on a cruise . . . or he must be on his way to New York."

Sometimes the shock waves of the Commodore's advent would precede him to the building on Park Row. He once took a liking to the young reporter sent to meet the liner on which he was traveling, and before they came up the bay Bennett had issued instructions that the reporter was to be given the city editor's job. The Commodore never deigned to explain himself. On another New York visit, he ordered George J. Taylor, the father of Bert Leston Taylor, who was to conduct the famous "Line o' Type" column in the Chicago *Tribune*, transferred from the highly responsible post of news editor to supervising the district reporters in Brooklyn, a comedown as dismal as it sounds, without ever giving a reason for the demotion.

One of the Commodore's associates, Thomas G. Alvord, claimed that there was a purpose behind his seemingly haphazard juggling of personnel, his endless effort to keep his staffs in turmoil and uncertainty. Alvord said that "the seemingly erratic, unjust, contemptible conduct now and then shown the most deserving members of the staff was designed to put to the severest test the loyalty of the individual whose seeming fealty, expecting a reward, had been proven a dozen times. Came he through demotion, reduction of pay, undeserved suspension, designed humiliation, and still remained steadfast in his devotion to the *Herald* and its master, taking his dose without complaint or the seeking of a place on some other newspaper, then Mr. Bennett believed he might be trusted in great temptation and relied on in all emergencies. In no other way, in his opinion, could a thoroughly reliable corps of news-paper employees be built up and maintained."

Yet those who survived this pulping process often were beaten men, zombies of the city room, fearful of making decisions, concentrating all their thoughts and energies on trying to anticipate the whims of their absentee master. Some who clung to their jobs through all the rough weather manufactured in the Commodore's study were, as Don Seitz observed, "never themselves again." Only the spineless would put up with such treatment for any length of time. The result was that while Bennett may have shaken a few clinkers out of his organization through such tactics, he also lost the services of many good and able men who refused to be deliberately humbled and degraded. And in the coming years of struggle against Hearst and Pulitzer, the Com-modore would stand in need of such men, and would find that browbeaten men who had "proved" them-selves were incapable of taking the editorial initiative.

Often the consequences of his whirlwind inspections of the *Herald* building were more ludicrous than tragic.

He swooped down on New York one year on his steam yacht *Namouna,* which his employees called the "Pneumonia" for obvious reasons. Accompanying him was Captain Candy of the Ninth Lancers, who was credited with having taught Bennett how to play polo and was frequently the Commodore's guest at New-port, where he was fondly known as "Sugar Candy."

The Commodore and the Captain decided to make a lightning descent on the *Herald* before continuing their journey to Newport. The *Herald's* water-front re-porter, however, was tipped off by his news sources that Bennett's yacht had just been sighted off the Am-brose lightship, and immediately alerted the city desk. There was the usual panicky reaction. Reporters were rounded up from Park Row saloons, bullied into sobriety, ordered to shave and put on clean collars. All through the building, in fact, the Commodore's satraps were frantically tidying up for his inspection.

Only one employee resisted the sprucing up, an old printer named Elmer who was crapulously drunk, refused to surrender his bottle, and proclaimed that he had been drunk under Bennett Senior and would remain so under Bennett Junior.

The Commodore, trailed one step by Captain Candy in the role of aide-de-camp, briskly marched through the various departments of the *Herald* and *Evening Telegram,* and for once he had no criticisms to make, no shake-ups to be ordained.

Down in the pressroom, however, he caught sight of Elmer, now comatose, who had been hidden behind some rolls of newsprint with just his legs sticking out.

"Who is that man?" Bennett demanded.

"Why, sir, that's old Elmer," the pressroom foreman said. "A very loyal and valuable employee. He worked for your father, sir."

The Commodore walked over and studied Elmer's recumbent form with benign approval. "By gad," he told the foreman, "this fellow is the only one around here who looks as though he's been doing any work. Everybody else is groomed to the nines—obviously haven't been doing a lick of work. This poor chap is suffering from exhaustion. Foreman, you're fired. Elmer will take your place as soon as he finishes his nap."

9: Sam the Elegant, Sam the Drunken

If one were to believe the tales of old newspapermen, there never was and never will be another like Sam Chamberlain. Park Row produced many brilliant craftsmen, but none, apparently, to equal the Chamberlain legend, not only for his journalistic performance but his easy attainment of a baronial style of living. Who but Sam Chamberlain could have been the intimate friend and collaborator of both Bennett and Hearst? Who but the brilliant Chamberlain could have supervised, within one decade, an assortment of newspaper births like those of Hearst's San Francisco *Examiner* and New York *Journal,* Bennett's Paris *Herald, Le Matin* of Paris? Who but Chamberlain could have accomplished all this while putting away enough liquor to send any six men to the Keeley Cure for extended stays? Who but Chamberlain could go off on a bender, wind up in Amsterdam (Holland), and return to his desk a month later as though he'd stepped out for a cup of coffee? On nostalgic evenings at the Silurians, an organization of veteran New York newspapermen, Sam Chamberlain's name is still recalled with awe and reverence, though any sober history of American journalism would grant him a footnote at best. Samuel S. Chamberlain never rose above the rank of managing editor but his influence on the evolution of the American newspaper, his exploitation of news in the style of a

Barnum, his bold forays to the outer limits of sensationalism all marked him as the cynical genius of the "new
journalism."

Not the least of his distinctions was his ability to get
along with James Gordon Bennett. With most subordinates, particularly those on the editorial side, for whom
he may have had a deep-seated envy, Bennett's manner
was generally dictatorial, often contemptuous. Chamberlain, who could charm the birds out of the trees, was
not only his employee but his friend; he had the rare
grace, rarer than may be supposed, of being able to
forgive Bennett's inherited wealth without at the same
time becoming a sycophant. With an aristocratic ease
that was the envy of his colleagues, Chamberlain managed to combine the functions of amanuensis, editor,
collaborator, drinking companion, playfellow, and tact-
ful adviser to two of the most spoiled and willful men
ever sired by American millionaires.

For Sam Chamberlain had the one attribute most
admired by the men of his generation: style. His dress,
his manner and his bearing, not to mention the ease
with which he could move from a Fifth Avenue drawing room to the grimiest saloon on Park Row, all
stamped him as a man of parts.

He was a true child of the newspaper business, ill-
educated but well informed, as obsessed with his calling
as any Trappist, yet able to move in any kind of society.
His father was Ivory Chamberlain, an editorial writer
on the pre-Pulitzer *World* who had also worked for the
elder and younger Bennetts. Born into the newspaper
business, young Sam cut his teeth on copy pencils and
went to work as a reporter about the time he graduated
from short pants. Before joining Bennett in Paris, he
labored as a reporter, correspondent, news and city
editor on a dozen papers. In those years he gained two

distinctions among his fellows, aside from professional brilliance. He drew fewer sober breaths than any of them, and he was the best-dressed man on Park Row until Richard Harding Davis came along, wearing English tweeds, frock coats with flowered cravats, and evening dress with the air of an English duke. Thus his nickname on Park Row: "Sam the elegant, Sam the drunken." Booze and dandyism, however, did not interfere with his cool handling of the news. Once while he was serving time on the city desk of the old *Morning Journal,* a young reporter rushed in with the news that there had been a murder on a streetcar.

"What streetcar line?" Chamberlain calmly asked.

"Bleecker Street cross-town," the reporter told him.

Chamberlain shook his head sadly. "What happens on a cross-town car never attracts any attention. Now, if it had only been a Broadway car. . . ."

During a political upheaval in the Sandwich Islands, now Hawaii, he was sent to Honolulu with a number of other correspondents, all of them instructed by their editors to do their best to get an interview with the native queen. His rivals were sternly excluded from royal society, but Chamberlain, whose reckless manipulation of expense accounts shortened the life of more than one editorial auditor, wangled his way into the court's inner circles by giving champagne suppers at which he presided with an ambassadorial magnificence. The queen herself was soon attracted to Chamberlain's midnight routs and fell under his sway. Chamberlain got himself not only an interview, but Her Majesty's whole life story. By the time Chamberlain left Honolulu with his thoroughly beaten colleagues, it was reported that he had passed all the tests for royal consort with full honors, and only his loyalty to the newspaper business prevented him from sharing the Hawaiian throne.

Beneath all his insouciance, his more perceptive fellows noted evidences of stress and a well-camouflaged melancholia. "Always brilliant, always erratic," wrote Joseph Clarke, "the phantasmorgia of Sam Chamberlain's mind would be a wonder-ground for the psychoanalyst. Slim, elegant, blue-eyed, genial, he could change in an hour to one of the distraught."

Bennett, fascinated by all he had heard of Chamberlain, summoned him to Paris to act as his "secretary," actually as his executive assistant, a year or two before he began publishing the Paris edition of the *Herald*. The two men hit it off immediately. Bennett was a lonely man, with few friends aside from Captain Candy and the Jerome brothers. Most men shied away from his lurid reputation—the respectable ones, at any rate —or sucked around him in hope of reward. Others were appalled by his tantrums, his recklessness, and his unpredictability.

Chamberlain, whose appetite for the high life was all but insatiable, was able not only to keep pace with his employer, but to view his most outrageous antics with aplomb. Both were of about the same age, both were bachelors, and neither of them, really, gave a damn: they shared a quality of despair and rootlessness which they chose to conceal under a carnival spirit.

One day, inspired by brandy, Bennett decided to launch an editorial campaign against the Catholic Church in the New York *Herald*. One of the few prejudices he had inherited from his father was the latter's all but lifelong anti-Catholicism. He called on Chamberlain, as the interpreter of his thoughts, to get it all down on paper.

"Sam," he said, "I'm tired of all this talk of the *Herald* being controlled by the Roman Catholic Church and of the number of Trinity College men on its staff."

The *Herald,* as a matter of fact, had provided a refuge for a number of men who had fled Ireland after coming in conflict with the British authorities. Bennett was completely sympathetic to the British aristocracy, yet he could not forget that his mother was Irish-born, and contributed $100,000 for the relief of Irish famine victims—just as he established free-ice stations in the New York slums during the summer despite his often expressed contempt for the lower classes. Few men so perversely combined philanthropy and misanthropy.

"Now," Bennett continued, "I want you to write an editorial that will put us right before the public and show that we have no affiliations with Rome.

"Attack the Catholic Church, its monasteries, nunneries and schools and make it as strong as you can. Write the editorial and bring it to me this evening."

Chamberlain thought he knew how to handle this latest brainstorm. On many previous occasions he had dutifully complied with the Commodore's instructions—to oppose them was fatal—and then delayed matters until his employer sobered up and could be reasoned with, if he had not already forgotten all about what vexed him.

So he spent the afternoon composing a vitriolic assault on Catholicism and all its works, recommending that all of the Church's institutions be razed to the ground, their servitors deported, and all their spiritual and political influence rooted out like noxious weeds. He made it so strong, in fact, that even the slavish executives on the New York end of the cable would not have dared to publish it.

It was headed, "To Hell with the Pope."

That evening Chamberlain brought the editorial to Bennett, hoping that the Commodore would be appalled by its strong language.

On the contrary, Bennett was delighted with it and said it conveyed his sentiments exactly.

"Now, Sam," he added, "you've fooled me many times before but you're not going to do it this time. We'll get this on the cable tonight."

At Bennett's insistence, Chamberlain accompanied him to the office of Commercial Cables and fearfully watched while the Commodore stood over the operator who transmitted the editorial. Bennett returned to his apartment on the Champs Elysées highly pleased with the night's work. By way of celebrating his victory over the Church, he extended his spree to ten days.

On the eleventh day Bennett began sobering up and fumbling through a hazy backlog of memories. One bleary recollection was the anti-Catholic editorial. Good God, if those servile and spineless wretches in New York had carried out orders, the *Herald* building might now be a heap of rubble, a fate it had narrowly escaped at the beginning of the Civil War. Bennett, in a fearful sweat, sent for Chamberlain.

"Uh . . . Sam . . ." he faltered, "some days back didn't we send a piece attacking the Church to New York?"

"Yes," Chamberlain said, "so you did."

"And it was published?"

Chamberlain let him suffer for a moment, then replied with a straight face, "No, Commodore, it wasn't. On second thought, I didn't think it was strong enough and told 'em in New York to hold up on it until we could rewrite it."

Bennett almost fainted with relief.

The simple phrase "thank you" always stuck in his craw, but that afternoon he took Chamberlain to a jewelry shop, picked out an expensive cat's-eye ring, and wordlessly shoved it in Chamberlain's hand.

For more than two years it was an amiable and fruitful partnership. Chamberlain helped establish the Paris *Herald,* and undoubtedly, if their collaboration had withstood the stress of Bennett's temperament, he would have succeeded in tactfully steering him away from the dangerous shoals of Boulangism. While they worked on plans for the Paris paper, Chamberlain also expounded to the Commodore on his own great ambition—the establishment of a chain of newspapers throughout the United States. Bennett was then the wealthiest of the newspaper magnates, and Chamberlain hoped that he would back the project, which may have been one reason Chamberlain was willing to suffer through their association. The Commodore liked the idea but could never be pinned down, lacking that final touch of the grandiose which was necessary to such empire building, and which Chamberlain was to find ultimately in William Randolph Hearst.

Helping Bennett run the New York *Herald* by cable and directly supervise the Paris edition simply didn't provide enough stimulus for Chamberlain, who missed the excitement of metropolitan journalism just a little more than he loved the boulevards of Paris.

Perhaps he had already decided to leave Bennett when a yachting incident curdled their relationship.

Bennett, Chamberlain, and a number of guests were aboard the *Namouna* on a cruise along the Greek coast, relaxing from the ardors of establishing the Paris edition of the *Herald*. Bennett's willfulness displayed itself early in the cruise when the Commodore and his guests debarked to inspect a monastery which claimed to have a lamp which had been kept burning for more than a thousand years. That votive flame fascinated Bennett; it also presented a challenge to his sometimes destructive temperament.

When one of the bearded monks led him to the sacred lamp, Bennett roared in his best quarterdeck tone, "Are you sure this thing's been burning for a thousand years?"

The monk affirmed that it had.

Bennett leaned over the rail and blew out the flame. "Well," he observed, "it's out now."

Down the coast, just outside the harbor of Piraeus, the *Namouna* approached an American warship on maneuvers with its squadron in the eastern Mediterranean. One of the Commodore's nautical obsessions was never to change course; every movable object in the path of the *Namouna,* whether it was an ocean liner or a bumboat, had to make sea room for him. As Albert Stevens Crockett picked up the story later, the *Namouna* and the American cruiser were plunging ahead on a collision course which would send the yacht crashing into the warship amidships.

The yacht's sailing master pointed this out to Bennett, who was standing stone-faced beside him on the bridge. Sam Chamberlain, chalk-white with fear, was hanging onto the rail nearby.

"Keep right ahead," Bennett snapped to the helmsman. "That ship has no right to cross my bow."

Chamberlain protested that deliberately colliding with an American warship would have repercussions of the most serious nature, aside from smashing up the yacht.

"Keep her on course," roared the Commodore.

A few hundred yards away from the cruiser Chamberlain leaped for the helm, swung the wheel over, and avoided a collision.

Bennett was outraged. Chamberlain's insubordination, he shouted, was unforgivable and merited condign punishment. Later in the day, according to the story that subsequently drifted back to Paris and New York, Bennett marooned Chamberlain on a tiny uninhabited island, leaving with him only a few days' supply of food and water and a white shirt to wave at any passing ships. Off sailed the *Namouna,* but only a short distance away. The other guests of the Commodore by then had protested so strenuously that he ordered a small boat lowered and Chamberlain returned on board. Neither man would apologize. At the next port of call Chamberlain left the *Namouna,* and Bennett's employ, and returned to Paris.

With the backing of John Mackay, whom he had met through Bennett, and several French businessmen, Chamberlain established *Le Matin,* which became one of Paris' leading journals. After leaving Europe and going back to New York, a sort of reconciliation via cable and letter was arranged between him and Bennett, one of the few times the latter ever choked back his wrath. Chamberlain thereupon took over as editor of the *Evening Telegram,* the pink-papered sensation-monger which Bennett could barely bring himself to read.

Ralph D. Blumenfeld, an ambitious young man from Wisconsin who had made himself a reputation on the *Morning Journal,* was ordered to assume the post of city editor at the *Telegram.* His first conference with Chamberlain, whom he described as approaching fifty but looking a clear-eyed thirty for all his dissipations, was brief but ominous. "Heaven help you," Chamberlain told him, "if you fall afoul of the Commodore's lightnings. And make sure that even a scrubwoman is a lady, or must be in the columns of the *Telegram,* because we have so many lady readers who are scrubwomen."

It was not long before Chamberlain finally wearied of dodging Bennett's lightning bolts via cable from Paris. Bennett, he could see, would never help him realize his slightly alcoholic dream of founding a chain of newspapers. But one day, at the bar of the Hoffman House, he met a young man who just might do it, a tall, diffident fellow with what Ambrose Bierce described as "a long horse face, close-set eyes and a peculiar strained smile with a manner that was a combination of Harvard and a faro-bank lookout." He was the son of a United States senator from California who had made millions out of a Dakota gold mine. His name was Hearst.

The two men swapped names, expanded on their ambitions in the newspaper field, and took an immediate liking to each other. William Randolph Hearst, recently expelled from Harvard, was impressed by Chamberlain's knowledge of the newspaper business, his boulevardier's manner, his worldliness and, not least of all, by the fact that each of the Hoffman House's seventeen bartenders knew him and came up to pay their respects. Young Mr. Hearst wanted to take over and build up his father's San Francisco *Examiner,* a project which Chamberlain encouraged.

A short time later Chamberlain quit Bennett for good, went west, and took over as Hearst's principal adviser and managing editor of the San Francisco paper. With Hearst's money and Chamberlain's whipcracking over a journalistic circus, they made San Francisco sit up and take notice; circulation boomed, and one of the most spectacular careers in American journalism was launched. The portents of that career, with the weight of the Hearst millions and Chamberlain's journalistic genius behind it, were ominous for James Gordon Bennett.

To all but Bennett, who looked down on Hearst with a lordly contempt, that threat was made visible on September 25, 1895, the day the Californian bought the *Morning Journal*. Hearst brought with him from San Francisco not only his millions but his wrecking crew, headed by Sam Chamberlain. His first objective was to cut down the circulation of the *Morning* and *Evening Worlds*, which by then had passed up the Bennett morning-evening combination in readership, advertising, and prestige.

Hearst poured out his millions, captured an audience with his six-inch scareheads, lured away Pulitzer's ablest editors and reporters with higher salaries, and proceeded to revolutionize journalism with his flamboyant methods. Hearst sensationalism was proving as effective in the nineties as Pulitzer's crusading in the eighties, Bennett Junior's creation of exclusive news in the seventies, and Bennett Senior's widening of journalistic horizons in the decades before that; it was superficial, manufacturing what one of his editors called the "gee-whiz" emotion with tall headlines and taller adjectives, but it was loud, boisterous, and compelling. And to the Commodore, far away in Paris or cruising the Indian Ocean in his yacht, it was merely a noisy bore.

The Commodore still believed that "nothing can hurt the *Herald*." Let Hearst and Pulitzer battle it out in the gutter—the *Herald* would remain aloof, would maintain its standards and continue catering to the better people.

Even when the New York *Herald's* circulation slipped below the 100,000 mark, Bennett remained haughtily indifferent. The public would weary of watching Hearst and Pulitzer trying to outdo each other, of such circus stunts as those emblazoned "Stephen Crane in the Tenderloin," "Why Young Girls Kill Themselves," "Anna Held Receives Our Dramatic Critic Attired in a Nightie," and "Strange Things Women Do for Love." Penny-paper vulgarity might appeal momentarily to the immigrant masses in the New York slums, but the people who mattered would continue to read the *Herald*. And comic strips? They were obviously designed for morons and illiterates.

More vexing to the Commodore than the competition from Hearst and Pulitzer were the defections in his own ranks. For years the New York *Herald* had been the mecca of every ambitious journalist in the country, and even the Byzantine atmosphere of that newspaper had not repelled them. As Don Seitz wrote, they found "something compelling about the tigerish proprietor with his fickleness and brutality." Now, with his rivals paying higher wages and offering a great deal more consideration and opportunity to the stars of Park Row, Bennett was finding it difficult to hold onto his best men. Even Edward T. Flynn, a friend since boyhood, could not put up with his tyrannical whims. Julius Chambers had been managing editor of the *Herald* for three years but his nature was too "strenuous" (as Joseph Clarke noted) to allow him to suffer under the Bennett lash. Then Ballard Smith, a highly competent managing editor, defected to Pulitzer, and Bennett came raging across the Atlantic to find out what was going wrong at the *Herald*.

Smith had wisely departed by the time Bennett arrived, but the latter decided to "humiliate him in absentia."

Rampaging through the executive offices, Bennett bellowed that he would strangle Smith with his bare hands if he ever caught up with him; furthermore, he proclaimed, the post of managing editor was highly overrated, a mere puppet manipulated by the publisher.

"Any man can fill that job," Bennett shouted at his cowering executives. "Why, I'll make my stenographer managing editor, I'll make the baseball reporter managing editor. It's no trick to be managing editor. . . . By God, I'll have no managing editor. I'll abolish the job!"

And thus, by fiat, Bennett abolished the most responsible post in a newspaper's editorial department; henceforth the city room would be bossed by the city editor, on the local side, and the news editor on the national and international side. As city editor, and his principal satrap, he installed William C. Reick, who actually took over the functions of a managing editor. Though his hours were from noon to midnight, Reick stayed on this hot spot for eighteen years. "He was a very able man," according to Seitz, "who could transform the owner's orders into action without demoralizing the staff." Bennett, for once, treated this talent more gently than was his custom, and even rewarded Reick with a block of uptown real estate that made him rich when the subway was extended there.

With the post of "editor-in-charge"—a designation indicating that the incumbent was merely a caretaker for the real editor in Paris—Bennett also experienced difficulty. He wanted Charles Nordhoff, the *Herald's* distinguished Washington correspondent, to take over the job, but Nordhoff proved understandably reluctant. Finally Bennett cabled him an ultimatum: "You can either now leave Washington and go to New York as editor-in-charge or, if you decline this, I will give you the alternative to retire on pension on condition that you will live in California." Nordhoff chose California and retirement. A gentleman named E. S. Drone filled the post of editor-in-charge without any of the brilliance which might have attracted the Commodore's "lightnings." For all his difficulties with personnel, for all the evidence that some of the best ex-*Herald* men were happily laboring for Hearst or Pulitzer, Bennett was still convinced that he could hire the best brains for twenty-five dollars a week.

What really engaged him during this period when Hearst and Pulitzer were turning the journalistic world upside down was enhancing the *Herald's* prestige, not by any bold editorial maneuvers, but through architecture. As though to remove himself from the undignified brawling of Park Row, Bennett decided that the *Herald* would be the first to leave the old journalistic homestead of Park Row and join the movement uptown. Always real estate conscious, he realized that the center of commercial gravity was moving toward mid-Manhattan. And there were other considerations. He was exceedingly irked that there were a number of tenants who shared the building at Broadway and Ann Street through leases granted in perpetuity by his father. Furthermore, Pulitzer was building a fourteen-story, gold-domed skyscraper near the Brooklyn Bridge, which Bennett considered to be in ostentatious bad taste. The Commodore would house his *Herald* in a building which would be a model of architectural beauty.

So the hundreds of thousands which he might more realistically have appropriated to circulation promotion and strengthening his editorial staff were devoted to building a minor masterpiece at what was then known as Dodge Place, on a triangle formed by Thirty-fifth Street and the intersection of Broadway and Sixth Avenue. Ever afterward it would be called Herald Square, though its name was changed without any municipal sanction. Without doubt it was one of the most beautiful buildings erected in New York up to the turn of the century. It was not functional in the ordinary sense, except that its function was to gladden the eye of the Commodore; certainly it was ill-suited to the publication of a metropolitan newspaper.

The celebrated Stanford White of the firm of McKim, Mead & White was engaged to draw the plans. The robust and redheaded Mr. White had already fulfilled several commissions from Bennett: the Newport Casino, the interior of the old building at Broadway and Ann, the interior of the *Namouna*. The *Herald,* in reporting plans for the Columbus celebration, referred to White as "the one man in New York who seems to be omnipotent in matters pertaining to structural beauty." He was, in fact, the most famous and successful of American architects. For all his "omnipotence," however, Bennett did not hesitate to differ with him on the plans for the new *Herald* Building. The Commodore wanted it modeled after the Doges' Palace in Venice. White thought that idea a little too grandiose and argued that the Palazzo del Consiglio of Verona, a more modest structure, would serve as a more appropriate model. For once Bennett yielded to another's opinion, but it cost him such an effort that he never recaptured his original enthusiasm for the project. It had become White's building, so the hell with it!

As conceived by Stanford White, the *Herald* was to be housed in a long, two-story building with an arcade, supported by slender white columns, running around three sides. There were to be Bennett touches to the exterior. Bronze owls, with wings protectively outstretched, were to be placed all around the cornice at regular intervals, guarding the Bennett luck as always. A huge clock costing $200,000, with two heroic bronze figures to strike the hours, was imbedded in the face of the building. And by way of added extravagance, and additional affront to the architect's sense of the seemly, the Commodore insisted that the bronze owls be equipped with electric eyes that blinked eerily through the night on Herald Square.

While medieval Verona was being recreated in mid-town New York, Bennett performed his usual repertoire of conflicting orders, querulous criticisms, and ill-considered recriminations. Stanford White was driven to his wit's end by the flow of contradictory messages from Paris. The architect, unable to attune himself to the Commodore's sudden transitions from extravagance to parsimony and back again, recommended that the *Herald's* business manager buy a $14,000 antique silver desk set from Tiffany's to enhance the restrained elegance of the publisher's office. The business manager bought the set without consulting Bennett. When the latter learned of the purchase, he immediately cabled his strenuous objections, adding, without quite meaning it, that the executive could pay for it out of his salary. The business manager quit immediately rather than spend years paying off the obligation. Occasionally aware that his temper betrayed him into committing an injustice, Bennett made post-mortem amends by remembering, many years later, to leave the desk set to the ex-business manager in his will.

When the building approached completion, he came over to inspect it, by now thoroughly convinced that he had been foolish in allowing White to have his way, gloomily remarking to Ralph Blumenfeld, whom he had appointed as his personal watchdog on the project, "I fear privately our Italian renaissance palace will look like a fish market."

Blumenfeld tried to reassure him, pointing out, however, that it might have been a mistake to erect the building on ground which Bennett had obtained through a lease extending only thirty years. On that point Bennett had no qualms. "Never mind, Blumenfeld," he said, "thirty years from now the *Herald* will be in Harlem and I'll be in hell."

Despite his forebodings, the *Herald* building turned out to be one of the city's show places, coolly disputing the architectural taste and wisdom of the towering structures then being thrust into the Manhattan skyline. "It was a show, an exhibition, a palace," the New York *Times* conceded years later, "which drew strangers and sojourners for many years." And the *Journalist,* a trade magazine, commented, "A tremendous lot of talking has been done about the *Herald* Building; yet the half of it has not been told. It breathes independence, and bears upon its face the stamp of enterprise, ambition and foresight. Its broad roofs, spacious apartments, generous architecture and massive decorations tell a story of success. . . . Though rich and royal, there is nothing bizarre about it. A newspaper palace it was intended to be, a newspaper palace it remains, a monument to the wisdom of James Gordon Bennett." The terminals of the Pennsylvania and Long Island railroads were located near by; hotels, theaters, department stores, and fashionable shops quickly sprang up on the periphery of Herald Square, and the whole neighborhood boomed.

But to most newspapermen, the Veronese palace was the Commodore's Folly. It was beautiful, it added to the Bennett prestige just when he needed it, and it attracted tourists with its huge plate-glass windows opening into the pressroom under the arcade, but it was ill-suited to newspaper publication. The traffic around Herald Square made it difficult for circulation trucks to move out in a hurry with the latest editions. Furthermore, according to old-timers who worked there, the composing room was located under the hip roof and was abominably hot and cramped, particularly in the summertime. In addition, the building was located on a narrow island of real estate which would not permit expansion.

Bennett himself lost interest in the project long before it was completed. Four years after the *Herald* began publishing in the new building, he finally brought himself around to looking it over. Arriving one morning on a liner from Europe, he decided to stop at the Union Club for lunch on his way uptown from the docks. He ordered his favorite dish, mutton chops, but they came to his table deplorably overcooked and sent him into a towering rage. He upbraided the waiter, denounced the steward as a saboteur, and stomped out of the club.

The *Herald* Building was only a dozen short blocks away, but the infuriated Commodore canvassed the steamship lines until he found a ship leaving that afternoon, engaged the captain's cabin for the journey back to France, and went back downtown without pausing to see the building, the construction of which had caused the expenditure of so much time, thought, and spleen. It was another couple of years before Bennett finally consented to inspect the masterpiece.

In the meantime he had turned enthusiastically to another project which was conceived as an even more enduring self-monument—a statue 200 feet high which was to be erected on Bennett property in Washington Heights looking down on Manhattan. It was to be a gigantic owl, which Stanford White was commissioned to design and Andrew O'Connor, a Massachusetts sculptor, to execute.

The great stone owl, 125 feet high on a 75-foot pedestal, was to contain his sarcophagus. As Bennett outlined the project to White, the owl would be hollow, with a circular staircase leading up to its eyes, which were to be windows looking out on the city. Two steel chains would be suspended from the head, to which his coffin would be attached. Thus tourists, wending their way upward on the staircase, would be able to pay their respects to the monument's creator in addition to obtaining a magnificent view of the city. The Commodore would not be lonely in death. He worked excitedly over the plans: the owl must *glower* "quite ferociously"; it was to be fashioned of glazed granite; it was to be finished as soon as possible and constitute a landmark even before his death. Few of his many costly possessions so delighted Bennett in prospect as that projected monstrosity. Not the least of its wonders would be the fact that it would overshadow Grant's Tomb on Riverside Drive (Bennett had always considered General Grant a national disaster and had vigorously opposed his second term in the White House). In June of 1906, however, a pistol shot punctured the Commodore's dream of resting through all eternity in the head of an owl. Stanford White was killed by a bullet fired by Harry K. Thaw. Sculptor O'Connor had already completed a clay model of the owl and White had finished his plans, but Bennett apparently took the architect's murder as an ill omen and ordered all work on the monument halted.

In the several years leading up to the Spanish-American War, Bennett seemed to be losing heart for the struggle to maintain his New York papers in the white-hot competition engendered by Hearst and Pulitzer. The Paris *Herald* had a deficit of more than $100,000 annually, the brief existence of the London *Herald* had been an even heavier financial burden, and the New York *Herald* lagged far behind the *World* and the *Journal* in circulation and advertising. Some of his best men were now employed by his rivals. A soundly edited newspaper—and the *Herald* was always that, despite its publisher's crotchets—no longer seemed to command a large audience. Bennett seriously considered selling his New York properties, though he threatened libel suits when a European news agency circulated a report to this effect.

Then a Chicago baker named H. H. Kohlstaat, who dropped a fortune publishing the Chicago *Herald,* sold all his interests and announced that he was going to invade the New York newspaper field. He approached Bennett and offered him a good price for the *Herald* and *Telegram;* the Commodore not only accepted but signed an agreement listing the terms of the sale. Bennett was then staying at his father's old house on Washington Heights (formerly Fort Washington), and perhaps the old man's ghost walked those dreary chambers. Bennett spent a sleepless night trying to fight off second thoughts about that agreement. The *Herald,* after all, had been a Bennett property for almost sixty years, and his father had literally invested his life in the paper. Shortly after dawn he bounded out of bed and hurried downtown to Kohlstaat's hotel. Fortunately, as a baker, Kohlstaat was accustomed to unseemly hours and was in a good mood. He listened to Bennett's pleas, nodded, and agreed to tear up the contract.

No such pious reflections need have inhibited him regarding the *Telegram,* "that pink drab," as it was known. It was still losing money, and many of its readers had deserted to the *Journal,* which had blacker headlines and more illustrations. One Saturday afternoon in Paris he cabled an editorial which was to be published in the *Sunday Herald* and read:

"The *Evening Telegram* ceases to appear from yesterday . . . in accordance with Abraham Lincoln's wise saying that 'you can fool all of the people some of the time, and some of the people all of the time, but you can't fool all the people all the time.'

"And he was right. The public also can fool publishers all the time and the advertisers can fool publishers some of the time, and they seem to be continuing to fool them all the time. But the *Evening Telegram* doesn't propose to be fooled all the time.

"An up-to-date evening paper at one cent doesn't pay. Therefore those who are publishing evening papers at one cent [by which he meant the *Journal* and the *Evening World*] are either fooling the public or fooling themselves. As the *Evening Telegram* doesn't intend to fool itself or fool the public it has ceased publication until the time becomes ripe when it can stop being fooled and stops fooling."

This fair sample of the Commodore's rhetoric was published as ordered on November 21, 1897, certainly one of the oddest fulminations to appear in a New York newspaper in a long and eccentric history.

If it read as though the Commodore was on a colossal bender, the suspicion may well have been justified.

Next day, however, the executives in New York argued with Bennett via cable against the summary execution. They promised that the *Telegram* could be made to pay its way if the newsstand price were cut to one cent and the classified-ad columns fattened by offering advertisers twice the space for the same rate charged by the *Herald*. Bennett allowed himself to be persuaded, although his business instincts in this case were keener than those of his advisers; the *Telegram* eventually achieved a measure of prosperity, but largely at the expense of the *Herald*.

Monday's *Herald,* therefore, displayed the abashed announcement: "In view of its many outstanding advertising contracts and large circulation and for other considerations, the several editions of the *Evening Telegram* will continue to appear as usual every day, with all the latest news and the numerous bright features that have made the *Telegram* the favourite evening paper of Greater New York."

Fortunately Bennett recovered from his depressed state of mind by the time the war against Spain broke out, a war which Pulitzer's *World* and Hearst's *Journal* attempted to convert into a national carnival of shrieking headlines and gaudy exploits. At the Commodore's insistence, the *Herald* was going to play it straight, cover the war news thoroughly and objectively and make the *Herald's* running account of history as soberly credible as Hearst and Pulitzer sensationalism were not.

Now the Bennett of the Stanley-MacGahan years came back to life. He spent $300,000 covering the war, hiring the best and most authoritative correspondents, rushing their stories of Santiago and Manila Bay into print, and within a year making the *Herald,* once again, the number one American newspaper.

Before the first month of the war was over, in fact, the *Herald* was proudly publishing a box just under its masthead which read:

HIGH WATER MARK
Circulation. . . . . .503,200.

Not only *Herald* expertise in handling this kind of hard news, but the overly aggressive methods of the *World* and the *Journal* in exploiting their hourly sensations turned the newspaper public back into the Bennett fold. It took years of effort, in fact, for the *World* to rid itself of the "yellow journalism" label it earned trying to compete with Hearst for circulation in the nineties. Moralists decried the warmongering of both papers, whose "only purpose was to sell papers." Hearst was "that blackguard boy." In a celebrated denunciation in *The Nation,* Edwin L. Godkin declared the *World* and the *Journal* were "newspaper firebrands scattered broadcast throughout the country. . . . A better place in which to prepare a young man for eternal damnation than a yellow-journal office does not exist." The Hearst eagle screamed in triumph as a crew of *Journal* reporters snatched Evangeline Cisneros, a seventeen-year-old political prisoner of the Spanish, from a Havana jail and smuggled her to New York dressed as a boy; it condemned President McKinley and the "Wall Street Cabinet" for hesitating to plunge the country into war, and offered a $50,000 reward for information on just how the battleship *Maine* was sunk. If Pulitzer was not quite so flamboyant in whipping up interventionist sentiment, it was only because he lacked a Sam Chamberlain and an Arthur Brisbane to whoop it up for him. Many days both the *Journal* and the *World* grew so hysterical over the situation that practically their whole front pages were covered with exclamatory headlines.

Meanwhile the *Herald,* though hardly less jingoistic, set about arranging for war coverage calmly, efficiently, and expertly. Many of its correspondents, while less famous than Mr. Hearst's Stephen Crane and James Creelman, were former navy officers who had turned to journalism and would be able to write authoritatively of what became mostly a naval war. Thus, while Havana swarmed with Hearst and Pulitzer men largely occupied with spying on each other, the *Herald* correspondent on the scene when the *Maine* blew up was Walter Scott Meriwether, who had served with several officers on the ill-fated battleship. When the Spanish closed the cable office in Havana to the clamoring correspondents, Meriwether chartered a boat which took him to Key West. At the telegraph office in that port he instructed the operator to start sending the Bible while he composed a precise and detailed account of what had happened to the *Maine*. He tied up the wire—supposedly it was the first time this stratagem was used in competitive journalism—to keep any of the other correspondents on his heels from getting their stories in ahead of him. The *Herald* was thus enabled to publish the first reliable account of that event.

Bennett directed every detail of the *Herald's* wartime operations, mostly by cable from Paris. Late in April, 1898, he chartered the steamer *Avery Hill* to shadow the Spanish squadron at Cape Verde Islands as it lifted anchor for Cuban waters. He also signed the foremost correspondent, Richard Harding Davis, the glamour boy of turn-of-the-century America, to cover the expeditionary force landed in Cuba. Davis had quit Hearst's employ the preceding year after one of his dispatches had been twisted out of shape in the *Journal's* city room and he had publicly disavowed it in a letter published in the other newspapers.

When Commodore Dewey sailed into Manila Bay after cutting the Manila-Hong Kong cable to prevent any interference from Washington, Joseph L. Stickney, a former naval officer, was standing on the bridge beside him as a *Herald* correspondent. The first intimation of an American victory at Manila, in fact, came in a bulletin received by the *Herald,* which did not hesitate to proclaim:

HERALD GIVES THE
NEWS TO PRESIDENT

During the Asiatic Squadron's engagement with the Spanish hulks, Stickney was pressed into service as volunteer aide to Commodore Dewey on the flagship

Olympia, and one of that officer's first dispatches to the mainland was a cable congratulating the *Herald* on its foresight in assigning a correspondent of Stickney's background and capability to the squadron. And thus it was Stickney who reported in eloquent detail Dewey's calm competence as his warship plowed through broadsides from the Spanish fleet and shore batteries, and the *Herald* which first printed his historic order:

"You may fire when you are ready, Gridley."

Even during the most exciting days of America's venture into colonial expansion, the *Herald* continued its practice of printing its classified ads on the first four pages, with Page Five the first to display news. But its coverage was superb; on May 3, heralding the Dewey victory on the basis of Spanish communiqués, it carried four full pages of stories and illustrations on that event, including detailed drawings of the Spanish fortifications around Manila Bay, and two more pages on the preparations for the expedition to Cuba. All dispatches were carried under the slug "Copyright by James Gordon Bennett"—there was to be no doubt about who was commanding the *Herald* forces in the war against Spain, which included a small fleet of dispatch boats zipping around the Caribbean and dogging every movement by the American fleet.

And Richard Harding Davis, immaculate as always, performed under the Bennett colors with his usual excellence in the Cuban campaigning, despite the New York *Sun's* jibing quatrain:

> O, sweetly Dickey pens the tale,
>   And how he loves to pen it,
> And sends it off by wire or mail,
>   To Jimmy Gordon Bennett.

Well groomed and imperturbable as one of his own fictional heroes—Chesterton, the war correspondent, for choice—Davis strolled into the fire from the Spanish rifle pits above Santiago with the first wave of American infantry, and on July 1 the *Herald* banner lines proclaimed his calm, precise account of the great victory, beginning, "After hours of fierce fighting the American Army has succeeded in driving the Spaniards into the city of Santiago. . . . The city may fall tomorrow. . . ."

Nor was military aviation neglected:

WAR BALLOON IS
USED BY SHAFTER
From It Was Reported
Every Move Made by
Spanish Troops
and Ships

A week later, under Davis' byline, the *Herald* was revealing in exclusive dispatches "the precarious situation at Santiago" brought on by feuding between the army commander, General Shafter, and the officer leading the United States fleet off that city, Admiral Sampson. The admiral refused to bombard the Spanish forts around Santiago, Davis disclosed, without orders from the Navy Department. The *Herald* revelations caused a storm of criticism to break over the navy and contributed considerably to Admiral Sampson's unpopularity. Bennett, as an ex-third lieutenant of the Union Navy, considered himself the journalistic spokesman for that branch of the service, but that did not prevent him from sternly criticizing some of its actions.

The army also came in for its full share of editorial denunciation by the *Herald*, particularly when the matters of corruption in the War Department, the open scandal over spoiled and wormy army rations, and the use of blackmail in obtaining military contracts were revealed by its correspondents in Washington, at the army bases in Florida, and with the forces in Cuba. The *Herald's* charges, in fact, stirred up almost as much excitement as the brief flurries of fighting on land and sea against a tottering Spanish Empire; Bennett seemed to regard Secretary of War Russell A. Alger and his bureaucrats as worthier enemies than the Spanish captain-generals—and undoubtedly they were. "The charges," according to Margaret Leech (*In the Days of McKinley*), "weighed so heavily against the credit of the administration that James Gordon Bennett . . . was emboldened to attempt a little blackmail on his own account. Colonel Boynton of the Associated Press wrote General Grenville Dodge in April that the President had been given to understand that the *Herald's* attack would stop if Alger were replaced by a candidate named by that newspaper." Great as the *Herald's* prestige then was, however, the Commodore was not allowed the privilege—if he sought it—of naming his own Secretary of War.

Perhaps the best evidence of the *Herald's* success in covering all phases of the war was a long blistering editorial dictated by the Commodore and flaying a number of newspapers throughout the country, particularly the Pittsburgh *Dispatch,* for reprinting its dispatches without even crediting their source.

So the brisk little war against Spain had done wonders for the *Herald,* bringing a circulation of over half a million, restoring the old million-dollar-a-year net profit, and even reviving its publisher's flagging interest in his newspapers. The way the public had rejected Hearst-Pulitzer sensationalism and had responded instead to the solid authority of the *Herald's* coverage of the war news convinced him that there was a market for a good newspaper, an audience for a cool, reasoning voice.

Now in his late fifties, the Commodore was so rejuvenated by his successes that he began taking an interest in a new method of communication. The electric impulses which sped along the news had fascinated both of the Bennetts. Development of the electric telegraph had been seized upon by Bennett Senior, first among all the newspaper publishers, as a means of more quickly informing the public and incidentally beating his rivals. His son similarly had utilized the cable to awaken American interest in foreign affairs.

Now Bennett heard of the experiments a young Italian named Marconi was making with the wireless, trying to beam messages from Ireland to Newfoundland on the radio waves. The Commodore immediately assigned Milton Snyder, a young man in his London bureau, to join Marconi and report back on the progress of his experiments. Snyder's report was enthusiastic. So Bennett commissioned Marconi to provide wireless communications for coverage of the America's Cup yacht race in 1899, and paid the Italian $5000, which helped him perfect his system just when his capital was running low. Subsequently Bennett established his own wireless station at Sankaty Head, assigned the *Herald's* naval expert, Lieutenant Commander J. D. Jerrold Kelly, to assist Lee J. De Forest in his experiments along the same lines, and supplied De Forest with funds to improve the transmission of news by wireless. . . .

A rather comic aftermath of the Spanish-American War was the engagement of James Creelman, a star in the Hearst constellation, to act as roving correspondent of the New York *Herald*. For years the Commodore had been looking for another Stanley, and his search had not been successful. Richard Harding Davis stayed on the Bennett payroll to cover the Boer War in 1900, but he was too spoiled by fame, from his employer's standpoint, too concerned with becoming a literary figure. For a time Bennett held high hopes for Aubrey Stanhope, the cousin of an English earl, an amateur prize fighter of some renown, and the man whom the Commodore had sent to ask Stanley whether he was beating his wife. Drawn into the intimacy of court circles in Berlin and Saint Petersburg, however, Stanhope was developing a swelled head, had even hired a ghost writer for a time, and was given to submitting dropsical expense accounts. The Englishman was on his last legs with the Commodore. His final offense in Bennett's eyes was committed some years after he was detached from the payroll: he turned up in Berlin during the World War, edited a German propaganda sheet called the *Continental Times,* and served as the model for Lord Haw-Haw in a later war.

The black-bearded Creelman, energetic and dashing, promised to add luster to the *Herald's* foreign correspondence. In the Cuban campaign he had suggested a bayonet charge to the officer commanding an infantry battalion at El Caney, and the Spanish blockhouses had been captured in one fell swoop. Creelman was wounded in the shoulder during the charge, and came to with his employer, William Randolph Hearst, who was personally directing the operations of his correspondents in the field, bending over him. "I'm sorry you're hurt," Hearst said, his face "radiant" with enthusiasm, "but wasn't it a splendid fight? We must beat every paper in the world!" Possibly dismayed by his employer's lack of solicitude, Creelman quit Hearst a short time later and signed on with Bennett.

The correspondent was ordered to report to Bennett on his yacht in the harbor of Leghorn, and clambered up the companionway expecting a warm welcome from his new employer. On deck he was halted by the yacht's quartermaster, who told him, "You can't come on board, sir."

"Why not?" Creelman demanded. "I've been ordered here by Mr. Bennett."

"You'll have to go back ashore and take off your beard. The Commodore will permit no one on the ship who isn't clean-shaven."

A few years before, according to Ralph Blumenfeld, the Grand Duke of Russia had shaved off his beard "by orders" before he was permitted to join Bennett's other invited guests aboard the yacht.

Creelman, however, possessed a more than ducal pride.

Obtaining the yacht's itinerary, he followed it down the Italian coast, presenting himself at each stop and each time being turned away. Finally, in Fiume, he gave up and went back to Paris to await Bennett's pleasure.

Weeks later the Commodore summoned him to his apartment on the Champs Elysées. Neither man mentioned Creelman's unsuccessful attempts to obtain an earlier interview. Having a grudging respect for those who resisted his whims, Bennett (and, of course, the resident Pekingese) took a liking to Creelman and invited him to stay for lunch.

The main dish, which Bennett fancied almost as much as mutton chops, was plovers' eggs, a delicacy imported from the upper reaches of the Orinoco and Amazon rivers at a cost which fluctuated between $200 and $400 a dozen. Bennett received half of the entire European supply; the other half, much to the excitation of his already considerable anti-German prejudice, went to Count Herbert Bismarck, the Iron Chancellor's son.

Creelman had never tasted the delicacy before, but he was willing to educate a palate hitherto accustomed to the coarser fare available on a newspaperman's salary. Before the lunch was over, Creelman had consumed a dozen of the marble-sized eggs, a whole week's supply, at a cost approximating a month's salary, while his employer smiled grimly and congratulated him on his refined tastes.

Bennett forgave him for both his beard and his unseemly appetite for plovers' eggs, and Creelman worked for the *Herald* for several years until he was lured away by the *World*.

No less bizarre was the experience of another reporter summoned to a job interview by the Commodore. He was received by Bennett in the library of his Paris apartment, both of them sitting before the briskly burning fireplace. As they talked, the reporter noticed that Bennett was squirming around in his chair, as though something were digging into his backside.

Finally the Commodore jumped up with a roar of exasperation and dug a huge roll of bills from his rear pocket, mostly twenty- and fifty-dollar bills, as the reporter had occasion to observe a moment or two later. Bennett, swearing violently, hurled the roll of bills into the fire.

While Bennett's back was momentarily turned, the unemployed newspaperman reached into the fireplace and retrieved the burning money. After slapping out the flames, he handed the roll to Bennett.

The Commodore tossed the money back into the fire. "Perhaps that's how I wanted them," he said.

The saddest part about this anecdote is that those

who told it were unable to say whether the reporter
was given the job he sought. It seems unlikely. Bennett
couldn't abide the helping hand, even if it was slightly
scorched in his service.

10: The Commodore Afloat

If he was a problem to his friends and a tyrant to his associates and employees on land, the Commodore at sea, with his own deck beneath him and a hundred clean-shaven crewmen jumping to his orders, was a mettlesome combination of Captains Bligh, Kidd, and Katzenjammer. At the helm of his own vessel—and the Commodore never went yachting with anyone else—he considered himself godlike. No other ship, whether it was a transatlantic liner or a battlewagon, could be permitted to cross his bows. The chief professional sailor aboard was never addressed as the captain but as the "first officer"; the Commodore's authority must be absolute. Bennett never actually marooned or keelhauled anyone or ordered a flogging with the cat-o'-nine-tails, but those who sailed with him sometimes got the impression that such measures would be taken if necessary.

Several rules had to be obeyed by anyone, guest or crew member, who sailed with Bennett:

1. All men had to be clean-shaven—except, of course, the Commodore. Even he trimmed his large mustache for all maritime occasions. He once explained this fetish to George A. Cormack, secretary of the New York Yacht Club, as having grown out of his admiration for the whiskerless officers and men of the British Navy. The crew members received extra pay for shaving off their beards and mustaches.

2. No one must address the Commodore until he spoke first. At sea he was subject to deep thinking, or so he said, and must not be distracted.

3. No cardplaying aboard. He never explained his reason for this shipboard rule. Possibly he considered it an insult for guests to hole themselves up in the salon or a cabin playing bridge or poker when they should be enjoying the sea air. At any rate the luggage of all guests was searched, no matter how august the personage, and any decks of cards found were taken to the Commodore, who removed the aces, tore them up, and then returned the remaining cards to their owner.

For some years during his self-exile in Europe, he was nautically content with the 900-ton *Namouna* and with experimenting on the Thames and the Seine with speedboats. In 1900, however, flush with the profits from the New York *Herald's* resurgence during the Spanish-American War, he decided that he must have a larger, swifter, and more palatial craft at his disposal. He commissioned G. L. Watson, the prominent naval architect, to design a steam yacht, which was built by Denny and Brothers, at Dunbarton, for $625,000. Experts said it was more palatial than any royal yacht then afloat. Bennett had a suite on each of her three decks, reserved for himself alone, so he could sleep as the fancy took him; it was just possible, too, that his amorous proclivities dictated the necessity of having several different sleeping quarters at his disposal, though at sixty even the Commodore's fires were being banked. Quarters for a score of guests were only a little less expansive.

Bennett named her *Lysistrata*, "for a Greek lady reputed to be very beautiful and very fast."

Several features of the *Lysistrata* were unusual even for millionaires' steam yachts in their most opulent period. One was a Turkish bath set aside for the Commodore's use only. When he was sweating out a hangover, he did not fancy company. Another luxury item was a padded stall outfitted for a milk cow, an Alderney, whose duty it was to supply milk and cream for the Commodore and his guests. Aside from Bennett himself, the cow was the most pampered creature aboard. An electric fan was installed to keep her quarters cool when the yacht was sailing in tropical waters. One of the first electric milking machines was also purchased for the private dairy.

One Alderney proved to have a tendency to seasickness and her replacement became necessary. Bennett sent word to the Paris *Herald* office that a certain young reporter was to meet him at Villefranche, where the *Lysistrata's* anchorage was located, a few miles from his villa at Beaulieu. Deeply flattered by the invitation, the reporter had visions of himself sailing off into the blue Mediterranean with lords and ladies and pretty actresses as his fellow guests. When he arrived at Villefranche, the Commodore took him on a long tour of the inland farms, searching for an Alderney with the proper butterfat ratio in her milk. The reporter, of course, was pleased by the fact that his employer chose him for a companion on this important mission.

He was still dazzled by dreams of a romantic cruise when they found a suitable cow and Bennett brought him back to earth by shoving the creature's lead rope into his hand and crisply ordering him, "Here, you'll have to lead the cow back to the yacht." The Commodore whisked away in a cloud of dust. The reporter trudged many miles back to Villefranche, leading the cow which would be his proxy on the forthcoming cruise.

Aboard the *Lysistrata,* Bennett ranged beyond the Mediterranean. Several times he cruised the Indian

Ocean, going as far as Ceylon. He also steamed to
Bermuda and New York a number of times. One of
his favorite cruises, however, was into the eastern
Mediterranean, among the bone-white islands of Greece
whose austere beauty in a fabled seascape endlessly
enthralled him. Venturing into these waters, he invariably stopped off in the Golden Horn for a visit with the
Sultan of Turkey, internationally notorious as Abdul
the Damned. An odd friendship had sprung up between
the two men years before, when Bennett had interviewed him for the *Herald*. In contrast to the large,
rawboned, self-confident American publisher, the ruler
of the decaying Ottoman Empire, soon to be swept into
exile by the Young Turks' revolution, was a small,
sallow, furtive man so terrified of assassins that he never
slept in the same bed twice and kept loaded revolvers
in every drawer of every room of his sprawling Yildiz
Palace. Abdul's only sure-fire political remedy for his
tottering empire was an occasional massacre of a
Christian minority to take his people's minds off their
troubles. What the two men found to talk about (in
French) was always a mystery to the Commodore's
associates. As the last of the absolute tyrants, however,
Abdul-Hamid exercised a strong fascination for the
Commodore, who was enough of a romantic to be
impressed by harem beauties peering through lattices,
eunuchs padding down marble corridors, courtiers
salaaming so low their foreheads touched the floor, and
bodyguards lurking behind every silken drapery.

On his long voyages the Commodore kept in touch
as best he could with his New York and Paris offices.
News summaries were cabled from the New York
Herald and waited for him at every port. Once when he
took the *Lysistrata* up the Nile, he had dispatches awaiting him at every telegraph station along the river. Often

when he suddenly took a notion to go voyaging he
ordered his headquarters to send all the mail at the
Paris *Herald* to the yacht while she was being commissioned for the cruise—everything: letters, mail dispatches from correspondents, checks, advertising copy,
contracts, and publicity handouts, whether addressed to
him or not. Large sacks of mail would then be stacked
on the *Lysistrata's* decks. "If," as Albert Jaurett, the
Commodore's chief liaison with the Paris operation, told
Laney (Paris *Herald*), "the Commodore got up in the
morning feeling good and the weather was fine, things
would not be so bad. He would call his secretaries and
they would go through the mail, sending it back where
it belonged. If, on the other hand, the Commodore got
up with a hangover, or the weather was foul, he would
kick the sacks into the Mediterranean, say the hell with
it, and go off to a favorite restaurant along the Riviera.
. . . If, at some later date, an advertiser would complain that the copy he had sent to the *Herald* had not
appeared, Bennett was quite capable of blaming someone in the office and firing him without further notice."

He was too proud to admit to loneliness, of course,
but he liked to move, on land or sea, surrounded by
people. Most of them were idlers, spongers, social butter-
flies who flitted from resort to resort, luxuriating in a
hospitality available only in those pre-World War years,
elegantly worthless figures playing out their last carefree
hours in a world soon to be destroyed by the crash of
guns from the North Sea to the Bosporus. To them
"M. Gordon-Bennett" was the most lavish, if unpredictable and idiosyncratic, host then offering himself
to the parasitic throng; no other American helped to
fix so firmly in the European mind the image of the
wealthy American as an international sucker. "Paris
and the 'high world' of Europe," as Albert Stevens

Crockett wrote, "were always looking to him to do in the most elaborate fashion everything he did in the way of entertaining. . . . He knew they expected eccentricity from him, and he played the part."

Even the Commodore, dazzled by every flash from a tiara, spellbound by every tale of life in a remote, verminous court, sometimes wearied of their pretensions. He once gave a dinner party at his Paris apartment at which he sardonically notified his hangers-on that he recognized the greed that sometimes shone in their languid gaze. From Appay's, the jeweler on the Rue de la Paix to whom he gave his patronage, he borrowed a trayful of costly baubles for the occasion. His butler and other servants were instructed to wear the diamond, emerald, star sapphire, and ruby rings on every finger when they served dinner. Eyes popped, but no one said a word, as each course appeared at the table. His guests were so overcome by conflicting emotions that they hardly had the energy to attack the grouse imported from their host's shooting box in Scotland. Bennett, it was observed, "thoroughly enjoyed the amazement that ordinary politeness forbade them to express in words."

Those who partook of his hospitality on the high seas were even more likely to be amazed, discomfited, or confounded by him. Aboard the *Lysistrata* he was as highhanded as any pirate captain. Sometimes, overcome by his passion for the sea, he would disappear from sight of his guests for days at a time. He held a master's license and charted his own courses. An instrument connecting the bridge with his sea cabin would alert him when the helm was unduly shifted, which generally brought the Commodore raging up to find out what the hell was going on. In this ascetic, seafaring mood, he shunned the company of the landlubbers on the decks below.

Bennett did not take kindly to complaints from his guests about their accommodations. A finicky bachelor annoyed him by complaining that the steward had not called him at the proper time in the morning, and furthermore his bath was improperly drawn. "Should be just tepid, old boy," the guest explained to Bennett. "Not hot, not cold. Just tepid."

"Tomorrow morning," Bennett said, smiling grimly, "you shall not only be called early but your bath will be brought to your stateroom."

"If it wouldn't be too much trouble——"

"Not at all, my dear fellow."

At the crack of dawn the next morning, Bennett ordered the biggest fire hose aboard rigged up and its nozzle poked into the open porthole of the fussy bachelor's stateroom.

A torrent of water washed the guest right out of his bunk and half drowned him.

When he came up to the bridge to complain, Bennett bellowed at him, "I had you awakened early this morning, didn't I? Your bath was brought to your cabin, wasn't it? Now get off my bridge or I'll give you another dose of tepid water!"

Every time the *Lysistrata* lifted anchor at Villefranche, continental society could count on a steady flow of anecdotes, scandal, outrage, and recrimination to come wafting back from every port the *Lysistrata* touched.

While cruising the North Sea on one occasion, Bennett and his guests got bored with each other's company. The weather had been squally, the sea rough, and the guests had largely been confined to their cabins. The Commodore ordered the yacht to put in at Amsterdam, where entertainment might be found and boredom alleviated. Some of his guests wanted to go ashore when the *Lysistrata* dropped anchor, but Bennett wouldn't hear of it. Perhaps he suspected that they intended to jump ship. Entertainment would be brought aboard, he ordained.

Later that day the members of a theatrical troupe playing at an Amsterdam theater were invited to join a party aboard the yacht.

Toward dusk Bennett took the impresario aside and inquired whether every member of his company had accepted the invitation. The manager said they had. Bennett nodded and hurried out of the salon.

A short time later everyone was surprised to learn that, while they were dancing, frolicking, and guzzling champagne, the *Lysistrata* had quietly lifted anchor and was pushing out to the open sea. The performers were almost hysterical; the impresario shrieked imprecations in nine languages, pointing out, in lucid intervals, that the company was scheduled to give a performance that evening before a sold-out house. Only the Commodore was calm.

"Never mind," he said. "I have decided to engage the company for tonight's performance. Tomorrow morning you will be returned to Amsterdam. A little sea air will do all of you a world of good."

After what may have been the first seagoing presentation of a theater-in-the-round, sans costume, make-up, and scenery, the company topped off the night with wassail and next morning was returned to the quays of Amsterdam. Bennett handsomely rewarded each player, stifled the impresario's outcries with further applications of cold cash, and reimbursed the theater several times over for the canceled performance.

Yachting brought him in social conflict with the third man whom he particularly detested among his contemporaries, Kaiser Wilhelm of Germany. The Commodore had always refused to join in his generation's admiration for the German race, to begin with, because he was too ardently pro-French to spare any good will for the nation which had snatched away Alsace-Lorraine. Wealthy Americans at the turn of the century often preferred Germany to the rest of the continent because of its clean, orderly cities, its disciplined people, and its somewhat American passion for efficiency and material progress, as well as its rich contributions to music, philosophy, and culture in general. Germany was not yet an ogre among nations. Socially conscious Americans competed as eagerly for presentation at the imperial court in Berlin as for the privilege of curtseying to British royalty.

Bennett, however, was inclined to the French view that the Germans had a dangerous streak of barbarism likely to burst civilized restraints at any moment. Years before the World War broke out he was pointing to the danger of German aggression and editorializing against German attempts at colonial expansion, particularly after the Samoa affair and the German Navy's attempt to muscle its way into the Philippines. Admiring as he was of the aristocracy, Bennett disliked the Prussian brand; among the few exceptions he made, according to Crockett, were the Duke of Mecklenburg-Schwerin, who was "a warm personal friend," and his daughter, the Crown Princess, of whom he was "extremely fond." But that lady's father-in-law, Kaiser Wilhelm, was anathema to him.

A right royal snub incurred his hostility in the German Emperor's case. Bennett sailed his yacht to attend the German royal regatta at Kiel and naturally expected to be received by the Kaiser. Both Queen Victoria and her son, Edward VII, had granted him audiences; he was a friend of Abdul-Hamid of Turkey, and on easy terms with most of the lesser royalty of Europe. Naturally he expected to be welcomed graciously by the German Emperor, both as a leading yachtsman and as one of the world's leading newspaper proprietors. "It was no secret," Crockett noted, "that Mr. Bennett considered himself just as important a personage as the Kaiser."

Somehow the Kaiser, on his yacht at Kiel, was not thoroughly briefed on the social and journalistic importance of this American Commodore Bennett. When Bennett, through an intermediary, advised the Kaiser's aides that he would not object to being invited aboard the imperial yacht, his hint was simply ignored. And Bennett sailed off in a rage.

Several years later Bennett took the opportunity of snubbing the overbearing Wilhelm in return. The Commodore's yacht was tied up in the harbor of Beirut when the imperial yacht *Hohenzollern* sailed in with an escort of several German warships.

Bennett was ashore when the German ships dropped anchor, and when he was rowed back to his yacht he found that his first officer had dressed the ship with pennants honoring the royal visitor. So had every other craft in the harbor with the proper pennants in its locker.

As soon as he reached his own deck, Bennett pointed aloft and shouted at the first officer, "What the hell are all those rags strung out for?"

"The German Emperor is in port, sir," the first officer replied.

"I don't give a damn if he's walking across the water."

"I thought, sir, that if you had been aboard, you would have ordered it done."

"Don't *think!* Hereafter when you are in the slightest doubt as to what I might want done, do nothing. Now have those flags hauled down—and up anchor!"

Bare of bunting, the Bennett yacht haughtily put out to sea within an hour, leaving one or two guests stranded in Beirut.

The Commodore's action was so unmistakably an affront that even the Kaiser became aware of it. In aggrieved tones, he demanded of his courtiers why the American gentleman had taken such an abrupt and impolite departure. No one could tell him. The Kaiser ordered that an investigation be made through diplomatic sources. Finally he was advised that he had unintentionally snubbed the influential American at his regatta.

Amends must be made, the Kaiser ordered. A few months later an important function was scheduled at Potsdam, and Wilhelm sent Bennett a personal message asking him to attend.

The Commodore did not even answer, although this was regarded as an unthinkable insult.

For years afterward, deeply hurt by the countersnub, the Kaiser brought up the matter with every American, private or official, to whom he was introduced. He had never been insulted before. The Americans could have told him that he was merely one of a long procession of people who had felt the rough edge of the Commodore's temper.

Stiff-necked and spoiled as he was in his relations with the rest of humanity, Bennett was not entirely incapable of righting a wrong. Many would have found this hard to believe, particularly former employees who had been sent packing on some unworthy pretext or other, but when he attempted to make amends for an injustice he went all the way. Or so Emma Eames, the celebrated American soprano, discovered to her amazement. The singer, born in Maine, was described by William Lyon Phelps as possessing the "finest soprano voice I had ever heard," ranking her above such prima donnas as Calvé, Lehmann, Ternina, and Nordica. Furthermore, according to Dr. Phelps, she had "a noble physique, ravishing beauty of face and expression, and a voice of apparently unlimited power and freshness." Her performance as Marguerite in *Faust* at the Grand Opera House in Paris in the summer of 1890 had made her as famous on the continent as she was in her homeland; and, again according to Dr. Phelps, she was a "charming woman with a particularly well-furnished and interesting mind . . . she has a Continental brain and an American heart."

Miss Eames, then the wife of Julian Story, a portrait painter, first met Bennett when she came to Paris in 1901 from her place at Vallombrosa, in Italy. In her memoir (*Some Memories and Reflections*) she recalled that one afternoon Bennett's card was brought in to her, and "I read his name unbelievingly as it was a matter of common talk that he did not like me—although no one knew why, least of all myself—and had given the New York *Herald* emphatic instructions to dismiss any operatic success of mine with a bare mention, and not to print my name if it could be helped."

Bennett, with his "hard, austere face" and "unapproachable" manner, came striding into Miss Eames' drawing room, announcing "I have come to make you my deepest apology."

A jealous rival of Miss Eames, he said, had been "chagrined at her reception in New York" and informed Bennett that Miss Eames' intriguing had caused the critical coolness. Bennett had thereupon cabled the New York *Herald* to give Miss Eames as little favorable publicity as possible. "He went on to say that he had just learned by merest chance, and from a person who neither knew me nor was particularly interested in me, that this singer had deliberately lied, and therefore he had come that afternoon to 'place the *Herald* at my feet.' I could have told him that I could not see that its attitude had materially hindered my career, but refrained from doing so. . . . One of the *Herald* men told me later that the reporters had known the facts [of her rival's scheming] all along, but none of them dared to go to Bennett about it."

As she grew to know him better, Miss Eames said, she discovered that he possessed a "keen sense of justice" and a "tender heart," in support of which she wrote, "He adored animals and perpetuated his affection for them in a motley array of china and painted iron figures of every size which took up a large part of his lawn at Beaulieu. Every time he went to Nice he added to this collection by purchasing a new specimen from a poor old woman who sold such wares."

In the following spring, Bennett commissioned the prima donna's husband to paint his portrait and invited the Storys to visit him at his villa in the South of France. While the Commodore posed and her husband painted, Bennett regaled Miss Eames with stories about her malicious rival. "She had the habit, so he said, of always doing something to put him in her debt, usually seating herself at his piano and entertaining his guests by an impromptu song recital after a luncheon or a dinner, and immediately afterwards asking some favor of him which he often found difficult to grant and hard to refuse.

"At last one day when he received word from her that she was coming up from Nice to lunch with him, he sent the piano out of the house to forestall her generosity. When she arrived and found it gone, she was perfectly nonplused and asked anxiously what had become of it. All Bennett told her was that it had been sent away for repairs as it was out of order."

The Commodore appointed himself Miss Eames' guardian against her rival's venomous gossip. When she skipped a season, her "dear enemy and colleague" vigorously propagated rumors that Miss Eames was paralyzed and would never sing again. "Mr. Bennett pointed out that it was impossible for me to deny this, as no one ever believed a denial under any circumstances. He also said that any answer I made to this rumor would only call attention to it, even as a denial of any statement in the public press only served to call attention of the thousands who had not read the original article. . . . I asked: 'But what can I do? I am far from well, although I am equally far from being paralyzed, and had planned to do nothing this year.'" The Commodore advised her to give a series of parties at which she could publicly demonstrate that the rumors were wrong. "I felt as much like giving a party as I did like climbing a steeple, but nevertheless I did give four musicales in the studio of our house on four consecutive Thursdays. . . . At each party I sang. . . . After each one Bennett had a lengthy article, including a list of the brilliant company and the names of the famous musicians who took part in the program, cabled to the *Herald* in New York."

The Commodore's sense of fair play was a variable quality, tempered by his whims, prejudices, and perversities. An artistic celebrity like Emma Eames or a social figure like William K. Vanderbilt, Sr. was much likelier to make its acquaintance than a member of the lower orders. When Vanderbilt took a second wife, Albert Stevens Crockett, then attached to the Paris bureau of the New York *Herald*, was assigned to interview him as he and his bride arrived from England.

Vanderbilt, however, was not eager for publicity, evaded reporters at the Gare du Nord, and sped away in an automobile. Crockett borrowed a twelve-horsepower Panhard, showing a spirit of enterprise that ordinarily would have been highly praised, and chased the millionaire socialite to his château beyond Saint Cloud. Had it been a Gould he was hounding, Crockett would probably have been rewarded with a fat bonus, but William K. Vanderbilt was a friend of the Commodore's.

When Vanderbilt protested the reporter's unseemly zeal, Bennett sent Crockett a telegram reading, "Consider your hounding Vanderbilt to earth as worst possible type of yellow journalism." Furthermore Bennett ordered that Crockett henceforth would be reduced to the job of opening the mail at the Commodore's Paris apartment. Several days later Bennett summoned him to Beaulieu for a further dressing down. Then Vanderbilt insisted that Crockett be fired, and Bennett exploded, "I'll be damned if anybody is going to dictate to me who is going to be hired or fired!" And Crockett was immediately restored to his correspondent's rank.

The Commodore's own love affairs were, of course, kept out of the papers as much as possible.

Perhaps the most unfortunate was his romance with Camille Clermont, a beautiful and fairly accomplished actress, with whom he began an affair not long after moving his headquarters to Paris. It was in her memoir, (*Confessions of Gentle Rebecca*), that Bennett was most tellingly ticked off as a "barbarian" and an unfeeling lover concerned only with his own appetites and amusement. Mlle. Clermont apparently had some reason for ripping into him several years after his death. Her role was that of the woman scorned, which few play gracefully and fewer still *sotto voce*.

The unhappy aftermath of Bennett's affair with Mlle.

Clermont was disclosed in a series of lawsuits in the Paris courts brought by the actress' daughter, Mlle. Juliette Schettler, who sought to have the Commodore named as her father and demanded that he support her in the style of an American millionaire's offspring. The girl's petitions dogged him for years, but she was never successful in legally proving that Bennett was her father.

A rather startling glimpse of Bennett's amatory tactics, which were inclined more to the peremptory than the subtle or tender, was provided by the Countess Balsan (Consuelo Vanderbilt) in her memoir *The Glitter and the Gold*. The glamorous Consuelo's father and mother, Mr. and Mrs. William K. Vanderbilt, were "great friends" of the Commodore, and she could recall visits to his seaside villa at Beaulieu which were often full of surprises but seldom dull. She remembered in particular that the railroad tracks ran close to the outer boundary of his gardens and "Mr. Bennett invariably ran to his windows to watch the trains pass. I thought it unusual for one who had his yacht, the famous *Lysistrata*, anchored in the quiet bay at his feet to find so much to excite him in passing trains."

Countess Balsan told of one incident which illustrated his attitude toward the ladies and which occurred when three pretty Americans were visiting him at Beaulieu. They were a Mrs. Moore, whose malapropisms provided much amusement in Paris society; Lady Lily Bagot, and Adele, the Countess of Essex, the latter two married to English noblemen. One or more of his guests captured his fancy, and since he could not disengage her from her friends he invited all three to dine with him aboard the *Lysistrata*, which was anchored at nearby Villefranche. The ladies, believing there was safety in numbers, accepted the invitation.

Dinner was decorous enough, but the Commodore

seemed to be fuming inwardly as he bolted down champagne and brandy.

Then he suddenly disappeared from the table. The three ladies, aware of his changeable disposition, continued their conversation.

Just as they were about to seek out the Commodore and suggest that the party return to dry land, they became aware of the fact that the *Lysistrata* was putting out to sea. Smoke was pouring out of its huge single funnel and the yacht was moving briskly out of the harbor as though a long voyage were in prospect. Worse yet, the sky was clouding up and the yacht seemed to be heading into a rough sea.

The three ladies searched the decks for the Commodore but he couldn't be found; then they hurried up to the wheelhouse and demanded that the officer in command turn around and head back to shore.

"I'm sorry," the first officer told them. "I have Mr. Bennett's orders to proceed to Egypt."

"But we can't go to Egypt!" the ladies wailed.

"Nothing but Mr. Bennett's word," the first officer said, "will change that order."

Bennett had locked himself in one of his three suites and refused to pay any attention to the clamor outside his door. Apparently, in his befuddled state, he had concluded that kidnaping was the only solution to his amorous problem.

His guests, at any rate, spent a miserable night on the *Lysistrata* as it plowed through heavy seas toward Alexandria.

Next morning the Commodore recovered his senses and ordered the yacht to put back to its home base, but breakfast was an unhappy affair with three ruffled, sleepless, and indignant ladies venting their anger on his aching head.

At Villefranche, amid much smirking from by-standers on the dock, "the furious and outraged guests were disembarked in broad daylight still wearing their evening clothes," as Countess Balsan has recounted. "Profuse apologies accompanied by extravagant presents finally restored more friendly relations, but in the future visitors were less easily persuaded to dine on the *Lysistrata*."

Bennett's longest and stormiest affair involved a Russian woman whose name was not mentioned in the various memoirs of the period but who was described as being as formidable in her way as the Commodore was in his. She was the wife of a Russian general living in Paris, a gentleman either so wrapped up in memories of old campaigns or so indifferent that he did not object to her extramarital activities. Apparently she was a handsome woman, or she would not have caught Bennett's eye in the first place, but what impressed most people was her size, her loud voice, and her domineering manner. She was built like a guardsman and had a temper to match. Bennett had literally caught a Tartar, it appeared, and what bewildered his friends was the fact that this relationship continued for years, possibly because Bennett was afraid to attempt breaking it off. Then, too, Bennett had such a perverse and sardonic outlook on life; she was reputed to be the "most unpleasant woman in Paris"; he was well aware of his own reputation for being wildly unpredictable when he was not downright difficult—and it was quite in character for him to conclude, with a bitter humor, that they deserved each other.

Noisily contemptuous as he was of conventional taboos and bourgeois morality, his mixture of Celtic strains bred in him a typical tendency toward self-punishment. None can be more publicly defiant than the Celtic renegade, and none so secretly apprehensive, so darkly aware of the retribution to come. Like his father, he was the sort of stubborn sinner who holds out for a deathbed absolution, hanging onto a devilish pride until the last feasible moment.

So "Mme. A," as she was discreetly referred to, served, perhaps, as Bennett's hair shirt, his tithe of penance performed on a private pay-as-you-go plan.

Apart from the early moments of delirium, there could not have been a great deal of pleasure in the relationship for the Commodore. "Mme. A" was a constant embarrassment, the sort of woman who delights in causing scenes. Bennett was not exactly shy about attracting attention himself, particularly when drunk, but he winced and flinched and was appalled when someone else behaved in the same way, or worse. As time went on, they were seldom seen together in public.

Crockett told of a curious incident that occurred when he took a vacation at a Bohemian resort, leaving on the Carlsbad Express at a time dictated by the Commodore. He had just been shown to a table for two in the dining car when a "large, imperious-looking" woman swept in, "talking at the top of her voice and gesticulating wildly. . . . Never have I seen a woman order men about more vigorously."

The seat opposite Crockett was the only vacant one in the car. "She looked at it, she looked at me; her lip curled; then she flounced down upon the chair and began to order her food in a loud tone and with a rasping, disagreeable accent which made it impossible for me to enjoy the rest of my meal, for she did not cease talking to the waiters and to anybody and everybody when she selected her food."

Several days later, at the Savoy West End Hotel in Carlsbad, Crockett again caught sight of the woman and asked the manager who she was. "I am surprised that you do not know the lady," Crockett was told. "That is Madame A, whom everybody in Europe knows as the *cher amie* of your chief."

It then occurred to Crockett that sending him on the same train as "Mme. A" was "one of those ironic little touches of which Mr. Bennett was very fond. . . . He knew quite well that the lady whose finances were still a subject for his consideration was journeying on that train; he himself had selected that particular Carlsbad Express for me; and it is my guess that he passed the word to Madame A that he was sending a *Herald* correspondent along to keep an eye on her."

That encounter took place in 1906, as Crockett recalled, when the Commodore was sixty-five years old. The latter's relationship with the Russian general's wife was to continue almost until 1914, when Bennett escaped into the sanctuary of marriage. Until then, Bennett was as browbeaten while Mme. A was around as any impoverished bookkeeper with a vixenish wife. "It is to the hold she exercised over Bennett for many years," Crockett said, "that I believe may be ascribed the carrying out of many whimsicalities and curious fads which helped to bring the *Herald* of that day into disrepute—at least she was so credited abroad." One of the *Herald's* "fads" which Crockett and others blamed on Mme. A was the paper's constant campaigning against the practice of vivisection, but the Commodore's almost zoophilic regard for small animals undoubtedly prompted that crusade. Likewise the *Herald's* other eccentricities. Bennett was too jealous of his newspapers to share them with anyone, even a mistress so domineering as the Russian lady.

Perhaps it was just as well that he waited until he

was well into his seventies before marrying, because, in some ways, he clung to adolescence longer than most men hang onto their hair, teeth, and muscle tone. This long-lasting immaturity, along with his alcoholic tendencies, his irascibility, and his huge income, produced some of his lordliest gestures, the effects of which were not always bad or harmful. His appreciation of good food, for instance, encouraged many Americans visiting Europe to educate their palates to something more exotic than ham and eggs and other American staples; at least a dozen good restaurants throughout France, it was said, owed their success to Bennett's praise in the columns of the Paris *Herald* and his countrymen who consequently patronized them. His own tastes were simple but demanding, which led to such occasional tantrums as that which resulted in the establishment of the famous Ciro's of Monte Carlo.

He often lunched at a restaurant with an outdoor terrace sloping down towards the sea at Monte Carlo. Aside from the sun-drenched view, the restaurant performed splendidly on mutton chops.

One day he arrived for lunch and found that all the terrace tables had been reserved for drinking, with those guests who ate their lunch moved inside.

He flew into a rage, and before the afternoon was over he arranged to buy the restaurant and fire the manager who had segregated the eaters and drinkers.

Then he sought out his favorite waiter, an Italian-born Egyptian named Ciro, handed him the bill of sale, and told him:

"Now you own this place. Get those luncheon tables back on the terrace, and go cook my chop."

Ciro's of Monte Carlo became one of the great restaurants of the Riviera and incidentally made a fortune for the ex-waiter. Later it was sold to an English firm, which opened the still more famous Ciro's of Paris. Other Ciro'ses were established in London and Biarritz, but they had nothing to do with Bennett or his beneficiary. The name itself became so celebrated that as late as the 1940s a Ciro's was flourishing in Hollywood. Like the Ritz among hotel names, the Egyptian waiter's name, glorified by a Bennett whim, has been made synonymous with fashionable catering.

At times, however, the Commodore's behavior verged closer to the psychopathic, the self-destructive, than the angry caprice which led to the establishment of a celebrated restaurant. A New York *Herald* correspondent named William Dinwiddie, who had been covering the English forces fighting the Boer War while Richard Harding Davis followed the Boers, told of calling on Bennett late in 1900 while passing through Paris on his way back to New York. "I followed the usual policy demanded by Mr. Bennett of obsequiously calling his private secretary's attention to the fact that I was in Paris, and that I would esteem it an honor if I might, at Mr. Bennett's convenience, see him personally. Mr. Bennett was a great stickler as to the form of approach made by men who were on his payroll."

An hour later Dinwiddie was informed that he was to dine with Bennett that evening at his country estate in Versailles. Percy Mitchell, then the Commodore's private secretary, later his editor-in-charge at the Paris *Herald,* was to drive him down in an automobile, then a daring experience even for a war correspondent. "I still rather vividly remember the horrors of that first early motor experience. The Commodore owned a French make of car said to be the most powerful of its kind, at that time. It had four cylinders, was chain-driven, had a rubber-bulbed horn, and was cranked by hand. The roaring engine was so badly balanced that when it was not moving forward it actually quivered and shimmied over the pavement. I think we touched the unheard-of speed of forty miles an hour, and I have a dazed recollection of women and children and pigs and chickens fleeing out of our path, in the narrow twisting streets, as we went roaring by with a spasmodically sounding horn.

"Two years of war and being shot at occasionally had not half the terrors of that trip.

"When the lodge gates had been thrown open and we had passed inside the huge gray and moss-grown walls which surrounded the Commodore's estate, a dialogue took place between Mitchell and one of the Commodore's manservants, in exclamatory French which I did not understand. Mitchell laughingly interpreted that the servants were all worried because Mr. Bennett had climbed on top of the wall, at a broken-down place, and that they could not get him to come down.

"Following the man, under the shade of the huge trees of the park, we reached the spot on the wall where the Commodore was precariously teetering along the narrow top, some twelve feet off the ground. An old gardener, carrying a light ladder which barely reached to the top of the wall, was begging the Commodore to descend by its aid. Mr. Bennett was protesting that he would never come down until he found the place where he went up. I personally never did see the breach in the wall where he had ascended.

"As he caught sight of me, he exclaimed, 'Hello, Dinwiddie, I am glad to see you.'

"Then the excited, trembling old gardener placed the

ladder, and the Commodore, nimbly if a little un-
certainly, climbed down to shake hands with me. . . ."

At the time the Commodore courted a broken neck
by flywalking the high walls of his estate, he was going
on sixty years of age.

16. A passionate chef once was thrashed by Bennett in this kitchen of his Versailles menage.

17. A procession of mutton chops passed over this table in the dining room at Versailles. Bennett considered the mutton chop, along with plovers' eggs, the finest of foods.

18. The Commodore and his guests are togged out in gaiters, bowlers, even an umbrella for a day's shoot at Versailles.

19. Pour le sport. Cigarette dangling from his lips, Bennett is ready for lawn tennis. Those are Turkish slippers on his feet. He always wore them on the court.

20. Tallyho. Bennett and two understandably nervous companions before setting out on a cross-country dash.

21. Aboard the *Lysistrata*. Two requirements of the Commodore for a successful cruise were in evidence here—sightly females and a full complement of his small dogs. Bennett is seated to the left.

22. Seaside villa at Beaulieu, the most tenderly regarded of all the homes Bennett kept fully staffed and awaiting his awesome tread.

23. The new Herald Building designed by Stanford White. The flags, bunting, and placards proclaim that the *Herald* has sided with the United States during its difficulties with the Spanish empire.

24. Sanctum on Herald Square. Here, at infrequent intervals, the Commodore confronted his trembling janissaries.

25. The Herald lobby. Here, too, Stanford White's impeccable taste and Bennett's impeccable money were apparent. Over the counters to the left passed those notorious *Herald* "personals."

26. At Beaulieu. The Commodore proudly displays two of his horde of small dogs. The dogs were allowed to drink only Vichy water. Bennett was not so choosy about his own liquid intake.

27. Expatriate returns. This shipboard photograph was taken on one of his last visits to the United States.

28. The Garden at Beaulieu in which Bennett calmly waited for death, certain he would die on his seventy-seventh birthday. He did. The Commodore liked to have his own way, even with death.

29. Bound for Passy. A restless voyager all his life, the Commodore is borne from the church after funeral services in Paris. His last trip was to a small cemetery in the suburb of Passy. He preferred to rest eternally in the soil of France.

Credit for all photographs: BROWN BROTHERS

Part Three:

The Years of the Scotch Miser

11: The Commodore vs. the Chief

From the moment William Randolph Hearst invaded New York, he incurred the enmity of James Gordon Bennett. His methods, although they resembled the elder Bennett's efforts to gain a foothold on Park Row for the infant *Herald,* were regarded by the Commodore as loathsome and degrading to the newspaper profession. Socially and journalistically, Mr. Bennett looked down upon young Mr. Hearst as an insufferable parvenu.

During the Spanish-American War, Bennett had taught both Hearst and Pulitzer an elementary lesson in journalism, that covering even such a comic-opera war required a serious approach, since American lives were being lost and American aspirations were involved. You couldn't treat a war as you would a good juicy murder. The *Herald's* circulation, as a result, rose to an all-time crest of 511,000 (which, incidentally, is higher than any of today's afternoon papers in New York), and for a few years after that Bennett's organ maintained its recaptured supremacy.

In 1902 Hearst, unaware of any personal animosity on Bennett's part, and having heard rumors that the Commodore was weary of newspaper publishing, cabled him the hopeful query:

"Is the *Herald* for sale?"

Bennett, according to his aides, exploded in wrath at the very idea of the upstart Hearst's buying him out.

The pale-eyed Californian, in his opinion, was hardly equipped to publish a scratch sheet for race track followers, let alone such an ancient and honorable institution as the *Herald*. So he fired back the insulting reply:

"Price of *Herald* three cents daily. Five cents Sunday. Bennett."

From then on, it was war to the knife between Hearst and Bennett, and the result was that the former's political ambitions were ultimately ruined and the latter's finances seriously impaired.

At the time of his attempt to buy the *Herald*, Hearst's prestige had suffered several serious blows. He badly needed the solid respectability afforded by a paper like the *Herald* to bolster the fortunes of his small but growing newspaper empire, which now included the San Francisco *Examiner*, the New York *Journal*, and the recently established Chicago *American*. Ever since President McKinley had refused to initiate hostilities against Spain as quickly as Hearst demanded, the latter had attacked the President with an unprecedented bitterness. After Governor Goebel of Kentucky was assassinated, the New York *Journal* had published a particularly violent and suggestive quatrain from the pen of Ambrose Bierce:

> The bullet that pierced Goebel's breast
> Can not be found in all the West;
> Good reason, it is speeding here
> To stretch McKinley on his bier.

And then on April 10, 1901, a *Journal* editorial had been even more explicit in suggesting a remedy for the evils its publisher found resident in the White House: "If bad institutions and bad men can be got rid of only by killing, then the killing must be done." Several months later an anarchist fired the bullet fatal to President McKinley. Many blamed Hearst for having planted the idea in the assassin's mind, and both he and his newspapers were assailed from coast to coast. Huge bonfires were built from Hearst newspapers. Hearst, a rusty revolver in one hand and the other handcuffed to a figure representing Emma Goldman, the anarchist, was burned in effigy in a dozen cities. His newspapers were boycotted as "anarchist sheets." And McKinley's successor, Theodore Roosevelt, was indicting William Randolph Hearst and his papers (so he made clear later), when he told Congress in his first message that McKinley's slayer was "inflamed by the teachings of professed anarchists, and probably also by the reckless utterances of those who, on the stump and in the public press, appeal to the dark and evil spirits of malice and greed, envy and sullen hatred. The wind is sowed by the men who preach such doctrines, and they cannot escape their share of responsibility for the whirlwind that is reaped."

Thus Hearst sorely needed whatever rehabilitation might be afforded his reputation by acquisition of a respectable organ such as the *Herald*, especially since he was then embarking on a political career which he hoped and believed would land him in the White House.

Bennett had insulted him in turning down his offer to buy the *Herald;* now he added injury to insult by opposing, with effective editorial campaigns, every phase of the Hearst political career.

Forming an alliance of convenience with Tammany Hall, Hearst was elected to the House of Representatives from the Tammany-controlled Eleventh District in November 1902. In celebration of that victory, the *Journal* sponsored a "monster" fireworks display in Madison Square on election night. A mortar used to set off rockets exploded, ignited a pile of fireworks, caused a panic, and turned the square into a shambles in which seventeen persons were killed and almost a hundred seriously injured. Hearst not only refused to accept responsibility for the disaster but buried the story about it on Page Five of the *Journal,* while every other paper, of course, played it for all it was worth. He fought suits charging him with carelessness in arranging the fireworks display for twenty years before finally settling them. On the very night of his first political triumph, by his apparent indifference to the death and injury of his supporters, Hearst effectively killed off his own chances for higher office, particularly in New York. By way of distracting attention from this ugly affair, he began attacking the "criminal rich" and posing as the friend of the "common man" to the point where he was veering to the left of socialism; these tactics attracted a certain amount of national support for his presidential drive. In 1904 he received as many as 263 votes at the Democratic National Convention, but the much more conservative Alton B. Parker won the nomination on the final ballot.

Two years later he ran for governor of New York, obtained the Democratic nomination, and was considered the favorite over the Republican candidate, Charles Evans Hughes. He spent $265,000 and threw all the resources of his organization into the campaign; the governor's mansion at Albany, after all, was the last way station on the road to the White House.

In the journalistic chorus raised against him, none was more vituperous than the New York *Herald.* Bennett ordered his editors to hammer away at Hearst every day until the election, and *Herald* editorial writers were still masters of invective. Hearst was charged with having accepted a bribe from the Southern Pacific

Railroad, with having employed convict labor in California, and with having moral deficiencies strikingly similar, as a matter of fact, to those of the *Herald's* publisher. This campaign was not at all deterred by an offer from Hearst of $42,000 worth of advertising to be placed in the *Herald*. When the matter was brought to Bennett's attention, he replied, "I would not admit that man's name to the *Herald* for the full value of the Hearst estate." Daily the electorate was reminded of every misstep in the Hearst career, from his expulsion as a student at Harvard to his inflammatory editorials preceding President McKinley's assassination.

Although the Democratic slate otherwise carried the state, Hearst lost the governorship to Hughes by less than 60,000 votes. And for that defeat, by such a narrow margin, he held Bennett and the *Herald* largely responsible.

The *Herald*, furthermore, gloated over his humiliation and promised in an editorial, written in the sledgehammer style of Bennett himself, to oppose Hearst's candidacy "if he so much as dares to run for dogcatcher."

Hearst, still hopeful of coming to terms with a man he had never met and who could not reasonably hold any personal grudge against him, sent one of his executives, Thomas T. Williams, to Paris with a proposal that they settle their differences peaceably. Bennett practically kicked the Hearst emissary out of his office.

Now Hearst, his political ambitions thoroughly doused, turned his attention to avenging himself on Bennett.

It did not take the Hearst editors long to find a vulnerable spot in the Commodore's operation. Ever since the Reverend Dr. Charles H. Parkhurst's celebrated anti-vice crusade of 1894, which impelled the police reluctantly to clamp down on the Tenderloin and which drove prostitution off the streets, the *Herald* had been publishing four to six pages of "personals," which brought in an estimated quarter of a million dollars a year revenue. The classified ads, but mainly the personals, were the *Herald's* financial mainstay. They were also the business directory of the houses of prostitution and assignation, the "massage parlors," Turkish baths and "rooming houses with female clientele," which had to operate more discreetly after a legislative investigation had shown how closely the police co-operated with organized vice. Along Park Row the *Herald's* personals columns were known as the Whores' Daily Guide and Compendium. Yet the local authorities did nothing to interfere with their publication; the new reformist district attorney, as a matter of fact, was the crusading William Travers Jerome, who happened to be the son of Bennett's old friend, the late Lawrence Jerome.

Bennett, of course, was aware of the purpose which his otherwise respectable journal was serving. Flynn, Chambers, Reick, and other *Herald* editors had warned him that some day the personals would get him in trouble with the postal laws, that they were a constant affront to decent people and a target for professional moralists. The Commodore swept aside their warning memos. Those little ads kept him in yachts, champagne, and country estates, as well as helping to pay for the *Herald's* costly foreign correspondence. Besides, a lusty fellow himself, he contended that they performed a worth-while, if covert, service to the public. In addition they made interesting reading, even for those without lascivious intentions.

Some of the personals, of course, were innocent of any flesh-peddling purposes, such as:

"CRAFTSMAN!— Oh, Lord! Oh, My God! Is there

none to help the widow's son to some employment to prevent starving?"

"42nd Street— Gentleman noticed lady taking Boulevard car, will pass Wednesday, 11:30, same place."

"Any person knowing of impending business failures or having any other valuable information can make big money by communicating with smart lawyer."

On the other hand, there was no mistaking the purpose of such invitations as:

"Is there a TRUE man who would help and care for a SWEET girl?"

"Attention! Is there a man of honor and sterling worth who can appreciate the cruelty that impels a gentlewoman, superior mental and physical attractions, age 34, to adopt this means of release from hated bondage? No Shylocks or triflers."

"Refined young woman desires immediate loan."

"A woman finds paddling her own canoe dreary task, seeks manly pilot."

"The Little Girl cannot meet expenses this month. Hopes Mr. W. will see this and embrace opportunity he requested at lunch."

"Young lady, good figure, wants to pose for artist."

"LADY: loyal, loving, lovable, with famished heart craves devotion of but one man financially worth while."

And there were the dollar-a-line allurements of the "chic Parisian ladies with cozy suites," "masseuses with highly magnetic manners" and "witty affectionate ladies possessing beautiful figures, hair, teeth" craving the companionship of "jolly sports" and promising "pleasant possibilities."

Hearst himself was reaping a similar fortune from almost identical advertisements in his San Francisco *Examiner,* but in New York "The Chief," as he now preferred to be addressed by his underlings, played the stern public moralist. Hearst reporters under the direction of Victor Watson, later one of his more ruthless editors, rented post-office boxes under assumed names and began investigating the *Herald's* advertisers. Watson himself spent a whole year visiting massage parlors where the biceps were rarely brought into play, rooming houses with unusually sociable inmates, manicurists who weren't quite sure where the cuticle was, artists' models whose poses were uniformly horizontal, Turkish baths steamy with all sorts of unorthodox revelry, and other aspects of the *Herald's* guide to Venusberg.

Hearst then began publishing a long series on Watson's findings in the New York *American* (the *Journal* was now his afternoon paper).

S. S. Carvalho, a Hearst executive, simultaneously presented the evidence to the federal grand jury in New York.

All this, of course, was journalistically dirty pool. Publishers generally abide by the rule of overlooking each other's private little enterprises, such as "charity" funds raised by blackjacking promoters for slices of their proceeds and other lucrative activities. Hearst's exposé of the *Herald* personals was, in fact, unprecedented, but "The Chief" was aroused as never before or afterward by Bennett's successful attack on his political ambitions.

Henry L. Stimson prosecuted the government's case against Bennett and secured an indictment on charges of sending obscene matter through the mails.

Bennett immediately announced that he would never return to the United States to stand trial, and cabled Hearst from Paris:

"I will never forgive you for this."

To which Hearst cabled in reply, "I hope you never will."

A few months later Bennett realized that the *Herald* could hardly continue to operate with the federal indictment hanging over its head. The personals had already been discontinued. On April 10, 1907, he returned to New York, went immediately to the criminal branch of the United States Circuit Court, pleaded guilty, and was fined $25,000. The *Herald* itself was fined $5000 and its advertising manager $1000.

Bennett, with a casual and contemptuous gesture, removed a large wad of currency from his pocket, hurriedly counted out thirty-one one-thousand-dollar bills, and stalked out of the courtroom. Later that day he boarded ship back to France.

Once again his prudish, prurient native land had let him down. France and its easy, gracious ways, its tolerance, and sophistication became all the more attractive. To hell with the bluenoses. Thereafter Bennett's visits to America occurred only when business affairs made them imperative.

A few months after he paid the fines, he was gratified by an announcement from Hearst that "It is no longer necessary for me to be a candidate." At least he had succeeded in quelling what must have been a nightmarish possibility to all right-thinking Americans— President William Randolph Hearst chiefing it over the whole damn country.

But the high-principled cause had been ruinous. The *Herald* had lost prestige, circulation, and advertising; it had been struck a blow from which it would never recover, and Bennett, deprived of a quarter-million in annual revenue from the personals, would never again be the free-spending Commodore of the years before he decided to tackle "The Chief." Their little war had been only an episode in Hearst's picaresque career; to Bennett it was fatal, so far as his overriding ambition—to establish the *Herald* beyond challenge as the greatest newspaper in the world—was concerned. His enemy had succeeded in disproving the Commodore's adage that "Nothing can hurt the *Herald.*"

Bennett's only available means of retaliation was rather pathetic. To him the direst possible punishment was to order that a man's name never be mentioned again in his newspapers; this to Bennett was excommunication from human society. This anathema he pronounced on Hearst—who was perfectly delighted.

The financial bruises and ego lacerations he suffered in the clash with Hearst did not crush the Commodore's spirit—nothing could do that, not even the onrush of the Kaiser's armies on an all but defenseless Paris several years later—but he was never the same man again. After that, one long-time associate noted, his judgment showed signs of being "impaired." If anything, he became more capricious, demanding, and arrogant toward his editors in New York, just when he should have been rallying their utmost efforts to rehabilitate the *Herald.*

"Distrusting everybody whom he had reason to trust," Crockett observed, "not concerning himself with employees he did not personally know, he was now vesting his confidence somewhat after the fashion of a senile monarch throwing his jewels to the jester who made him smile; he had no means, if any desire, for reaching out and claiming for his own some of the men who had been building up the *Herald's* rivals."

The *Herald* organization, as Ralph Blumenfeld wrote after leaving the London bureau for the managing editorship of the London *Daily Telegraph,* was a "group of unhappily mortised yes-men, the victims of a system of office politics and jealousies which promotes disloyalty and produces a general decline of prosperity."

Blumenfeld decided to quit, he said, despite the fact that he was a personal favorite of the Commodore's, because he foresaw that "forceful competition and lax control from afar" had doomed the paper. Meanwhile, in the New York morning field, Hearst's *American* was booming; the *Times* was revitalized under the management of Adolph S. Ochs; the *World* was becoming what it had promised to be before its essay in sensationalism—the best newspaper published in the United States.

Men of pride and ability were being driven away from the *Herald* by Bennett's jealousy and suspicion. Among several cases in point were the departures of such men as James L. Ford, William C. Reick, and Joseph I. C. Clarke, the latter having returned to the *Herald* after service on other papers.

Clarke quit again after writing a play, *Prince of India*, news of which enraged Bennett, because he believed that his hirelings should devote all their time and energy to the newspaper, and caused him to order that no mention of the play be made in the columns of the *Herald* or *Evening Telegram*.

Ford received what he called the "kiss of death" after he was appointed Bennett's personal representative on the editorial council, which was designed to carry out his cabled instructions on policy. A jealous rival, Ford said, circulated the report that he had been appointed because he was "a close personal friend of Bennett's," knowing how the Commodore reacted to any employee's claim to his personal regard. "Find out who circulated it," a friend told Ford, "and you'll know where at least one of your enemies lives." As predicted, the rumor reached the Commodore, who proceeded to make life so miserable for Ford that he quit and went over to Hearst.

Reick had been named president of the *Herald* Corporation but Bennett insisted on treating him, at times, like a rather lazy and stupid office boy. The publisher reportedly was irked by information that Reick had grown wealthy through real estate investments—partly, as a matter of fact, through the parcel given him by Bennett years before—and that he had been adopted by Mrs. Stuyvesant Fish as her social protégé. Obviously Reick was getting above himself, putting on airs, turning into a social climber. No matter how high a man rose in the Bennett hierarchy, its watchful pontiff insisted on regarding him as a member of the lower orders, only a cut or two above the latest drunkard hired for the rim of the copy desk. Worse yet, Bennett heard that Reick was widely credited with the paper's superlative performance during the Spanish-American War.

In the last year of Reick's connection with the Bennett interests, he was summoned to a conference in Paris with the Commodore. He was told to bring along the family, and the *Herald* would pay all expenses. Reick was rather surprised at the sudden return of cordiality, but complied with pleasure. He was instructed to stay at a certain hotel and await a summons from the Commodore.

After days of waiting he went around to Bennett's apartment on the Champs Elysées, where he was handed a note saying Bennett had been called to Beaulieu and Reick was to proceed to Nice, where the Commodore would get in touch with him. That was the beginning of a long, dizzying runaround. Every place Reick went, as ordered, he found a note from the Commodore waiting with instructions to go somewhere else. After some weeks Reick wearied of the chase and wrote Bennett a stiff letter demanding to know his purpose in shagging him all around the continent.

"Go back to New York, Reick," Bennett replied. "You

won't see me. I never wanted to see you. I just wanted to show you that the *Herald* can get along just as well without you."

Before returning to New York, Reick "expressed himself bitterly" to another *Herald* man and indicated that one day soon he would have his own "surprise" for the Commodore.

And Bennett was surprised indeed, unshakable in his belief that no real *Herald* man could bear to work for another paper, when Reick signed a contract to become associate editor of the New York *Times*. Reick's brusque announcement that he was leaving caused Bennett to grumble to an aide, "I thought I was doing the right thing by relieving him of a lot of detail work and making him president of the corporation." Then he added in a rather plaintive tone, "Do you know why he quit?" Crockett, to whom the question was addressed, could have told him but considered it more politic to shrug in puzzlement.

Sometimes Bennett's harassment of his employees took almost sadistic forms. One of his minor talents was an extremely acute sensitivity to forthcoming changes in the weather. He was reputed to be the best amateur forecaster in France. When he judged that a storm was brewing and would churn up the Channel, he would frequently summon a member of the London bureau notorious for his violent attacks of seasickness to Paris for an immediate conference. The sight of his underling's greenish face so amused the Commodore that he would be in high spirits for days.

And there were other disturbing elements in his absentee management of the *Herald*. His last effort to create exclusive news had been dispatching the DeLong expedition to the arctic almost thirty years past. Some of his schemes to win back readers were downright ridiculous, as when he tried to involve Sir James Barrie, the author of *Peter Pan* and other immensely popular plays, in a *Herald*-sponsored literary contest. He cabled his London bureau from Bermuda, "See Charles Frohman [Barrie's American producer] and ask if he will see Barrie and get him to compete with American authors for a serial novel in the *Herald*. If he wins, $25,000 prize; if he loses, $10,000. Later Frohman can use story as play. Answer at once here." Frohman had to be prodded into approaching Sir James with such a proposition, and when he did the playwright not only refused but wondered aloud if Frohman had taken leave of his sanity.

Many *Herald* men were irked by Bennett's personal representative in New York, G. G. Howland, who was also business manager of the *Herald,* "a very precise and punctilious gentleman, an aristocrat to his finger tips, who owed his place more to his social position than to his abilities." He was said to have clashed frequently with Reick and may have been a subsidiary reason for the latter's departure. Bennett, however, thought so much of him that he kept his house at Washington Heights open and fully staffed just so Howland and his two sons could play tennis on the Bennett courts every summer afternoon.

After Reick's departure the editorial management of the *Herald* was vested in a number of committees—eventually eighteen of them—which were supposed to decide how the Commodore's orders and policies were to be carried out. The system was a model of bureaucratic confusion, a "combination of despotism and puppet show," as Leo Redding, a former *Herald* reporter, described it in a disenchanted character study of Bennett (*Everybody's Magazine,* June, 1914). The committees "sit in solemn daily sessions to discuss routine affairs," Redding explained. "By this method five men take five times as long to determine to recommend that something be done as an ordinary managing editor would take." A Cable Committee, for instance, tried to decide in advance how much news would be cabled each week, disregarding the essential unpredictability of the substance called news and the fact that it can rarely be confined in a budget for more than a few hours. The whole operation was headed by an Executive Committee whose members were required to wear silk hats and frock coats whenever Bennett was in attendance and which looked, as Redding said, "like a convention of undertakers."

There was even a committee charged with overseeing the efficiency of the fire-extinguishing system in the *Herald* Building. Its efforts were tested one day while the Commodore was visiting New York. A fire broke out in a wastebasket in the library, and Bennett, a buff from 'way back, personally rushed up with a hose to put out the blaze. Rumor had it that Bennett himself had dropped a lighted match in the basket to test the alertness of his Fire Extinguishing Committee.

A separate editorial council grappled with the problem of translating the publisher's countless prejudices and contradictory attitudes into a consistent program. The *Herald's* bias was Republican, of course; it was strongly pro-navy; it favored American expansion in the Pacific, and it frequently warned of Germany's aggressive intentions on the continent. But sometimes his satraps of the editorial page had difficulty in keeping up with the Commodore's far-ranging intellect. On one occasion he turned up suddenly in the Far East to investigate what the Japanese were plotting after their victory over Russia in 1905. He concluded that Great Britain and Japan were conspiring to take over western Asia, and both the *Herald's* Far Eastern correspondents and the editorial writers back in New York were ordered to whip up enthusiasm for a precipitous alliance between the collapsing Chinese Empire and the United States to thwart this scheme.

During Theodore Roosevelt's Bull Moose campaign of 1912, his councilors were further harassed by the Commodore's outrage at the ex-President's break with the regular Republicans and his stern orders that Roosevelt's name was not to be mentioned in the *Herald*. Much awkward circumlocution resulted. The *Herald* had to refer to Roosevelt as the "Third Party Candidate."

Shortly after Woodrow Wilson won that election, his administration was vexed by a certain amount of meddling from Bennett in Paris, still riding his anti-Japanese hobbyhorse. Secretary of the Navy Josephus Daniels, according to his son (Jonathan Daniels, *The End of Innocence*) was amazed one morning soon after he took office to read in the New York *Herald* that the joint Army and Navy Board, a sort of forerunner of the Joint Chiefs of Staff, was planning orders for "a naval concentration at Manila" as a militant gesture toward Japan. Investigation showed that the admirals, who regarded the *Herald* as their principal organ, had "leaked" the information to Joseph K. Ohl, Bennett's former Far Eastern correspondent and now one of his principal editors in New York.

Another *Herald* pipeline into the Navy Department ran through the office of Assistant Secretary of the Navy Franklin D. Roosevelt, whose own assistant, Louis Howe, had been a *Herald* staff member for twenty years. "Howe often used the *Herald* as a paper in which to plant kind words and trial balloons about his ambitious young boss," according to Jonathan Daniels. Bennett and his editors, however, did not succeed in pushing the pacifistic Wilson and Daniels toward a showdown in the

Pacific. The days when newspapers could start wars, or think they did, had passed.

Just how the Bennett system of committee management could malfunction on occasion was cruelly illustrated by the *Herald's* farcical role in the Peary-Cook controversy over who discovered the North Pole.

Commander Robert E. Peary's earlier essays in polar exploration had been partly financed by the *Herald* in exchange for the right to publish his journals, so in 1908, when he was preparing to launch his final and triumphant expedition, he went to the paper to ask its support again. At the reception desk of the editorial department he requested an interview with Reick, with whom he had dealt before.

"Mr. Reick," he was informed, "is no longer with the *Herald*. He's over at the *Times*."

Commander Peary then recalled having had dealings with Reick's successor as city editor, Charles M. Lincoln, the only other member of the *Herald* staff he knew personally.

"Mr. Lincoln," said the receptionist, "is no longer with us. He's over at the *Times,* too."

"Who *is* in charge? May I see him?"

The receptionist racked his brain; city editors had been shuttling in and out so rapidly they hardly had time to introduce themselves. The present incumbent was finally identified, however, and came out to see Peary. He listened to the officer's proposals, then said, "I just don't think we want to be in on this trip, Commander, at least not for exclusive rights. If you make the Pole, we'll get the information through routine channels. Thanks just the same."

Peary headed straight for the *Times* Building, of course, and before the afternoon was out had come to an agreement with Reick and Lincoln. For a mere $4000 the *Times* secured the New York rights to his account of finding the North Pole.

The Commodore was not at all upset over losing the rights to Commander Peary's story. Wasn't the equally eminent Dr. Frederick Cook, a charming and persuasive gentleman from Brooklyn, who had served as expedition physician on Peary's 1892 survey of Greenland, working in the same field? Both men were, as the newspapers said, "racing for the Pole." Cook's stuff made better reading, anyway, than the Commander's sober naval prose. So the *Herald* paid Cook $25,000 for broadcasting his claims to discovery. On September 1, 1909, he cabled the news that on April 27, 1908, he had reached the Pole. Five days later the *Herald's* editors were somewhat dismayed when Commander Peary radioed the New York *Times* from Indian Harbor that he had touched base on April 6, 1909.

A violent controversy soon erupted over the rival claims, but it was generally agreed that, however authentic were Cook's *bona fides,* his descriptions of arctic conquest were far more thrilling and exultant than Peary's plodding narrative in the *Times*.

For *Herald* readers Cook told of the moment of triumph that capped a long winter's journey by sledge with only two Eskimos for companions: "We all were lifted to the paradise of winners . . . the ice under us seemed almost sacred. . . . At last we step over colored fields of sparkle, climbing walls of purple and gold—finally under skies of crystal blue, with flaming clouds of glory, we touch the mark!"

Sobersided scientists were willing to grant the doctor a certain amount of poetic license, but they were irritated by Cook's failure to produce the records of his expedition and inclined to agree with Peary's wirelessed advice to the Associated Press, "Cook's story should not be taken too seriously." A few days later Commander Peary assured the New York *Times* that Cook "has not been to the Pole on April 21st, 1908, or at any other time. He has simply handed the public a gold brick."

Dr. Cook, on the other hand, was publicly more magnanimous. "If Mr. Peary says he has reached the Pole, I am sure he has." He thought there was "glory enough for us all" and that "two records are better than one."

A Buffalo newspaper commented that "Dr. Cook is behaving like a man; Peary like a very naughty or ill-bred child."

Led by the New York *Herald*, naturally enough, a great deal of support was mustered for Cook's claims, along with scalding criticism of Commander Peary. Bennett was determined to defend his man's reputation with all the means at his disposal. His newspaper charged that Peary hadn't paid the members of his expedition, that he mistreated them in various ways, and gave prominent display to statements praising Cook's feat by two distinguished arctic explorers, General Adolphus W. Greely and Admiral W. S. Schley, neither of whom had any reason to adore his rival. On Dr. Cook's arrival in New York on September 21, 100,000 persons lined the docks to cheer him, partly through the exertions of the *Herald*. Peary's arrival ten days later was greeted with jeers and catcalls. Whatever the view of more detached and knowledgeable persons, the public considered Peary a "bum sport," and man-in-the-street polls ran ten to one, or more, in Dr. Cook's favor.

Eventually, of course, the experts prevailed. The National Geographic Society accepted Commander Peary's claims in their entirety, while the evidence produced by Dr. Cook was torn apart and discredited by various presumably disinterested authorities.

Bennett, predictably, refused to accept their findings or concede that Peary had won the race to the Pole. Cook's venture became known as the "celebrated gumdrop expedition," but his journalistic sponsor never gave up trying to prove him right. The outcome of the decision—not entirely Bennett's responsibility—to pay Dr. Cook $25,000, rather than Commander Peary only a fraction of that amount, was still further damage to the *Herald's* prestige.

Between then and the start of the World War, Bennett was to know one more moment of journalistic triumph, to seize upon and demonstrate how the *Herald,* under his personal direction, could brilliantly handle a world-shaking event. His news sense, when under the pressure of events and deadlines, which did not permit him time to indulge in his wayward fancies, was still sharp and inventive, still indicative of what he might have achieved if he had been forced to keep his nose pressed to the editorial grindstone.

The Commodore returned to the United States on his last prewar visit to his native city early in the spring of 1912. Newspaper photographs taken of him as his liner docked showed a lean, erect man of seventy-one, a bowler set at a jaunty angle on his white thatch, his eyes still fierce and testy, his face creased with wrinkles, but the nostrils of his imperious nose still flaring with the zest for combat.

A few days after Bennett's arrival in New York he had cause for rejoicing that he had changed his plans at the last moment and had taken an earlier passage rather than waiting to sail on the maiden voyage of the White Star's great new luxury liner—that ship being the R.M.S. *Titanic.* Aboard that floating palace, which had been advertised as "unsinkable," was the flower of

Anglo-American society as well as hundreds of immigrants in steerage.

The *Titanic* had sailed from Southampton April 10 and, hoping to set a new record for an Atlantic crossing, despite iceberg warnings had plunged ahead at top speed into drifting pack ice. At 12:45 A.M. April 15 an Associated Press bulletin was received in the *Herald* office from Cape Race, Newfoundland, stating that distress signals had been received from the *Titanic,* that she had struck an iceberg and was sinking, that passengers were being removed in lifeboats. The world held its breath for hours and days, as reports came in (later verified) that such millionaires as John Jacob Astor ($125,000,000), Benjamin Guggenheim, Isidor Straus, Henry E. and George D. Widener, Arthur Ryerson, George D. Wick, and Charles M. Hays had gone down with the liner, that 1517 lives had been lost, that only 706 persons had been taken off in lifeboats.

This was the Commodore's great moment. He hurried down to the *Herald* office to take personal charge of the story; if there was anything he knew thoroughly, it was the ships and the sea, and he was intimately acquainted with the icy waters of the North Atlantic. All the *Herald's* stories testified to that storehouse of knowledge. The *Times* had gotten the jump on the story by replating its final editions, but the *Herald's* over-all coverage from the day after the sinking until the last survivor came down the *Carpathia's* gangplank surpassed all its competitors.

Bennett's sizable contribution was seizing upon the passenger list of the *Carpathia* as it steamed toward the *Titanic's* lifeboats, seeking someone who could be enlisted as the *Herald's* impromptu correspondent. He studied the list for an hour until he came across a name that jogged his memory, Miss May Birkhead. He recalled her as a young woman who had earned the money for a trip to Europe by making and selling shirtwaists. The *Herald* had published a story about her months ago. She might be just the type of enterprising female who could seize upon an opportunity like this. Bennett radioed her immediately: WIRELESS ALL OPERATOR CAN TAKE ON TITANIC. BENNETT.

Miss Birkhead was entirely innocent of any newspaper experience, but the Commodore's intuition about her native talent was quickly justified. She went about the job like an old pro. Within hours after the *Titanic's* passengers were taken aboard the *Carpathia,* she was sending a stream of interviews by wireless. She also persuaded several survivors who could draw to sketch scenes of the stricken liner's decks as the *Titanic* slowly nosed down. As a result, the *Herald* was able to publish vivid accounts of the disaster days in advance of the other papers. And there was a happy sequel to Miss Birkhead's sudden plunge into journalism. Bennett not only rewarded her handsomely for providing him with the *Herald's* biggest beat since the Spanish-American War, but made her society editor of the Paris *Herald.* She became one of that paper's brightest assets. During the World War, having cultivated the acquaintance of General Pershing, she was the only woman accredited as a correspondent with the A.E.F., and came up with a number of exclusive stories.

Bennett was still in command of the *Titanic* coverage when the *Carpathia* steamed into New York harbor April 18. Hundreds of newspapermen were waiting to pounce on the survivors as they were disembarked at the foot of West Fourteenth Street, but the Commodore was determined to steal a march on the competition. He hired a tugboat at $100 an hour and packed his star reporters and best photographers aboard her, and off she steamed to intercept the *Carpathia* off Sandy Hook—a familiar tactic of the *Herald's,* dating back to his first years as editor.

The *Herald's* tugboat made contact with the rescue ship, all right, but Bennett's men were not permitted to come aboard. From then on, they suffered through a comedy of errors while imagining the Commodore's rage at the failure of their mission. The tug developed engine trouble as it pitched and rolled in the liner's wake. Then it lay dead in the water while repairs were being made and the journalists aboard contended with seasickness. Finally a freighter came by and shot a line over, towing the tug for an hour until someone thought to inquire where they were headed. The freighter, they learned, was bound for Norfolk, Virginia, and the towline was hastily severed. By the time repairs were completed and the tugboat managed to limp back to the Battery, the *Titanic* survivors had been landed and the extras were on the streets.

Other reporters, of course, met the *Carpathia* for the *Herald* and escorted Miss Birkhead to the office with her notes and drawings.

Largely because of Bennett's masterly direction, the *Herald* outshone its rivals, even the brilliantly edited *Times,* in capturing all the details of the *Titanic's* fatal voyage. But it was the *Herald's* last shining hour, the final flicker of greatness in a newspaper which had enlivened and invigorated the journalistic scene for three quarters of a century. Just as the death plunge of the *Titanic* rang down the curtain on the Edwardian age, with all its foolish splendors and massive overconfidence, this was most fittingly James Gordon Bennett's last bow in the New York newspaper world.

12: The Commodore vs. the Kaiser

A *Herald* man returning to New York after years of service in the various European bureaus was asked by his colleagues how the Commodore was getting along, now that he was well into his seventies.

"Bennett is dead," the correspondent said. "The old drunken, money-spending Jim Bennett is dead. In his place has come a Scotch miser."

It was true that the Commodore had stopped throwing his money around, that his communications with his editors and business representatives in New York were now sober and restrained, that he had stopped drinking, that at long last he was taking a sustained interest in every detail of his newspapers' operations (no more kicking mail sacks off the deck of his yacht— no more yacht, in fact; it had been sold to the Russian Navy). The Commodore had stopped raising hell. All of a sudden in the summer of 1914 he came to the realization, along with much of the rest of the world, that the old days were gone forever; the lights were going out in Europe, and nothing would ever be the same again.

But in one respect the "old" Bennett was not dead. Even at seventy-three he was still stirred by the lust for battle. His arteries might be hardening, but the spectacle of Germans goose-stepping by the millions as their armies mobilized, the infuriating self-confidence of their detestable Kaiser, whom he now hated even more than William Randolph Hearst, rejuvenated him. War is said to be an old man's tonic, for various discreditable reasons, and certainly it revitalized Bennett. Only his age, it may be believed, restrained him from volunteering for the French Army.

Just before the war broke out, the Commodore's financial position was close to the point of disintegration. His fortune was gone and there was no prospect of making another one. So far as the New York *Herald* was concerned, the circulation count told the whole story. From its all-time "high-water mark" of 511,000 during the Spanish-American War, its circulation had now slipped to about 60,000, and it was losing hundreds of thousands of dollars annually. Even the war news failed to stimulate circulation sufficiently. By 1916 the *Herald* was selling 92,000 copies, and by 1918, 128,000, but this was nothing compared to the booming circulations of the *Times,* the *World,* the *Tribune,* the *Journal,* and other competitors.

Now it was the *Evening Telegram,* that "pink drab of lowest journalism," which Bennett himself detested, that was supporting the *Herald.* Of all his three papers, the *Telegram* was the most vociferously pro-Allied, and its sensational accounts of the fighting in Europe sold papers in much the style of Pulitzer's *World* and Hearst's *Journal* at the outset of the Spanish-American War. "During the war," wrote Oswald Garrison Villard, editor of the New York *Post* and a confirmed pacifist, "it was the soul of mendacity, killing off in a few months of the war more Germans than were ever in the Kaiser's empire and preaching the worst kind of bitterness and hate."

And the Paris *Herald,* which had been losing money for years, suddenly began to turn a profit. For the past fifteen years, Bennett said, it had cost him $2,000,000 to keep the Paris edition in operation. He could hardly believe the balance sheets.

Percy Mitchell, his chief assistant now, reported to him one day in 1914 that increased circulation (it was now selling almost 25,000 copies daily) and consequent increased advertising revenue were beginning to pile up money in the bank.

"Impossible," the Commodore snorted.

But Mitchell insisted that the money was accumulating and asked, "What shall I do with it?"

"Do with it? Why—er—just leave it in the bank!"

Bennett seemed almost embarrassed that his journalistic hobbyhorse, which he regarded as an indulgence, like his yachts or country estates, should now be making money for him. But it still wasn't enough to make up for the seepage of assets caused by the New York *Herald's* steady decline.

The Paris *Herald*, by the summer of 1914, had attained a considerable respect in European journalism and was far in advance of most continental newspapers. "It was the best, almost the only real newspaper on the Continent," as Al Laney, its historian, has written. Its coverage of international affairs was condensed but thorough and perceptive. On Sundays it published a supplement glorifying the creations of the Paris fashion houses, though even the French newspapers had not yet recognized that industry, and a section of full-page comics in color, including "Snapshot Bill," "Great Caesar's Ghost," "Pranks of Pierrot," "Tiny Tads," and "Mr. Tweedeedle"—much as Bennett had sneered at the "funny papers" when Hearst and Pulitzer began developing the comic strip. Before the war news crowded out such matters, the *Herald* also gave much space to automobiling, motor tours, and road races. Very precise

weather reports, an editorial fetish with the meteoro-
logical-minded Commodore, were telegraphed daily
from all the continental resorts. Society, of course, was
thoroughly covered in all the European capitals and
watering places before it was driven to cover by invad-
ing armies.

Although the Commodore had been warning against
Germany's aggressive tendencies for years, even he, if
the pages of his Paris edition were a true reflection of
his outlook, did not immediately believe that a major
war would erupt from the belligerent attitudes of that
summer.

At the time of the assassination of the Austrian Archduke Francis Ferdinand by a Serbian nationalist on
June 28, Europe was glorying in an early summer, the
most splendid in years, warmed by a gentle sun. The
days were so balmy it seemed incredible that anyone
could start a war to disrupt their serenity. The 1914
social season was the most brilliant in years, and the
continent was thronged with visiting Americans. Nobody could imagine that those long lazy days under
the lindens of Berlin or the blue skies of Paris would
soon be obliterated by the tramp of millions of feet
marching toward regimental caserns and mobilization
centers.

Even while Austria and Serbia were wrangling over
how the Balkan kingdom could make amends for the
death of the archduke and his morganatic wife, the
Paris *Herald* was devoting most of its front page to the
trial of Mme. Caillaux, wife of the former premier and
present minister of finance, who was accused of a murder
with peculiarly Gallic overtones. The lady's victim was
M. Gaston Calmette, the editor of *Figaro*. She had put
a bullet in him because he threatened to publish M.
Caillaux's love letters to Mme. Caillaux unless the

minister resigned. Unfortunately the letters had been written before M. Caillaux had divorced his first wife.

By mid-July, in fact, the *Herald* was assuring its American readers, worried over being caught in Europe when and if war broke out, that "the crisis is believed past." On July 25, however, the *Herald* had to relegate the Caillaux murder trial and all its spicy revelations to the bottom of Page One. The "brutal tenor" of Austria's latest note had brought the possibility of war in the Balkans. In a few days it became apparent that Germany was firmly aligning itself behind Austria, and Russia, France, and Great Britain behind Serbia.

The *Herald* announced that it "strongly condemned" the Kaiser's ambitions, and began publishing long lists of Americans in Paris, with their addresses, just in case they wanted to seek comfort from one another. Visiting Americans were urged to sign the register at the *Herald* business office in the event that evacuation became necessary.

Flaring headlines told the story of succeeding days. On July 28:

EUROPE ASKS ANXIOUSLY: IS IT PEACE OR WAR?

On August 2:

GERMANY DECLARES WAR UPON RUSSIA;
FRANCE ORDERS A GENERAL MOBILIZATION

On August 4:

GERMANY OFFICIALLY DECLARES WAR
UPON FRANCE;
BRITISH FLEET PLEDGED TO
SUPPORT FRENCH COAST

While Americans were taking every available ship home, Bennett and his newspaper stood firm. He was "roused like an old war horse," as one of his editors said later, as the German armies swept over their frontiers, invaded Belgium, and once more quick-stepped down the roads to Paris. "The spectacle of mighty Germany riding roughshod over little Belgium," a *Herald* editorial declared, reflecting the Commodore's concept of international sportsmanship, "does not comport with the American idea of fairness and justice."

In any event, the *Herald* assured its readers, the French, British, and Belgian armies would soon counterattack and hurl the invaders back to the benighted Fatherland. The "Boche," as Bennett always unneutrally referred to the Germans, would never prevail against the Allied Entente; the war would be over by Christmas. But the Germans were pressing their initially successful but fatally modified Schlieffen plan, and a whole army group was advancing on the Marne north of Paris. Defeated in the field, the Allied armies could only regroup and hope that the German offensive would lose its impetus while a counterattack was being organized.

On September 3 the *Herald* sadly announced:

FRENCH GOVERNMENT
REMOVED FROM PARIS

Along with the government in the flight to Bordeaux went all the Parisian newspapers, except for Clemenceau's fire-breathing political journal, and as many of the capital's citizens as could crowd themselves into evacuation trains or find other means of transport. It was a city of darkness and trepidation, populated mostly by the remaining soldiers of the garrison.

Bennett and the Paris *Herald* stayed. Somehow the Commodore decided it was his duty; he regarded the *Herald,* he said in an editorial, as the representative of "a neutral nation of 100 millions." Now, in his seventy-third year, he attained a full measure of dignity, after years of reckless self-humiliation, of self-indulgence and dissipation of his latent talents. He became, in fact, a rather heroic figure; it was the best hour of his life. Certainly the Germans, if they took Paris, would respect neutrality "notwithstanding the excesses attributed to them," as he pointed out to the few remaining Americans, but they were not likely to make it pleasant for a man who had insulted their emperor and who had been denouncing German ambitions for years.

In the first days of the French mobilization he had watched most of his labor force disappear. Only one stereotyper, two printers, and three or four men in the pressroom remained in the mechanical departments. Bennett had announced on the day they left to join their regiments that his employees could be assured that their full salaries would be paid their wives as long as they stayed in uniform.

At the same time he told the British and American members of his staff: "Those of you who wish to quit may do so. This place will be under the protection of the Stars and Stripes, and I will defy those Prussians to disregard it. If they come and you stay, I will do what I can to ensure your safety. In any event, the paper comes out."

By the time the German advance approached the outer ring of the capital's defenses and the *Temps* was announcing that it had been persuaded to join the flight to Bordeaux because "France needs an organ which can continue to be the interpreter of French thought both in this country and abroad," Bennett was left with only a handful of editors and reporters, among them the faithful Percy Mitchell, long his secretary and chief assistant. Every day one or two more silently departed for the safety of England as the thunder of the guns across the Marne echoed over the city on the clear autumn nights.

One editor had been given the assignment of placing little flagged pins on a huge wall map in the *Herald* editorial room, so the Commodore could look the situation over the moment he arrived. One morning, as it appeared that the fingers of the German advance were groping toward the suburb of Senlis, the editor dropped his box of pins, hurried out of the office, and did not stop until he reached the deck of a Channel steamer bound for Dover. Others, as Laney recorded, "were held, against their better judgment, by the force of his will, and forever after they counted it to their eternal credit that they stayed by the Commodore and helped him to what may very well have been his greatest achievement."

Harry S. Brown, of the New York *Herald's* London bureau, later recalled how his editors in New York and his representatives in London kept urging him to consider suspending the Paris *Herald* and leaving the capital before the Germans arrived.

But Bennett, whose vision was sometimes extraordinarily clear, kept assuring them that "the Germans are falling in a trap." Studying the war map in his office, he was convinced—as few neutral observers were—that the Germans were overextending themselves and leaving their flank open to a devastating counterstroke.

"He was a great student of military strategy all his life," Brown recalled (New York *Times,* May 15, 1918), "and he had the situation accurately mapped out. When attempts were made to induce him to leave Paris, he lost his temper and said he would keep on printing his paper until the Germans got there, and if they ever did get there he would keep on printing it if the Germans would let him."

Meanwhile, publishing the Paris *Herald* became more difficult with every passing day.

Shortages of newsprint, mechanical help, and of any reliable news from the front forced Bennett to reduce the *Herald* to a two-page flysheet, with much of the second page given over to French translations to keep the remaining residents informed of what was happening on the approaches to the threatened capital. Thus it was from an American newspaper that most of them learned the few censored details available of the tremendous struggle of the Anglo-French armies north of Paris.

The military governor of Paris, an old colonial soldier named Gallieni, preparing to rush the regiments garrisoning Paris to join Marshal Joffre's forces on the Marne and the Ourcq, seized every usable vehicle for the purpose, including taxicabs, buses, automobiles, horses and carriages, Bennett's various means of transportation among them. He had to walk over to the *Herald* office from his apartment, now located more modestly in the avenue d'Iéna, through blacked-out streets silent and deserted except for the tramp of an occasional patrol. He was resolved to keep the *Herald* publishing even if the German legions marched under his windows, with the Kaiser and all his field marshals at their head.

For the first time in his career, Bennett performed as an ordinary working newspaperman. He sweated over writing heads, preparing copy for the composing room, even going out on a story or two. And he kept telling his fellow diehards who refused to leave the city that the Germans would never again march down its boulevards. On September 4, the banner line read:

INVESTMENT OF PARIS IS
IMPRACTICAL ENTERPRISE

To bolster Parisian morale, and perhaps their own, the *Herald's* council of war pointed out that the "outer wing of forts have a circumference of 150 kilometres" and that "a complete siege is impossible with the French armies intact," since the German armies would have to spread themselves too thin to be effective. The *Herald* chose to ignore the fact that Paris' fortifications were long outmoded and would present no serious problem to a modern army. Next day the *Herald* had to admit:

GERMANS SPREADING
TO EAST OF PARIS

During these days, almost within sight of the Eiffel Tower, the Allied forces were rallying themselves for the supreme effort to hold off the right wing of the German advance. The enemy had already modified the Schlieffen plan by weakening that right flank and using elsewhere the divisions that its strategists of a previous generation had emphasized must be employed to slam the door on Paris. The British had finally maneuvered to strike the Germans in the rear while the French attacked frontally, and a great battle was being fought in the flat unharvested farmlands between the Marne and the Ourcq, where a disastrous gap had widened between the First and Second German Armies. The thunder of guns along a front stretching almost 200 miles, to the forts of Verdun, shook the capital. Hardly a creature stirred on the boulevards. Paris waited breathlessly to learn its fate. A rigid censorship prevented the *Herald* from telling what little it may have learned of the decisive battle.

Then, on September 10, Allied Headquarters announced that a wedge had been driven between the German armies, the enemy was retreating to the Aisne, Paris and the nation were saved.

And it was from the *Herald* that the capital first learned of its salvation, of the heroic role played by its "taxicab army." On September 11 a *Herald* banner line conveyed the news:

ALLIES PURSUING
RETREATING ENEMY

And two days later:

RETREAT OF GERMANS
BECOMES GENERAL

The Commodore worked himself to a frazzle during those ten agonizing days. Very belatedly he learned the facts of a newspaperman's life. Perhaps it would be too much to say that in those days he made up for fifty years of a playboy's whirligig existence, but they won for the Bennett legend an element of respect hitherto present in only minute quantities. For old newspapermen, particularly *Herald* veterans, Laney wrote, "it was the climax of all their Bennett stories and the old Commodore, for whom no one had much love, was made to appear a splendid and heroic figure."

Reading through the files of the Paris *Herald* during those days, one can find only one story that bears the unmistakable stamp of Bennett's style and personality. Not surprisingly it concerned the abandoned dogs running around Paris and it was placed on Page One; more space was devoted to it than the war on the eastern front. It was headed:

ROUTINE OF CANINE LIFE
IN PARIS UPSET BY WAR
Many Dogs Leave the City—Others
Fed at Barrack Gates and
Live with Soldiers

The Commodore was not particularly distressed by any human suffering during the ten days of military crisis—people could take care of themselves—but the sight of a homeless or masterless dog almost reduced him to tears. The dog population of Paris, he pointed out, was not allowed on board the evacuation trains and "only little dogs that can be carried in a muff were able to avoid the regulations by travelling incognito." Those left behind, he said, were "wandering day and night in search of their masters," though some of them had been "adopted" by the few remaining soldiers in the city's regimental depots. Canine nerves, Bennett warned, were "too delicate" for survival in a city under siege. "A King Charles spaniel known to the writer was so affected by gunfire that it fell ill at every royal visit." When the evacuees finally came trickling back to the city from the south, the *Herald* sternly advised them to search out their abandoned pets and "feed them up properly." The privations of war must not be visited upon animals, he held (with the true misanthrope's tender regard for the lower species), and he was damned if he was going to allow dogs, cats, and birds to suffer in a cataclysmic war which was to take millions of human lives.

Nothing of the Commodore's conduct during those days should have surprised any who knew him well. He had guts; he had never gone soft through all the decades of dissipation and self-indulgence, and his defiance of the elements, whether a storm at sea or an outbreak of German militarism, had been habitual.

But even his closest friends were amazed to learn that Bennett, after a lifetime of avoiding matrimony with the utmost skill and determination, had finally succumbed to a woman. He had been terribly fond of saying, with whatever is the masculine equivalent of coyness, "I suppose no woman who ever lived could get along with me as wife." But he found one right under his imperious nose, where she had been for many years.

The lady was the Baroness de Reuter, formerly Maud Potter of Philadelphia, the widow of Baron George de Reuter, whose family had founded the British news agency. She had married the baron in 1891 and lived with him in Paris until his death in 1909, was the mother of two grown sons, and was reputed to be one of the most beautiful middle-aged women on the continent. She was also gentle, understanding, tolerant. Bennett had known her for years and valued her companionship.

Just what it was that pushed him over the brink of matrimony was never revealed, but they decided to get married on September 10—the day it was announced that the German armies had been pushed back from the Marne. The baroness had stayed in Paris during the September crisis.

That afternoon, at any rate, they went to the American Cathedral Church and were married in the presence of several hastily secured witnesses. Thorough as the *Herald's* coverage of society news was, no mention was made in his paper of the event. The baroness moved into his apartment on the avenue d'Iéna (where, in fact, she continued to live after he died and until her own death in February of 1946), and their honeymoon in the South of France was deferred until he could be assured that the Paris *Herald* would be able to keep publishing.

Even more surprising to those who had heard his fulminations against all kinds of religion was the fact that Bennett was also immediately received into the Protestant Episcopal faith, although he had been born a Catholic, at Mrs. Bennett's prompting.

From then on the Commodore was a thoroughly domesticated man, dotingly attached to the lovely Maud, almost fanatically uxorious. If his life was full of startling turnabouts, this was the final and most surprising of all. The old Jimmy Bennett was, indeed, dead—or at least tamed. It was a dreadful loss to the cabaret, restaurant, and café proprietors of Paris and elsewhere.

Soon after their marriage Bennett received a large bill from Mrs. Bennett's milliner.

"Did you buy all these hats?" he inquired.

"Of course I did," she said.

"Very well then, in that case the Paris *Herald* will have to pay for them," Bennett said. He called in Mitchell and told him to raise the price of the newspaper to twenty-five centimes—he had supported the paper for almost a quarter of a century; now it could at least help clothe his wife.

Harry Lehr and his wife-biographer (*King Lehr and the Gilded Age*) saw the Bennetts frequently in Paris and several times during the war visited them at Beau-

lieu. Elizabeth Drexel Lehr wrote that they were so
comfortably married that they could afford to quarrel
in public, one of the few issues between them being the
worrisome fate of one of her sons, who was imprisoned
in Germany (her younger son was serving in France
as a second lieutenant in the Grenadier Guards).

Bennett, wrote Mrs. Lehr, "even quarreled with his
wife" over his intensely pro-Allied sympathies, "if indeed their disputes could be described as quarrels, for
they were devoted to one another and their marriage,
although made late in life, was one of true love. . . .

"During the first year of the war Mrs. Bennett was
distraught with anxiety over the eldest son of her previous marriage, Oliver, who had gone to Germany to
consult an ear specialist and as a naturalised Englishman had been interned in Ruhleben when war was
declared. As his letters from the prison camp became
more and more despondent she grew nearly frantic and
implored Gordon Bennett to use his influence to secure
the release of her son, at all costs. She pointed out
that as an international sportsman he had many influential acquaintances in Germany. . . . Surely something could be done.

"Terribly distressed at her grief, Gordon Bennett
wrote several letters, despatched them to Germany.
Weeks passed before they were answered. Then came
a diplomatic intimation that Germany was badly in need
of propaganda in the United States. If Gordon Bennett
would throw in the influence of his newspapers he
would be suitably rewarded.

"James Gordon Bennett indignantly refused, but his
wife was heartbroken. She almost went on her knees to
entreat him to reconsider his decision. He was an American. America was not in the war, she urged. How

could there be any harm in making propaganda for Germany when her son's liberty was at stake?

"But in spite of his love for her he was adamant. . . . 'My loyalty belongs to my adopted country. I will not sell my honour, whatever the price. Not even for you. . . .'"

Oliver de Reuter was soon released in an exchange of civilian prisoners, and joined the Bennetts on the Riviera to recuperate from his ordeal in the German prison camp.

Most of the war years, however, the Bennetts spent in Paris, along with a small but vociferously pro-Allied colony of American expatriates, including Mrs. W. K. Vanderbilt, whom Mrs. Lehr described as "gliding sinuously" through hospital wards, clad in a white piqué uniform that Worth had designed for her "with an impressive cap like a Russian headdress"; Herman Harjes, the American representative of J. P. Morgan; James Hazen Hyde, who had fled New York after the state began investigating his insurance company; James Stillman, the banker, who had lived in France even longer than the Commodore; Mrs. Whitelaw Reid, the widow of the New York *Tribune's* publisher; Mrs. William B. Leeds, and other members of international society whom even the war could not drive back to their stuffy, unamusing homeland.

Even for these wealthy exiles, according to Mrs. Lehr, the grim reflections of a war which was destroying the old Europe were disturbing, and sometimes menacing. Already war had become three-dimensional, and death could come plummeting out of the sky for soldiers and civilians, rich and poor alike. "The silent sobered people crept about, the women almost invariably dressed in black. A joyless city with all its youth at war, its children sent away to the safety of the

Riviera or the Pyrenees. After nightfall the streets were almost deserted; everyone dreaded at any moment to hear the sirens announcing the advent of German aeroplanes, not knowing when the first bomb would fall." At night, when the sirens sounded, Parisians took to their cellars until the zeppelins or bombers had departed. Fortunately the basement of the Bennetts' apartment house had a huge old-fashioned cellar, which even the heaviest bombs could not have penetrated, but the Commodore complained that if a German bomb didn't get him, his rheumatism, flaring up in the underground dampness, would certainly finish him off. Soon he refused to take shelter when an air raid was in progress.

He continued to put in a full day's work at the *Herald*, helping to plan each day's issue, going out to the make-up tables in the composing room in his shirt sleeves, writing editorials which assured the French that they would win the war, that sooner or later his native land would wake up and join the fight against German imperialism. French morale, it was said, was boosted tremendously by these assurances from "M. Gordon-Bennett," whom they regarded as an unofficial branch of the United States embassy.

Parisians were so convinced of the reliability of the *Herald's* war news, in contrast to that published by their own propaganda sheets and political organs, that the police had to be summoned to handle the crowds gathering around the paper's outside bulletin board.

Violently anti-union all his life, Bennett had to concede that it was the typographical unions, motivated by gratitude for the *Herald's* morale-boosting role as an American outpost, as a constant proclaimer of forthcoming intervention by the United States, which kept the paper publishing. There were only a few printers and pressmen left in his mechanical departments. The

Paris unions, however, always rounded up a small group of compositors and pressroom workers from the other newspapers to drop in at the *Herald* shortly before four o'clock in the morning and help Bennett get the paper out. This voluntary assistance continued throughout the war.

The Commodore's sympathy for the Allied cause was exceeded only by what he considered to be his duty as a newspaperman. When the French military censorship grew more rigid as the enormous futility of the war became apparent, with Gauls and Teutons simply bleeding themselves to death in the deadlock of the trenches, Bennett exploded with defiance. A censor's decision that such-and-such a story must not be printed was taken as a personal affront, a silent accusation that the *Herald* would publish news helpful to the enemy. Bennett regarded himself as the best judge of what should or should not be published. He went over the heads of the censors and argued with high government officials and officers of the French General Staff or the Deuxième Bureau; he stormed into ministers' offices and shook his finger at generals, and sometimes, when all else failed, he ran a story marked for deletion and let the censors gnash their teeth. Any other paper would have been suspended, but the government recognized Bennett's loyalty and let him off with "serious" warnings against further infractions of the censorship.

Late in the summer of 1916 he made his last trip to America, a rather perilous voyage now that the German U-boats were so active in the Atlantic.

Two serious concerns brought him back to New York. He wanted to find out just what the sentiment was in America regarding intervention, and he had to try to save the New York *Herald*. His investigations regarding the first were more cheering than his exploration of methods to revive the *Herald*.

The United States was then involved—or trapped—in a vexatious dispute with Mexico, having sent a punitive expedition under General John J. Pershing across the border to hunt down the guerilla leader Pancho Villa. For months United States cavalry units had been chasing over the mountains and plains of northern Mexico in a futile search for Villa, and had succeeded only in uniting the Mexican people against them. Soon Pershing's travel-worn regiments would return empty-handed to their own side of the border.

Bennett, of course, was highly critical of a venture which, it seemed to him, distracted the nation from a worthier project—avenging the sinking of American ships and other outrages by jumping into the war against the Central Powers. His attitude was expressed in a *Herald* editorial on November 24: "Through no fault of Pershing's the punitive expedition has become as much of a farce from the American standpoint as it is an eyesore to the Mexican people. Each day adds to the burden of its cost to the American people and to the ignominy of its position. General Pershing and his command should be recalled without further delay."

Before he returned to France, however, he gathered sufficient evidence to bolster him in his opinion that the United States would soon join the Allies. "Only a question of time," he said, spreading the gospel of intervention wherever he went.

Meanwhile he conferred endlessly with his executives over means of rejuvenating the *Herald*, but at each meeting they wound up in a blind alley. Resuscitating the paper would take hundreds of thousands, perhaps millions of dollars, and the Commodore couldn't lay his hands on that kind of money. It would have to struggle along somehow. For years it had maintained him on a scale of living rarely attained by any other American; it had supplied him with thirty to forty million dollars in the fifty years since he had taken over as editor and publisher, and now there was nothing he could do for it. There were even rumors along Park Row that he had proposed to Adolph Ochs that the *Herald* and the *Times* be merged, and that Ochs had turned him down.

He returned to Paris late in 1916 knowing that sooner or later, unless a miracle supervened, the New York *Herald*, the capstone of his pride, the thing he valued most in the world, might well die before he did.

13: The Commodore Accepts the Inevitable

At 6:30 P.M. on June 14, 1917, a hard-jawed American general stepped off the train at the Gare du Nord and was greeted by the cheers of thousands of Frenchmen, who until then had become very weary of cheering generals. The newcomer was General Pershing, accompanied by members of his headquarters, and he was not merely another grim-faced brass hat, but the symbol and representative of millions of Americans who the Allies hoped would soon be bolstering the Western Front. Russia was out, America was in, and hope bloomed once again like the roses of a trench-scarred Picardy. That it would take many months to train, organize, and transport an American Expeditionary Force was something few were willing to recognize; the situation, with German divisions now being transferred from the broken Russian front, was too desperate to permit any cautionary thoughts, even among professionals who should have known better.

A little later that evening General Pershing stepped on a balcony overlooking the Place de la Concorde, and the almost hysterical uproar which greeted his ramrod figure had not been equaled in the French capital since the gates were torn off the Bastille. Pershing and his hundred-odd Americans were treated like gods; they were the last hope of France, and on no other day in history would Americans be so adored and welcomed.

Bennett was too busy supervising an exultant issue of the Paris *Herald* to join the cheering throngs, but that June twilight was a triumphant hour for the Commodore. Right from the outbreak of war he had urged American participation. For almost three years he had been promising the French that the Yanks were, as their song promised, coming. And now they were here—young, strong, and untainted by war weariness. Bennett naturally regarded the arrival of Pershing and the A.E.F. vanguard, to be followed shortly by the First Division, as a personal vindication, something to throw in the teeth of scoffers who had maintained that America would stay out of the war and rake in billions out of a cagey neutrality.

Like almost everyone else, the Commodore believed that it would be a matter of only a few months before the United States Army was taking its place in the battle line and smashing through to the Rhine. He and Mrs. Bennett were seldom seen at parties during the war, but now they joined in joyously welcoming Pershing and his officers, attending balls given by the Herman Harjeses, the Harry Lehrs, and James Hazen Hyde. Bennett liked the Pershing style which, if it was as effective militarily as romantically, promised swift victory for American arms. He watched with approval one night late in June when Pershing, the handsome widower, took one look at Louise Brooks, an American divorcee (later Mrs. [General] Douglas MacArthur), and monopolized her for the rest of the evening on and off the dance floor, with none of the younger officers daring to cut in, as Mrs. Lehr observed, and "as he showed no sign of relinquishing his place beside her even at supper they could only look on enviously." Obviously Pershing possessed the proper cavalryman's dash. It shouldn't take him long to get the A.E.F. into action.

But weeks and months passed, and the inflow of U.S. troops was only a trickle, held up by Stateside delays and a shortage of shipping. Even those regiments on French soil, as Bennett learned to his disgust, Pershing refused to turn over to the French Army, although the Allied commanders were pleading that the war might be lost before the Americans could arrive in sufficient strength and be organized into the independent American Army that Pershing insisted upon. The hardheaded "Black Jack" maintained that he would be betraying his country if his troops were thrown into the French and British armies by the company and battalion to serve under foreign flags.

To the Commodore, this view was stupidly provincial; the main thing was to save the cause, to hold off the German offensives certain to be launched in the spring of 1918, and then worry about collecting American troops under their own commanders. Many other Americans were pleading in this vein, both in Paris and Washington, but Pershing would not be swayed.

One of the American commander in chief's toughest assignments was trying to mollify James Gordon Bennett. His press officers, of course, had briefed him on Bennett's importance as the number one American in France before Pershing's arrival, his services in bolstering French morale, and his indubitable, if wrongheaded, patriotism. Bennett and Pershing were on good terms socially, but the latter, whose temperament was anything but diplomatic, was hard put to hang onto his short-leashed temper while the Commodore told him how to run the A.E.F.

Furthermore Bennett had a bone to pick with Pershing over the way the general had snatched away the services of the man whom Bennett had decided would head his newspapers' coverage of the American forces at the front. The man was a veteran foreign correspondent named Frederick Palmer, who had made a name for himself as the accredited representative of the three American wire services at Allied Headquarters. Bennett had offered him $750 a week as chief A.E.F. correspondent, which was accepted. While waiting for the contracts to be signed, Palmer wandered around Washington, trying to size up the scope and direction of the war effort. One of the men he visited at the War Department was General Pershing, whom he had known for many years. Pershing, a scheme already forming in a craftier brain than many gave him credit for possessing, invited the newspaperman to accompany the A.E.F. vanguard to France. All the way over Pershing made Palmer his confidante: he was particularly worried about press relations; he himself had no talent for dealing with newspapermen; it was Palmer's patriotic duty to take over the Press Section under the G-2 of his staff.

Palmer pointed out that he had agreed to sign a contract with Bennett (which, incidentally, would bring him $40,000 a year compared to the $175 monthly of a staff major), but Pershing remarked that a patriot of Bennett's stripe would be only too glad to relinquish a man so desperately needed by his country's army.

The Commodore wasn't at all glad; he had hoped that Palmer's ability and prestige as a war correspondent would restore the New York *Herald* to the eminence it had known during the Spanish-American War largely because of the Olympian reliability of Richard Harding Davis' dispatches. But he released Palmer from his oral commitment.

All the troubled summer and autumn of 1917, when

they met over cigars and brandy at a dinner party, at Pershing's luxurious rented mansion in the Rue de Varennes (once the home of Napoleon's Marshal Lannes) or in the general's office at 31 Rue de Constantine, Bennett served as Pershing's gadfly—but for once the Commodore's forceful determination met an immovable object. The A.E.F. would fight as a self-contained army, eventually.

One rueful entry in General Pershing's war diary, for July 28, 1917, read, "Had luncheon with James Gordon Bennett and found him more aggressive than ever."

With both American troops and camp followers arriving by the thousands, the Paris *Herald's* circulation leaped upward, but the paper also acquired an American competitor, the Chicago *Tribune* establishing a Paris edition for the soldiers on July 4, 1917.

By early 1918 more than a hundred thousand copies of the *Herald* were being sold daily, and it was able to pay Mrs. Bennett's millinery bills and still show a healthy profit.

Bennett had been sinking money into the newspaper for so long he still couldn't believe it was turning a profit. He called in Jaurett, his business manager, and announced that he was in desperate need of cash; the New York *Herald* was borrowing all the money it could to keep afloat, and a loan must be arranged. His aides had given up trying to convince him that there was a cash surplus in the bank. So Jaurett went to the Rothschild Bank and arranged for Bennett to borrow 250,000 francs ($50,000) on his personal note. This was not at all difficult since the Commodore had several million francs on deposit there, the accumulation of three profit-making years.

It was the last time the once-wealthy Commodore ever had to scrounge around for money.

Late in November he caught a cold, a severe one that verged on pneumonia and heavily taxed his heart and lungs.

Several weeks later, when he had partly recovered, Mrs. Bennett took him to the gentler climate at Beaulieu.

He failed to throw off the effects of the illness, however, and, superstitious as always, he began brooding over the approach of his seventy-seventh birthday on May 10. His father had died of a stroke at the age of seventy-seven, and Bennett was convinced that he would die in the same manner and in the same year. These premonitions became an obsession with him, even as spring came and he sat, wrapped in a blanket, in the sunlit garden of his estate overlooking the Mediterranean. He loved Beaulieu more than any place he had ever lived, and he was content, he told his wife, to die there.

One day late in April he and Mrs. Bennett attended a charity fete in Monte Carlo at which a clairvoyant insisted on telling his fortune. According to Elizabeth Drexel Lehr, who got the story from Mrs. Bennett, the seeress "told him amongst other things that his two dogs would die, and that the death of the second would be followed by the death of some member of his household. When a little later the two Pekingese died, as she had foretold, one within a short time of the other, James Gordon Bennett was convinced that the rest of the prophecy would be fulfilled. He gave up all hope of fighting his illness from that moment.

"'It was my death she saw in the cards,' he insisted, 'I know that it will happen as she said. I have lived out my life.'"

There was some justification for believing that superstition, which had gripped him all his life as firmly

as it held any Stone Age savage of the regions which his
expeditions penetrated to bring the light of civilization,
was the death of him. He was so transfixed by the
clairvoyant's prediction, and by his own conviction that
he would die when he reached seventy-seven, that early
in the morning of May 10 he suffered a massive brain
hemorrhage. It was his seventy-seventh birthday; it was
time to die. And he never regained consciousness. Heart
specialists arrived from Paris the following day, but
they could do nothing to rally him. His heart was failing,
uremia was developing, and as the Paris *Herald* reported
in its black-bordered columns a few days hence "his
breathing gradually became fainter and fainter."

At 5:15 A.M. on May 14 his breathing stopped altogether, as Mrs. Bennett held his large, motionless,
waxen hand, the hand that had thrown away more
money than that of any other American of his time.

The Paris *Herald* announced its publisher's death in
an obituary as restrained and unsentimental as Bennett
would have wished, and almost as quickly "Old Philadelphia Lady's" plaintive query was dropped from the
paper and the names of people on his black list were
stripped from the walls of the editorial department. He
was, a *Herald* editorial rather grimly noted, "essentially
a commander." It cannot be said that his troops, except
those who had escaped from his employ and could look
back on their service with something like nostalgia, were
suffused with grief at his passing. The old Commodore
had never sought love or popularity, particularly from
"the hired help," and except for a few men who saw
something wryly affecting and rudely gallant beneath
his surface, they had not been bestowed upon him.

Continental journalism mourned him with what was
termed a "sincere emotion" in the Paris *Journal*, which
pointed out that his sponsorship of the James Gordon

Bennett aviation trophy helped enormously in the development of military aviation and in the design and construction of the Spad, in which Fonck and Guynemer had won their aerial victories over the German flying circuses. "For James Gordon Bennett," the Paris *Journal* said, "had seen clearly ahead. He knew that it was sport that created the intense energy which in peacetime wins races and in wartime wins battles." To *Excelsior,* "his foresight was remarkable. In his journalistic field of action, Napoleon's words could apply to him: 'I live always one year in advance.'" To *Epoca* of Rome he was the "greatest of the modern journalists." *Eclairer* of Nice, which regarded itself as his hometown paper, recalled that even as death approached, the Commodore called its editorial room every afternoon to inquire, "How many Boche were killed today?"

Of all the American newspapers, the New York *Times,* conceding that Bennett was "the founder of the modern newspaper," was predictably the most penetrating and objective in assessing his life. Bennett, a *Times* editorial said, was "one of the most vigorous and cynical of the great figures on the personal stage of American journalism." He was full of "humors," in the Elizabethan sense, but there was "systematic method in his madness"—an element never suspected, certainly, by the men who had suffered from his whims.

"There was a deeper sagacity in this man than was generally realized," the *Times* continued. "He had his own way through a long life . . . but he was not an 'idler.' What editor worked harder? He played hard as he worked hard. He got out of life what he wanted. A vivid figure, such as a novelist could not invent, and yet that seems too fanciful for actuality. He was a sort of Fairy Prince to the last."

Bennett was buried in the little cemetery at Passy,

just across the road from the house where Clemenceau lived, after brief services in Trinity Church in Paris. He lies there still, an expatriate to the end. No cross of his belatedly accepted Episcopal God, not even his name or his birth and death dates were engraved on the simple headstone which marks his grave. In each corner of the stone, at his instructions, small figures of owls were carved.

The owls, as always, would watch over the departed pagan.

His will, as might have been expected, was grandiose and complicated, quite unrealistic as to the remaining resources of his estate. Although the New York *Herald* had been foundering for years before his death, he had directed that it be maintained and published in perpetuity; furthermore, his executors, Rodman Wanamaker and the Guaranty Trust Company of New York, were ordered to pay out annuities totaling $142,500. (Mrs. Bennett had already been assured of more than enough income from her first husband's estate.)

In addition, Bennett had ordered that when his estate was finally settled, the residue be expended on establishing and maintaining a home for indigent newspapermen who had worked for a daily newspaper in Manhattan for at least ten years. For this last worthy project, there was not a sufficient residue available to operate on the scope he hoped for, and there were many *Herald* veterans who considered this a last rude joke on the profession he had always professed to value so low. Actually the Commodore's intention was perfectly sincere; the newspapermen's home was a memorial to his father, whose memory was no joking matter to him, and perhaps also a way of making up for his large failings as an employer. The James Gordon Bennett

Memorial Home for New York Journalists was finally established, and still exists, but it could never become the sizable refuge he had envisioned.

Some *Herald* veterans also were embittered by the fact that he did not leave the paper to them. He had often hinted that they would be rewarded for their loyalty, and in an interview published in *Figaro* of Paris some years before, he had been quoted as saying his newspaper properties would be left to his "faithful employees." However, as Albert Stevens Crockett wrote, this was something of a confidence trick, conceived during the years when Hearst and Pulitzer and Ochs were raiding his staff. "I had not been many years on the *Herald* before I began to acquit him of any intention of this recognizing the services of those who worked for him, and investigation showed that his statement to the *Figaro* reporter had been subjected to a very literal translation."

The *Herald's* fate was dismal: it fell into the hands of Frank A. Munsey, the renowned cannibal of American journalism.

To satisfy the annuities provided in Bennett's will, his executors soon learned that they would have to sell all his properties. The New York *Herald's* circulation was down to 55,000, and the *Evening Telegram,* once again, was losing money; only the Paris *Herald* was still in sound condition, aided by the postwar flood of American tourists.

On January 14, 1920, all three papers were bought by Munsey for $4,000,000.

Munsey, a horse-faced Yankee trader of sixty-six, had yearned for years to step into the Commodore's shoes. A native of Maine, once a grocery clerk and later manager of the Western Union office in Augusta, Munsey had made a fortune out of publishing magazines, then turned his attention to the newspaper business, buying, combining, selling and wrecking a number of properties but always somehow emerging from the ruins with a sizable profit. He was utterly devoid of the newspaperman's sentimentality about the newspaper as a living institution into which hundreds of people have poured their lives and hopes and energies. A newspaper to him was simply a set of ledgers, circulation tallies, and advertising figures. But the *Herald* was different; it provided him with the mantle of the Bennetts, he fancied, and he had been looking forward to succeeding the Commodore for a long time.

For his part, Bennett had always referred to Munsey with loathing as "that grocer." It was the culminating irony of his career that Munsey should be his successor; the talismanic owls on the cornice of that beautiful building in Herald Square must have shrieked with rage when the news got around: the lordly and worldly Commodore was giving place to a grasping, small-minded, cheese-paring merchant from a Yankee crossroads.

Late on the afternoon he acquired the *Herald,* according to his biographer (George Brett, *Forty Years— Forty Millions*), Munsey "sat up straight in James Gordon Bennett's chair, at Bennett's small old-fashioned French desk, beside the fire burning cozily on the hearth in Bennett's office in the lovely old *Herald* Building, and he permitted himself to sip temperately of that heady draught, the pride of ambition achieved."

Munsey was so obsessed with crawling into Bennett's skin that he brushed his hair and trimmed his mustache as the Commodore had, tried to dress like his predecessor and ape his autocratic manner—an inept impersonation, both hilarious and pathetic, which would surely have enraged Bennett almost as much as the thought of his newspapers' being operated by the most lamentable parvenu who had ever intruded upon the newspaper world.

Shortly after he assumed ownership of the *Herald*, Munsey asked Frank Flaherty, the business manager, "Who owns the bust of Bennett out there in the outer offices?"

Flaherty assured him that it came with the property, and cagily added, "As you know, that marble bust might be yourself, line for line, the very image."

"That's a strange thing," Munsey said, visibly swelling under the effects of this blarney. "I was at dinner the other night at Mrs. W. K. Vanderbilt's. Reick was there and some others. And do you know what Mrs. Vanderbilt said to me? She said, 'See here, Mr. Munsey. It's strange that so many of your characteristics are so like Mr. Bennett's. You are purchasing his papers now, and on top of that, there's more than a strong resemblance in your appearance.' "

Perhaps the best known of the Commodore's photographic portraits was taken of him in his prime; he is wearing a rough tweed suit, his thumb casually hooked in a vest pocket, and he is staring boldly into the lens—the epitome of casual, well-born assurance. Munsey posed for his official photograph in exactly the same costume and in a rough approximation of the same pose—but the result was caricature.

Exultant as he was over his purchase, Munsey could not stifle his impulse to tinker, amalgamate, and cannibalize. Several years before, he had bought the *Morning* and *Evening Sun*. He combined the *Morning Sun* with the *Herald* and published the *Evening Telegram* as well as the *Evening Sun* separately for a time. Then he bought the New York *Globe and Commercial Advertiser* and merged it with the *Evening Sun,* bought the *Evening Mail* and combined it with the *Evening Telegram*. Within a few years Munsey had succeeded in turning Park Row into a cuckoo's nest.

In 1924 he decided that there was room for only one Republican morning paper in New York. The *Tribune* was then being published by Whitelaw Reid's widow and her son Ogden, so he proposed that the *Herald* and *Tribune* be consolidated. What he really wanted, he made clear, was to buy out the Reids. They surprised him by insisting that the only way such a consolidation could be effected was for Munsey to sell them the *Herald,* and offered an equally surprising $5,000,000 for both the New York and Paris editions. Since he had acquired the properties for $4,000,000 and in addition had found $1,000,000 in cash assets nestling in the Paris *Herald's* coffers, which Bennett's executors had neglected to remove before the sale, he could turn a profit of $2,000,000.

Much as he valued the *Herald* and the incongruous mantle of the Bennetts, he could not indulge himself to the extent of resisting such an easy profit taking. The *Herald* was sold to be combined with the *Tribune.* Later the Scripps-Howard chain acquired the *Evening Telegram,* and eventually the *World* and the *Sun.*

All that survives James Gordon Bennett, besides a tradition long dimmed by mightier but less original press lords, is the ornate clock and the bronze owls which once adorned the façade of the *Herald* Building, tolling its numbered hours and blinking ferociously, which were given New York University's school of journalism and may serve as a reminder of how fleeting is journalistic glory, and those fractions of his former enterprises now represented in the New York *Herald Tribune,* the New York *World-Telegram and Sun,* and the Paris edition of the New York *Herald Tribune.*

A Note on Sources

The basic research for this book was contained in a small mountain of old newspaper files, those of the New York *Herald,* the *Evening Telegram,* and the Paris edition of the *Herald.* Fortunately all of them are available in the New York Public Library's newspaper annex in West Twenty-fifth Street. The files of other New York newspapers were also found valuable, including those of the *Times, World, Sun, Tribune,* and *Evening Post.* Also helpful were the recollections of a number of veteran New York newspapermen, including several members of the Silurians, an organization largely composed of men who can remember when there were newspapers on Park Row.

The author would also like to acknowledge, with gratitude, the considerable assistance, enlightenment, and amusement he found in the following books:

Balsan, Consuelo Vanderbilt. *The Glitter and the Gold.* New York: Harper & Brothers, 1952.

Bent, Silas. *Ballyhoo.* New York: Boni & Liveright, 1927.

Berger, Meyer. *The Story of the New York Times.* New York: Simon & Schuster, Inc., 1951.

Blumenfeld, Ralph D. *Home Town.* London: Hutchinson, 1944.

Britt, George. *Forty Years—Forty Millions: The Career of Frank A. Munsey.* New York: Farrar & Rinehart, 1935.

Bullard, F. Lauriston. *Famous War Correspondents.* Boston, 1914.

Carlson, Oliver. *The Man Who Made News*. New York: Duell, Sloane & Pearce, Inc., 1942.

Churchill, Allen. *Park Row*. New York: Rinehart & Co., Inc., 1958.

Clarke, Joseph I. C. *My Life and Memories*. New York: Dodd, Mead & Co., Inc., 1925.

Clermont, Camille. *Confessions of Gentle Rebecca*. London, 1922.

Creelman, James. *On the Great Highway*. Boston: Lothrop, Lee & Shepard Co., 1901.

Crockett, Albert Stevens. *When James Gordon Bennett Was Caliph of Bagdad*. New York: Funk & Wagnalls Company, 1926.

Crozier, Emmett. *American Reporters on the Western Front 1914–18*. New York: Oxford University Press, Inc., 1959.

Daniels, Jonathan. *The End of Innocence*. Philadelphia: J. B. Lippincott Co., 1954.

Decies, Elizabeth Wharton (Drexel) Beresford. *King Lehr and the Gilded Age*. New York: J. B. Lippincott Co., 1935.

Downey, Fairfax. *Richard Harding Davis*. New York: Charles Scribner's Sons, 1933.

Farwell, Byron. *The Man Who Presumed*. New York: Henry Holt & Co., 1957.

Fiske, Stephen. *Off-Hand Portraits of Prominent New Yorkers*. New York, 1884.

Ford, James. *Forty-Odd Years in the Literary Shop*. New York: E. P. Dutton & Co., Inc., 1921.

Fowler, Gene. *Skyline*. New York: The Viking Press, Inc., 1961.

Greenwall, H. J. *I'm Going to Maxim's*. London: Allan Wingate Ltd., 1958.

Herd, Harold. *Seven Editors*. New York: The Macmillan Co., 1955.

Hudson, Frederic. *Journalism in the United States*. New York, 1873.

Laney, Al. *Paris Herald*. New York: Appleton-Century-Crofts, Inc., 1947.

Leech, Margaret. *In the Days of McKinley*. New York: Harper & Brothers, 1959.

Leslie, Anita. *The Remarkable Mr. Jerome*. New York: Henry Holt & Co., 1954.

Lewis, Oscar. *The Silver Kings*. New York: Alfred A. Knopf, 1947.

MacGahan, Januarius A. *Campaigning on the Oxus*. New York, 1874.

Melville, George W. *In the Lena Delta*. New York, n.d.

Morris, Lloyd. *Incredible New York*. New York: Random House, 1951.

Mott, Frank Luther. *American Journalism*. New York: The Macmillan Co., 1942.

Ross, Ishbel. *Ladies of the Press*. New York: Harper & Brothers, 1936.

Seitz, Don C. *The James Gordon Bennetts*. Indianapolis: Bobbs-Merrill Company, 1928.

————. *Joseph Pulitzer: His Life and Letters*. New York: Garden City Publishing Co., 1924.

Swanberg, W. A. *Jim Fisk*. New York: Charles Scribner's Sons, 1959.

Tebbel, John. *The Life and Good Times of William Randolph Hearst*. New York: E. P. Dutton & Co., Inc., 1952.

Villard, Oswald G. *Some Newspapers and Newspapermen*. New York: Alfred A. Knopf, 1923.

Walker, Stanley. *City Editor*. Toronto: McClelland & Steward, Ltd., 1934.

Wecter, Dixon. *The Saga of American Society*. New York: Charles Scribner's Sons, 1937.

Winkler, John. *William Randolph Hearst*. New York: Simon & Schuster, Inc., 1928.

Index